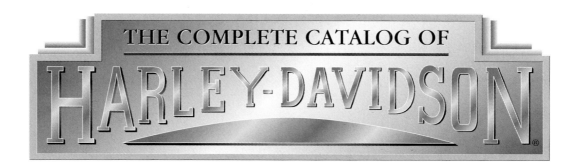

THE COMPLETE CATALOG OF
HARLEY-DAVIDSON

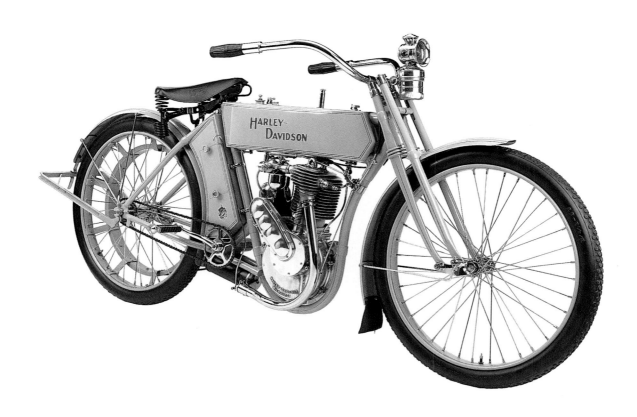

In memory of
Dorothy Jean
1917-1996

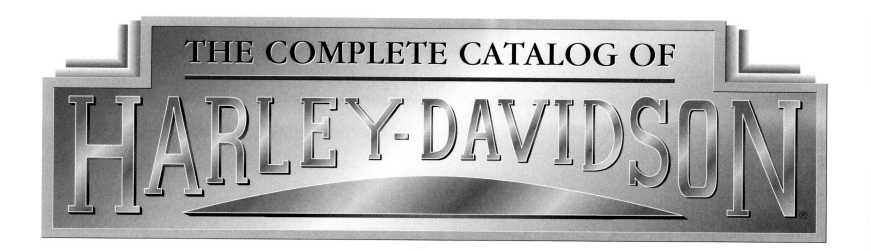

THE COMPLETE CATALOG OF
HARLEY-DAVIDSON

TOD RAFFERTY

Lowe & B. Hould
Publishers

Credits

This edition published in 1997 by Lowe & B. Hould Publishers, an imprint of Borders, Inc., 515 East Liberty, Ann Arbor, MI 48104. Lowe & B. Hould Publishers is a trademark of Borders Properties, Inc.

Simultaneously published in 1997 by Motorbooks International Publishers & Wholesalers, 729 Prospect Avenue, PO Box 1, Osceola, WI 54020, USA

CLB 4402
©1997 CLB International, Godalming Business Centre, Woolsack Way, Godalming, Surrey GU7 1XW, UK

Library of Congress Cataloging-in-Publication Data Available.

ISBN 0-681-21933-5

Thanks are due to all the owners and restorers who volunteered their motorcycles for photography. In more or less chronological order (bike's age, not owner's), our gratitude goes to Gene Calidonna, Joy and Marv Baker, Trev Deeley, Brian Holden, Fred Pazaski, Dave Bettencourt, Otis Chandler, Glenn Bator, Jeff Gilbert, Mike Parti, Bud Ekins, Armando Magri, Daniel Statnekov, Harold Mathews, Dave Royal, John Tosta, Mike Lady, Fred Lange, Oliver Shokouh, Ken Lang, Paul Wheeler, Doug Stein, Chuck Holenda, Ron Stratman, Bob Rocchio, Jim Kirchner, Bill Bartels, Jim and Mike Furlong, Tom Perkins, Randy Janson, Brad Richardson, Richard Brazas, Sam Williams, Chris Lamb, Dwight Yoakam, Gary Bang, Jr., Clay Osincup, Doug Holden, Jerry Warren, Steve Alamango, Dennis Huggins, Ginger Gammon, Duane Anderson, John Kingston, Howard Mahler, Val Bassetti, Ray Earls and Dave Ybarra.

Our appreciation also to the staffs of the Otis Chandler Vintage Museum, Petersen Automotive Museum, Trev Deeley Motorcycle Museum, Bartels' Harley-Davidson, Dudley Perkins Company, Los Angeles Harley-Davidson, Mathews Harley-Davidson, Harley-Davidson of Glendale, Harley-Davidson of El Cajon, Harley-Davidson of Atascadero, Harley-Davidson of Sacramento and Warren's Motorcycle Service. Thanks also to Marty Rosenblum and Susan Fariss of Harley-Davidson Archives, Mike Shattuck, Jay Westerbrook, Richard Messer, Philip Mitchell, Don James, Rick Cole, Jim McClure of Vintage Cycle Promotions, Reg Kittrelle of *Thunder Press*, Buell Motorcycle Company, Allan Girdler, Ron Hussey, Larry Kahn, Stephen Wright, Dennis Pegelow, Bronwyn Rafferty, Dan Argano, Chris and Sandy Sidah, Nanci Griffith, Little Feat and Sierra Nevada Stout.

And a parting wave of gratitude to William Harley and the Davidsons, Arthur, William and Walter.

Photographs identified as such in the text are copyright Harley-Davidson Motor Company and are provided courtesy of Dr. Martin Jack Rosenblum, Historian, Harley-Davidson Juneau Avenue Archives.

TOD RAFFERTY has been riding and racing motorcycles for 35 years. ("But I got a late start," he adds.) His previous book *Harley-Davidson: The Ultimate Machine* (CLB Publishing) was published in 1994 and appeared in English, Italian, French and German editions. Though primarily a dirt rider, the author keeps a sport bike for the road and hopes to add a touring motorcycle "if this book does well."

His other works in progress include *Harley Memorabilia*, a historical compilation of H-D collectibles, and *The Harley-Davidson Racing History* covering "ninety years of speed, skill and daring." A book on Indian motorcycles is also under consideration.

As a sideline, the author is proprietor of the American Garage, purveyor of vintage cars, motorcycles and related artifacts. The garage is also headquarters for his motorsports media production team, currently developing a feature film titled "Sunday Kind'a Love," a motorcycle racing adventure.

Rafferty dismisses the notion of spare time, comparing the concept to "other misnomers such as stadium motocross, extra money and rigid suspension." He nonetheless manages several skiing trips a year and plays some tennis. He also manages Team Geezer, an unorganized vintage racing group, and directs the activities of the Motor Jones Society, an association for recovering velocity addicts. The group's motto is "Make no haste to go slow." The official beverage is Guinness.

He continues to campaign for recognition of motorcycling as the world's most peaceful form of transportation. "Riding motorcycles develops a higher level of consciousness. The result puts our minds and souls into their natural rhythms, which match the tempos of the planet. And the universe. It's cosmic stuff."

Rafferty and his family live on the central coast of California.

Credits

Photographer
Neil Sutherland

Editor
Philip de Ste. Croix

Designer
Roger Hyde

Color artwork
Rod Ferring

Index
Amanda O'Neill

Production
Ruth Arthur
Sally Connolly
Neil Randles
Karen Staff

Director of production
Gerald Hughes

Page make-up
M.A.T.S.

Color reproduction
Pixel Tech PTE Ltd, Singapore

Printed and bound
KHL Printing,
Singapore

CONTENTS

Above: A 1955 KH, which was a longer stroke K model. Engine displacement was 54 cubic inches (883cc); top speed 95mph (153km/h).

Below: This is an extremely rare motorcycle – a 1915 Model 11K, one of the very few remaining examples of the original factory team racers.

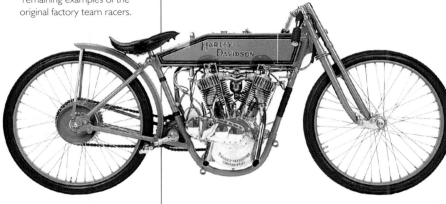

CONTENTS

Above: A 1995 Ultra Classic Electra Glide, Milwaukee's first fuel-injected tourer. Electronic cruise control is also standard.

Below: 1980 saw the re-introduction of belt-drive on the FXB Sturgis, some 65 years after its last appearance on a Harley-Davidson.

INTRODUCTION

"Harley-Davidson is the only motorcycle company in the world that gave its highest priority to tradition and succeeded."

Luigi Rivola
Racing Motorcycles, 1977

The motorcycle, a mechanized version of the horse, developed concurrently with the automobile, the motorized wagon. For reasons of safety, comfort and practical carrying capacity, most Americans put the wagon before the horse.

The steam locomotive preceded the motorcycle by a century, but it was more industrial elephant than iron horse. With the manufacturing economy of the twentieth century came the opportunity for personal transportation, and just about any young fellow or woman with some incentive could afford to go motoring on their own. And when Henry Ford made the motorcar obtainable for the average laborer, the motorcycle took a divergent path both socially and economically. A narrower path, to be sure, and the one less traveled.

The popularity of motorcycling in the 1920s faded with the Great Depression, but was revived in the mid-1930s. American riders could have the V-twin of their choice: the Indian of Springfield, Massachusetts or the Harley-Davidson from Milwaukee, Wisconsin. Available in any size, so long as it was large.

Hundreds of talented and enterprising young men had sought their fortunes in the new industry of the early 1900s. But four of them emerged as the dominant forces by the 1920s: George Hendee and Oscar Hedstrom of Indian Motocycles and William Harley and Arthur Davidson. Indian had a headstart by several years. As the market for the new machines grew, young Harley and Davidson called in the latter's big brothers and became The Harley-Davidson Motor Company. This book documents the hardware history of their enterprise.

We have included capsule histories on the design, engineering and manufacturing of all major Harley models from 1903 to the present. The most significant entries include the motorcycle's mechanical specifications, available colors, price and the number manufactured. Not in all cases are these figures absolutely accurate, but most are pretty damn close. Some records didn't survive as history, some figures were simply never recorded.

As a model history, this book represents the work of the pioneers in the motorcycle sport. From Bill Harley and the Davidson brothers to Bill Ottaway and the racers of the Harley Wrecking Crew; from Dud Perkins, Tom Sifton and Trev Deely to the second generation of Harleys and Davidsons; from Dot Robinson and the Motor Maids to Dick O'Brien and the third and fourth generations of Davidsons, the motorcycles pictured in these pages reflect the craft and enthusiastic commitment of all those who chose to make their careers in "the greatest sport on wheels."

Harley-Davidson was a family business for some 65 years. After ten years as part of a manufacturing conglomerate, the Milwaukee firm returned to private ownership in 1981. Throughout the years of boom and bust, Harley-Davidson was known almost exclusively as the builder of large, air-cooled V-twin engines, powering mostly large, heavyweight motorcycles. This remains true today.

Critics will say that Milwaukee has been building the same motorcycle for about two-thirds of the century. Fans, and stockholders, will say that's just fine.

This book cites the significant single-cylinder machines produced by Harley-Davidson, including the two-strokes and imported Aermacchi singles. But the bulk of this compendium features the V-twin as it spans 88 years of evolutionary change and development. The design principles have changed little over the years, but the engineering and construction are thoroughly contemporary.

And while some view the big-inch V-twin as an anachronism, others see it as the fundamental soul of motorcycling.

One thing is certain; no other motorcycle company, regardless of engine design, has been building motorcycles for 94 years.

Tod Rafferty
Atascadero, California 1996

INTRODUCTION

Notes on Terms, Numbers and Specifications

Numerous terms and names have been attached to motorcycle engines over the years. The early engines had an automatic, or atmospheric, or suction intake valve atop the cylinder, and a mechanical exhaust valve in a side pocket. These were designated pocket-valve or IOE (inlet-over-exhaust) engines. The latter term is used in this book.

With the arrival of mechanical intake valves in 1911, the term F-head describes the engine type. The valves are still arranged in the same fashion, but the system vaguely resembled the letter F and the label stuck.

The F-head is not to be confused with the Flathead (also known as the side-valve). This engine has the valves positioned parallel on the side of the cylinder and the head, as you might expect, is flat. The overhead valve (ohv) engine puts both valves at the top of the cylinder.

Motorcycle weights in the specifications include a half-full fuel tank. The production numbers cited refer to the number of motorcycles built for that model year. Production numbers, prices and colors were drawn from official Harley-Davidson publications and provided by the company archives.

Disputes and disagreements over some facts and figures are inevitable. Documented corrections, revisions and clarifications are welcomed, and will be incorporated in subsequent printings should they be warranted.

TR fax: 805/466-8248 e-mail: traff @ telis.org

1903-05 SINGLE

SPECIFICATIONS
ENGINE/DRIVETRAIN
Engine: IOE single
Displacement: 24.74ci (405cc)
Bore & stroke: 3 x 3.5in
(76 x 89mm)
Horsepower: Approx. 3
Carburetion: Approx. 0.88in
(22mm)
Transmission: Direct drive
Final drive: Leather belt
Brake: Rear coaster
Battery: 6-volt
Ignition: Coil/points

CHASSIS/SUSPENSION
Frame: Steel, single downtube
Suspension: None
Wheelbase: 51in (129.5cm)
Weight: 178lb (81kg)
Fuel capacity: 1.5gal (5.7lit)
Oil capacity: 2qts (1.9lit)
Tires: 28 x 2.5in (71.1 x
6.35cm)
Top speed: Approx. 35mph
(56km/h)
Color: Black, gold striping
Number built: 38
Price: $200

1903-05 SINGLE

The first prototype Harley-Davidson was actually begun in 1901. Since both William S. Harley, 21, and Arthur Davidson, 20, worked full-time for the same company, the after-hours project would consume most of the next two years. At the time, neither young man had any grand plans for a manufacturing company. Their first object, in fact, had been to produce an outboard motor, in order to reach their favorite fishing spots more easily. But soon they were captivated by the challenge of this newfangled device called a motorcycle. And their abilities, plus the support of friends and family, were to cast their futures in iron and steel. In 1903 they became The Harley-Davidson Motor Company.

Like many other pioneer motorcycle builders, William Harley had begun in the bicycle business. Arthur Davidson had trained as a pattern maker, and, with the added expertise of draftsman Emil Kröger, they set about the task of building a real motorcycle. Kröger had worked in Europe on the first renditions of the de Dion internal combustion engine, and brought the drawings with him to the U.S.

The premier machine was basically a bicycle frame fitted with a single-cylinder four-stroke engine, with direct belt drive to the rear wheel. Displacement was 10.2 cubic inches (167cc), with bore and stroke of 2.12 x 2.87 inches (54 x 73mm), producing in the neighborhood of 2 horsepower. This was sufficient urge to keep bike and rider rolling along on level ground, but not enough to carry any significant incline, so the rider still had to pedal up hills.

However, the engine did produce enough power, and added weight, to point up the shortcomings of the bicycle chassis. So

William and Arthur returned to the drawing table in search of both added power and durability. The second engine had bore and stroke of 3 x 3.5 inches (76 x 89mm) for a displacement of 24.74 cubic inches (405cc). The flywheel was more than twice the diameter of the original. Bill Harley designed a stronger loop frame to accommodate the new engine, and the first genuine Harley-Davidson motorcycle was born.

Arthur's older brothers, Walter and William Davidson, soon came to play larger roles in the company's fortunes. Arthur sent a letter about the project to Walter, then working in Kansas as a machinist for the railroad. Returning to Milwaukee in April of 1903 for the wedding of eldest brother William, Walter was also afflicted with motorcycle fever. He immediately took a job with the local railroad and devoted his spare time to the company.

Right: The first Harley-Davidsons had slight differences in handlebars, seats and belt tensioners. The tool box on the first model was fitted above the fender behind the rear frame section.

Above: The bicycle heritage is apparent in the frame and pedals. The oil tank is the D-section piece strapped above the top frame tube.

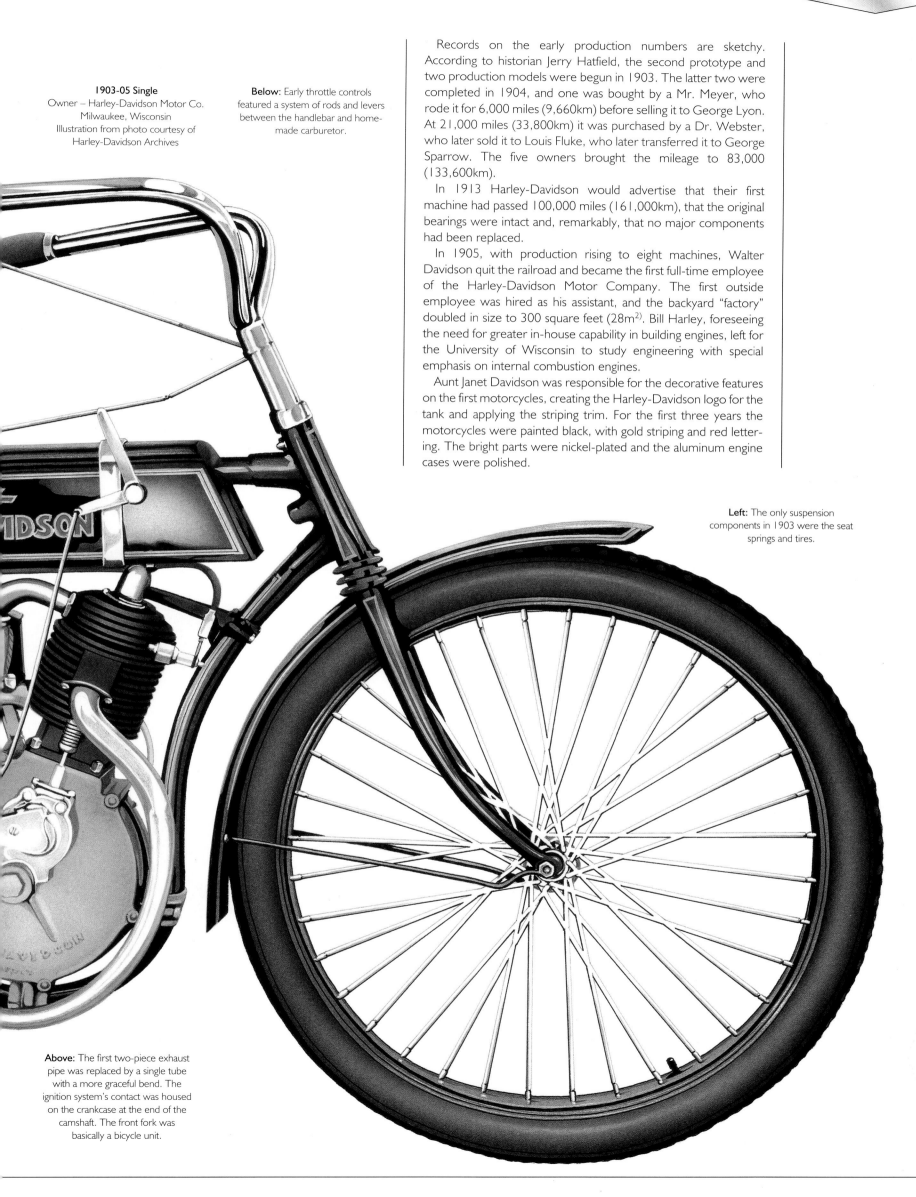

1903-05 Single
Owner – Harley-Davidson Motor Co.
Milwaukee, Wisconsin
Illustration from photo courtesy of
Harley-Davidson Archives

Below: Early throttle controls
featured a system of rods and levers
between the handlebar and home-
made carburetor.

Records on the early production numbers are sketchy. According to historian Jerry Hatfield, the second prototype and two production models were begun in 1903. The latter two were completed in 1904, and one was bought by a Mr. Meyer, who rode it for 6,000 miles (9,660km) before selling it to George Lyon. At 21,000 miles (33,800km) it was purchased by a Dr. Webster, who later sold it to Louis Fluke, who later transferred it to George Sparrow. The five owners brought the mileage to 83,000 (133,600km).

In 1913 Harley-Davidson would advertise that their first machine had passed 100,000 miles (161,000km), that the original bearings were intact and, remarkably, that no major components had been replaced.

In 1905, with production rising to eight machines, Walter Davidson quit the railroad and became the first full-time employee of the Harley-Davidson Motor Company. The first outside employee was hired as his assistant, and the backyard "factory" doubled in size to 300 square feet (28m[2)]. Bill Harley, foreseeing the need for greater in-house capability in building engines, left for the University of Wisconsin to study engineering with special emphasis on internal combustion engines.

Aunt Janet Davidson was responsible for the decorative features on the first motorcycles, creating the Harley-Davidson logo for the tank and applying the striping trim. For the first three years the motorcycles were painted black, with gold striping and red lettering. The bright parts were nickel-plated and the aluminum engine cases were polished.

Left: The only suspension
components in 1903 were the seat
springs and tires.

Above: The first two-piece exhaust
pipe was replaced by a single tube
with a more graceful bend. The
ignition system's contact was housed
on the crankcase at the end of the
camshaft. The front fork was
basically a bicycle unit.

1906-07 SINGLE

1906-07 SINGLE

SPECIFICATIONS
ENGINE/DRIVETRAIN
Engine: IOE single
Displacement: 26.8ci (440cc)
Bore & stroke: 3.125 x 3.5in
(79.4 x 89mm)
Horsepower: Approx. 4
Carburetion: Schebler
Transmission: Direct drive
Final drive: Leather belt
Brake: Rear coaster
Battery: 6-volt dry cell
Ignition: Coil/points

CHASSIS/SUSPENSION
Frame: Steel, single downtube
Suspension: Dual spring fork
Wheelbase: 51in (129.5cm)
Weight: 185lb (84kg)
Fuel capacity: 1.5gal (5.7lit)
Oil capacity: 2qts (1.9lit)
Tires: 28 x 2.25 in
(71.1 x 5.7cm)
Top speed: Approx. 40mph
(64km/h)
Colors: Black; renault gray
Number built: 200
Price: $210

By 1906 The Motor Company was well on its way to prosperity, which everyone agreed was just around the corner. Production increased to 50 motorcycles, and the first color option appeared on the order forms. Renault gray was the new hue, complemented by carmine red lettering on the tank and red pinstriping.

With new paint came a new nickname, and advertising slogan, for the Harley-Davidson motorcycle: The Silent Gray Fellow. Motorcycling was already straining for respectability, and Milwaukee meant to lead the way as a responsible manufacturer. The business had grown quickly, and Harley-Davidson was busy on all fronts, with research on new ideas and designs, a national advertising campaign and the first real factory on Chestnut Street, which would later become Juneau Avenue.

Building the bikes in a backyard shed was over. The new facility offered nearly 2,400 square feet (222m²) of work space. When the structure had been framed, the builders were informed that it was encroaching the railroad right-of-way by about a foot (30cm). This was according to surveyors employed by the railroad, which then wielded considerable authority. "So," according to Walter Davidson, "we got about eight or ten fellows, picked up the shop and moved it back about a foot and a half, so we were safe."

The motorcycle also showed signs that Harley-Davidson was in earnest about getting the job done. Having established something of a reputation for stout construction and durability, attention turned to making the motorcycle more user-friendly. The most prominent change came with the adoption of front suspension, in the form of the Sager-Cushion fork. The

dual-spring, leading link assembly helped smooth the rutted and rocky roads and absorbed a portion of the impact heretofore delivered to the rider.

With improved handling came a corresponding boost in power. An eighth-inch (0.32cm) increase in the cylinder bore brought displacement to 26.8 cubic inches (440cc), and the invigorating top speed of 45mph (72km/h). In 1907 production jumped to 154 motorcycles, and the Harley-Davidson Motor Company was incorporated, with sales of $35,000 in stock limited to the 18 employees.

Arthur and Walter Davidson quit their regular jobs to devote their full efforts to the family business. Their older brother William soon followed suit, and was appointed vice president and works manager. Bill Harley was chief engineer and treasurer, Arthur Davidson became sales manager and secretary, and Walter Davidson was the company's first president.

Walter and William Davidson were the most mechanically minded of the founding four, and paid close attention to the newest techniques in manufacturing and assembly. Together they went to Chicago to learn oxy-acetylene welding and trained their employees in the latest methods. Arthur was busy setting up a

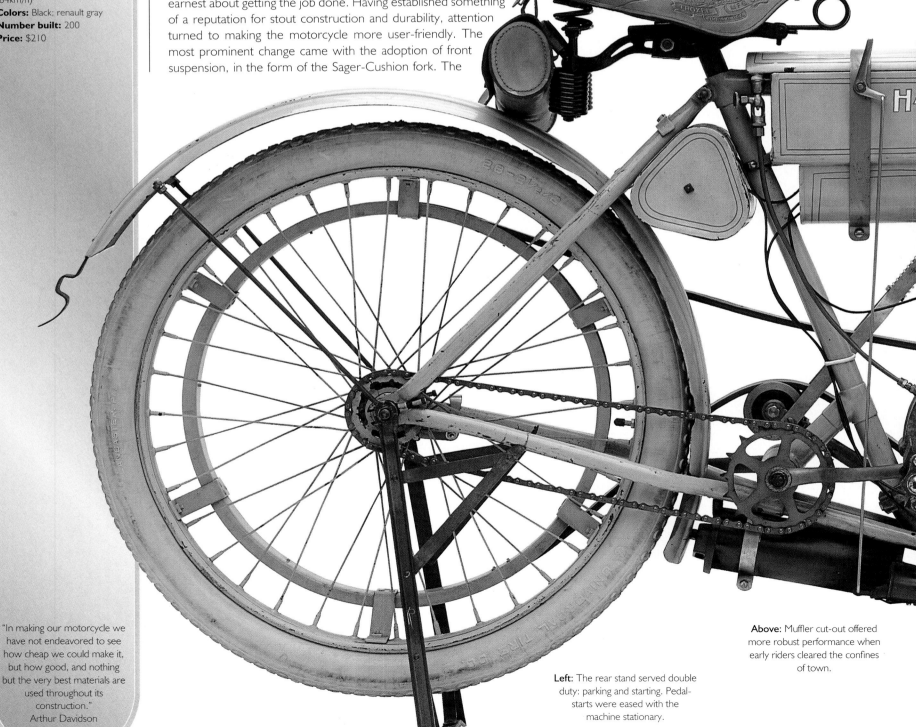

Left: The rear stand served double duty: parking and starting. Pedal-starts were eased with the machine stationary.

Above: Muffler cut-out offered more robust performance when early riders cleared the confines of town.

national network of Harley-Davidson dealers, while Bill Harley took time from his studies to start on the design of the company's first V-twin engine.

But it was Walter Davidson, the middle brother, who seemed to suddenly develop a talent that would gain a national reputation for the young company. The first of the Scots' immigrant family to be born in the U.S.A., Walter turned out to be one hell of a motorcycle rider.

At the age of 30, Walter entered a 2-day endurance run from Chicago, Illinois to Kokomo, Indiana and back. After more than 400 miles (650km) only three of the 27 riders finished with perfect scores, Walter among them. Endurance would become a key word in the Harley-Davidson sales brochure, the first of which was also produced in 1907.

Left: The triangular tool kit was mounted in the apex of the rear frame section. The seat-mounted leather pouch was an aftermarket accessory.

Above: The 1.25-inch (3.175cm) leather belt took engine power to the rear wheel. The leather-lined engine pulley was offered in three diameters.

Right: Early singles were securely clamped to the loop frame at four points, including the cylinder head.

Left: Renault gray was first offered in 1906. The Sager-Cushion spring fork premiered on the Silent Gray Fellow in 1907. The leading-link design would be employed for 42 years.

Above: Spring-loaded belt tensioner served as an early version of the clutch. The control lever was mounted at the cylinder base; the pulley rode on an arm anchored to the lower crankcase.

Right: Clincher tires were 28 inches (71.1cm) (outside diameter) by 2.25 inches (5.7cm) in cross-section.

1907 Single
Owner – Gene Calidonna
Seal Beach, California

**1908 MODEL 4
SINGLE**

SPECIFICATIONS
ENGINE/DRIVETRAIN
Engine: IOE single
Displacement: 26.8ci (440cc)
Bore & stroke: 3.125 x 3.5in
(79 x 89mm)
Horsepower: Approx. 4
Carburetion: Schebler
Transmission: Direct drive
Final drive: Leather belt
Brake: Rear coaster
Battery: 6-volt dry cell
Ignition: Coil/points

CHASSIS/SUSPENSION
Frame: Steel, single downtube
Suspension: Dual spring fork
Wheelbase: 51in (129.5cm)
Weight: Estimated 185lb (84kg)
Fuel capacity: 1.5gal (5.7lit)
Oil capacity: 2qts (1.9lit)
Tires: 28 x 2.5in
(71.1 x 6.35cm)
Top speed: Approx. 40mph
(64km/h)
Colors: Black; renault gray
Number built: 450
Price: $210

1908 SINGLE (MODEL 4)

The Harley-Davidson Motor Company now employed 18 full-time workers. And Bill Harley had apparently made considerable progress in designing the V-twin.

Officially, the 2-cylinder Harley didn't appear until 1909. But somehow a fellow named Harvey Bernard got hold of one engine in 1908, and wedged it into a single chassis. This became a matter of record when Harvey won the Algonquin, Illinois hillclimb in July. Milwaukee admitted to no chicanery in the deal, and to this day the story of Harvey Bernard and his backyard special remains shrouded in mystery.

Here also begins Milwaukee's first numbering system for the motorcycles. Using 1904 as the base production year, using the 0 designation, 1908 was listed as model #4. So starting in 1909, the number 5 precedes the model designation. The factory refers to the 1903-08 machines as 19–– singles.

The new factory, built with bricks, was growing steadily. Production tripled in 1908, with 450 motorcycles built. Technical improvements included graduated steel caps for the exhaust valve stem to facilitate adjustment. The front fork assembly was more stout, fenders were larger and the tires had grown a quarter-inch (0.6cm) wider. The price was unchanged at $210.

But the big news in 1908 was Walter Davidson's performance in the Federation of American Motorcyclist's national endurance run. The event was held on June 29, charted from Catskill, New York to New York City, a distance of 175 miles (282km). There were five Harley-Davidsons among the 61 starters, representing 17 manufacturers. Walter Davidson was listed as number 35.

Walter later noted that many entrants had 4-wheeled support vehicles carrying spare parts. He packed no spares, but finished the first leg with a perfect score. On day two, with the field whittled to 46 riders, he completed the 190-mile (306km) Long Island loop without losing any points. Davidson finished the meet with the maximum 1,000 points, and received the special diamond medal for consistency.

Below: The 1908 engine featured a steel cap on the exhaust valve stem. For purposes of accurate valve adjustment, the caps were available in six different sizes. Ease of maintenance was an early priority in Milwaukee.

Right: Renault gray or black remained the color choices for 1908. A stronger front fork and wider tires helped enhance Harley-Davidson's growing reputation for strength and reliability.

The impact of Walter's victory on Harley-Davidson sales was significant. Sales picked up in mid-year, and 450 machines were sold in 1908. In 1909 the company sold more than 1,100 motorcycles, and the figure jumped to over 3,100 in the following year. Milwaukee had turned the corner, and waiting there was Prosperity.

Despite this satisfactory turn of events, the founders knew that they would soon need a more powerful machine to compete with the twins and fours on the market. Indian, Excelsior, Merkel, Peugeot, Thor, Minerva and Reading-Standard all had twin-cylinder models, and the newly popular sport of board-track racing was bringing them plenty of publicity. Bill Harley had completed his work at the university, and turned his full effort to completing the V-twin engine which would appear in 1909. Americans wanted more horsepower to climb hills, carry passengers and pull sidecars. And, of course, to go faster.

So 1908 was a pivotal year for The Motor Company. The founders had advanced with cautious determination, not eager to rush development with unproven equipment.

But despite Harvey Bernard's early victory on the mysterious prototype V-twin, the following year's production model met with little success. However, it did force the company to bring more design and engineering effort to bear on the project. And when the twin was reintroduced in 1912, Milwaukee would reach the upper level in the growing motorcycle market, and seriously undertake running with the big dogs.

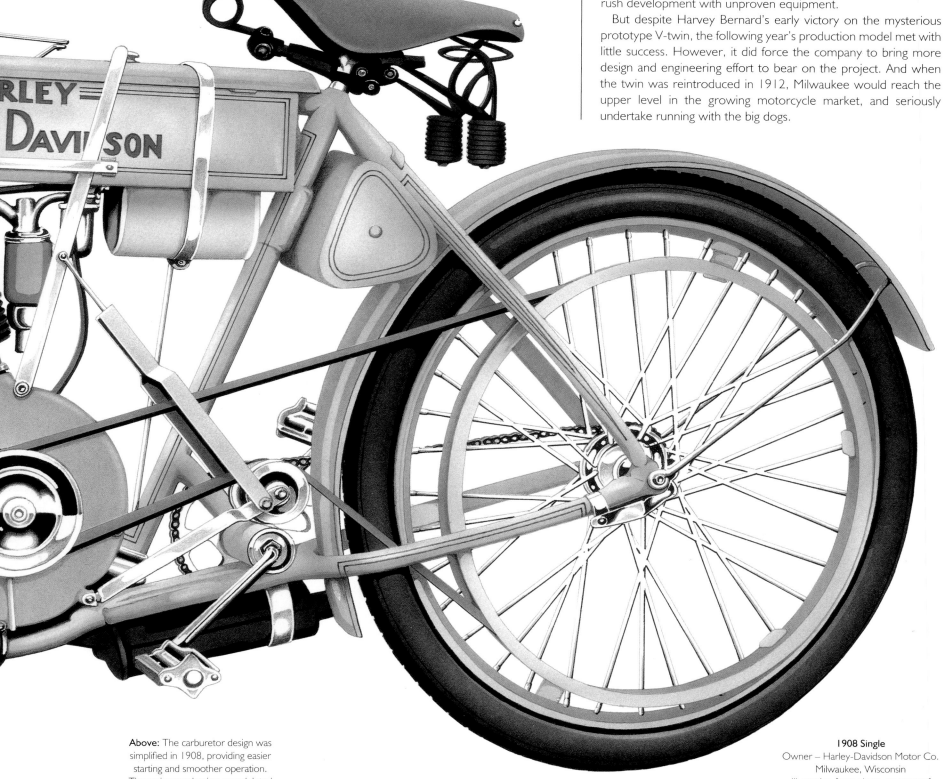

Above: The carburetor design was simplified in 1908, providing easier starting and smoother operation. The spring mechanism was deleted from the belt-tensioner yoke. Pedal starting was still standard procedure.

1908 Single
Owner – Harley-Davidson Motor Co.
Milwaukee, Wisconsin
Illustration from photo courtesy of
Harley-Davidson Archives

1909 MODEL 5A SINGLE

SPECIFICATIONS
ENGINE/DRIVETRAIN
Engine: IOE single
Displacement: 30.16ci (494cc)
Bore & stroke: 3.31 x 3.5in (84 x 89mm)
Horsepower: 4.3
Carburetion: Schebler
Transmission: Direct drive
Final drive: Leather belt
Brake: Rear coaster
Battery: 6-volt dry cell
Ignition: Battery/coil or magneto

CHASSIS/SUSPENSION
Frame: Steel, single downtube
Suspension: Dual spring fork
Wheelbase: 56.5in (143.5cm)
Weight: 235lb (107kg)
Fuel capacity: 1.5gal (5.7lit)
Oil capacity: 2qts (1.9lit)
Tires: 28 x 2.5in (71.1 x 6.35cm)
Top speed: 45mph (72km/h)
Colors: Black; renault gray
Number built: 54 (totals: 1,222 singles; 27 twins)
Price: $210 (battery), $250 (magneto)

Above: The "clutch" lever featured a spring-loaded thumb release and notches on the gate to ensure constant belt tension. The new simplified system moved the drive and tensioning pulleys closer together.

Above: The diagonal cover houses four gears carrying power from the crankshaft to the magneto. A new cylinder casting gave exhaust gases a more direct exit, and added finning meant a cooler and longer-lived exhaust valve.

MODEL 5 (1909)

After five years in the motorcycle business, Harley-Davidson was ready to take its place as an industry leader. The combined strategies of cautiously deliberate development, a network of trustworthy dealers and increased advertising were beginning to pay off.

The single, now designated the model 5, was the basic version; with battery and 28-inch (71cm) wheels, it was still priced at $210. The 5A pictured here, equipped with a Bosch magneto, was a hefty $40 more and only 54 were built. The factory also offered B and C models (battery or magneto) with 26-inch (66cm) wheels for shorter-legged riders.

The engine was slightly more powerful. With bore and stroke of 3.31 x 3.5 inches (84 x 89mm), displacement was up to 30.16 cubic inches (494cc) and a rating of 4.3 horsepower. Top speed was about 45mph (72km/h).

The big, if not necessarily good, news was the arrival of the much anticipated V-twin. The 45-degree inline twin was built on a beefed-up bottom end, with the magneto gear-driven off the crankshaft. The 3 x 3.5 inch (76 x 89mm) bore and stroke put displacement at 49 cubic inches (810cc). Rated at 7 horsepower, the 5D was reportedly good for 65mph (105km/h).

But at the price of $325, with no drive belt tensioner, the new twin didn't perform as Milwaukee had hoped. The engine was not easy to start, and the atmospheric inlet valves were at odds with the crankcase pressures of a V-twin. Only 27 of the twins were built, of which only two are known to remain in existence today.

The battery-equipped single accounted for the bulk of production in 1909, with more than 1,030 manufactured. The factory produced only 90 singles fitted with the magneto.

Linkage control rods for the throttle and spark advance had been replaced by wires routed through the handlebars. The oil tank was no longer strapped above the fuel tank. The new twin backbone frame carried a single tank with shared compartments; 1.5 gallons (5.7lit) for fuel and 2 quarts (1.9lit) of oil. The oil was delivered to the engine with a drip-feed line equipped with a sight glass. Wheelbase, as a result of development on the twin, had grown to 56.5 inches (143.5cm).

The Milwaukee motorcycles also received new styling touches in 1909. The longer fuel tank was tapered at both ends, and fitted flush with the rear downtube. The space between the rear fender and frame held a fitted compartment for tools, parts and riding accessories. The color choices remained renault gray or piano finish black.

Above: Once out of the city, the rider could lift the exhaust flap for higher performance.

1909 5A
Owner – Joy Baker
Vallejo, California
Restored by Marv Baker

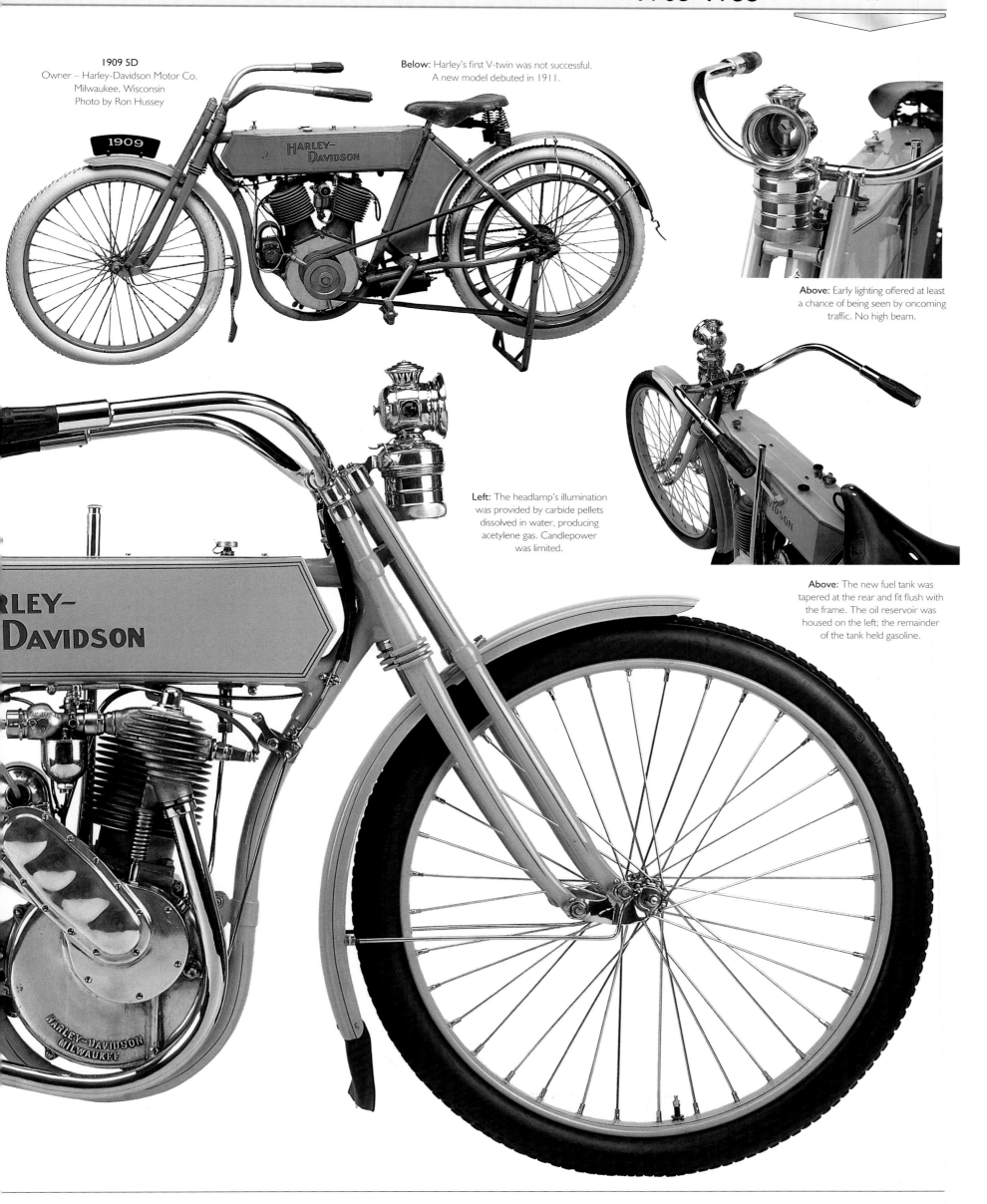

1909 5D
Owner – Harley-Davidson Motor Co.
Milwaukee, Wisconsin
Photo by Ron Hussey

Below: Harley's first V-twin was not successful. A new model debuted in 1911.

Above: Early lighting offered at least a chance of being seen by oncoming traffic. No high beam.

Left: The headlamp's illumination was provided by carbide pellets dissolved in water, producing acetylene gas. Candlepower was limited.

Above: The new fuel tank was tapered at the rear and fit flush with the frame. The oil reservoir was housed on the left; the remainder of the tank held gasoline.

MODELS 6 AND 7 (1910-11)

The singles went largely unchanged in 1910, but for the addition of an idler arm, allowing the rider to let the engine idle without disengaging the belt. Black paint was no longer offered, so all the Silent Gray Fellows were now gray. The V-twin was absent from the line, undergoing redesign for its reappearance in 1911.

But despite Milwaukee's disappointment with the results of its first twin, the overall picture for 1910 was hardly grim. The factory had grown to nearly 10,000 square feet (930m²), 149 workers were employed and production nearly tripled.

In four years there had been no increases in price. But in 1910, for the first time, a special model appeared on the roster. The 6E stock racer was priced at $275. A few 6E models, prototypes of the revised twin, were sold to bona fide racing customers.

Racers, and race-minded dealers, had for four years been badgering Milwaukee to produce a competition model. By 1909 the American motorcycle racing scene was booming, with board-track motordromes popping up all over the country, and fairground tracks hosting two-wheelers as well as equestrians.

Some half dozen manufacturers were building racing V-twins and singles by then, and several were achieving considerable success and subsequent publicity. Indian, Excelsior, Cyclone, Thor and Merkel were at the forefront, with European marques like J.A.P. and N.S.U. adding international flavor.

The more conservative elements in Milwaukee management (Arthur and Walter Davidson) were not interested in a factory-supported Harley-Davidson racing team. But pressure from customers, and the sentiments of Bill Harley and William Davidson, did result in the limited production of competition mounts built for sale to privateer racers. Only a few of the 3,168 motorcycles made for 1910 were racers, and no twins were put on the market.

However, the V-twin was back in 1911. Displacement remained at 49ci (810cc), but the new engine featured mechanical intake valves and a belt tensioner. Horsepower was rated at 6.5, just over two more ponies than the single. The cylinder heads on both singles and twins now had vertical rather than horizontal finning. The new twin's frame was reinforced and slightly lower than the original, and the front downtube was now straight on both the single and twin. Frames and bodywork remained gray, but broad striping in red or dark gray had replaced the pin stripes of earlier years.

Production numbers for 1911 are missing from the factory archives. Some early records were destroyed by a flood. Historian

1911 MODEL 7D

SPECIFICATIONS
ENGINE/DRIVETRAIN
Engine: IOE 45° V-twin
Displacement: 49.48ci (810cc)
Bore & stroke: 3 x 3.5in (76 x 89mm)
Horsepower: 6.5
Carburetion: Schebler
Transmission: Direct drive
Final drive: 1.75in (44mm) leather belt
Brake: Rear coaster
Ignition: Bosch magneto

CHASSIS/SUSPENSION
Frame: Steel, single downtube
Suspension: Dual spring fork
Wheelbase: 56.5in (143.5cm)
Weight: 295lb (134kg)
Fuel capacity: 2.5gal (9.5lit)
Oil capacity: 1gal (3.8lit)
Tires: 28 x 2.5in (71.1 x 6.35cm)
Top speed: 60mph (97km/h)
Color: Renault gray
Number built: Unknown
Price: $300

Right: Both the tires and belts had grown a bit wider by 1911. The coaster brake remained the sole stopping device. The new frame had a longer rear section, and the pedal sprocket had moved forward.

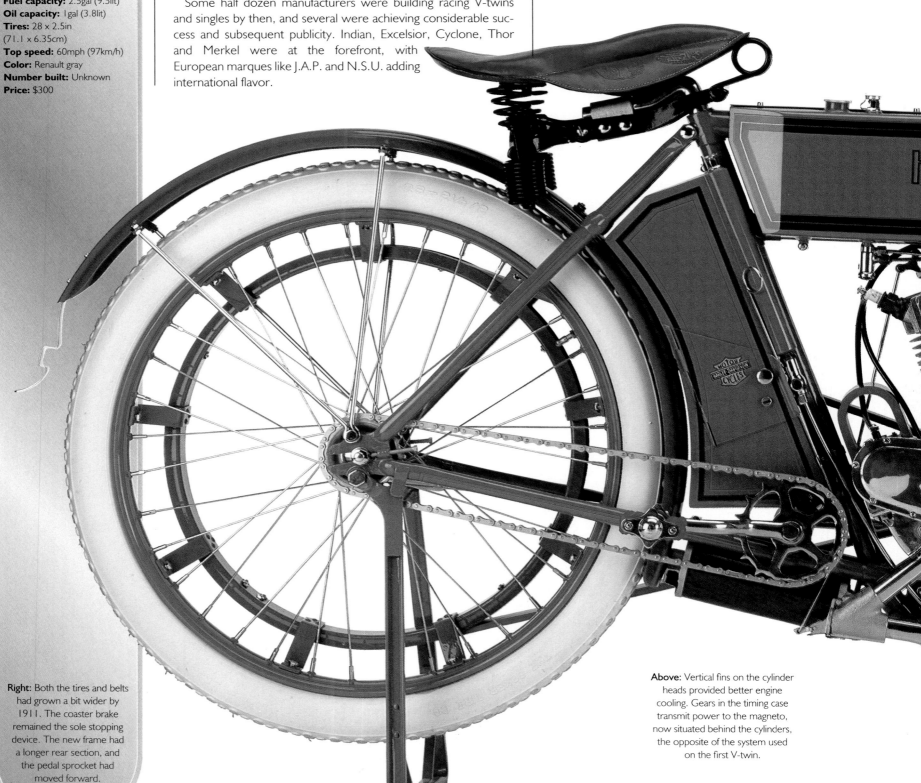

Above: Vertical fins on the cylinder heads provided better engine cooling. Gears in the timing case transmit power to the magneto, now situated behind the cylinders, the opposite of the system used on the first V-twin.

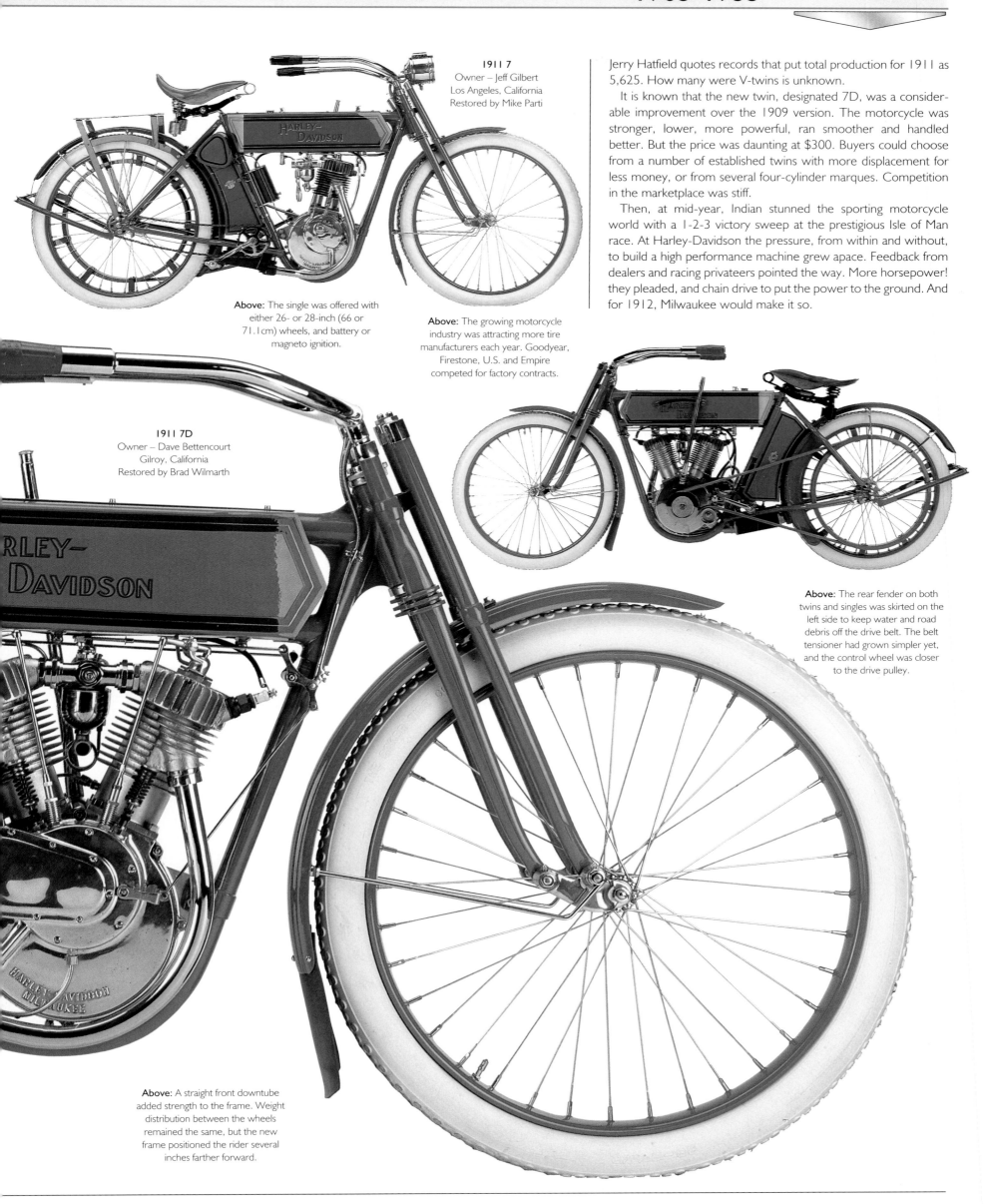

1911 7
Owner – Jeff Gilbert
Los Angeles, California
Restored by Mike Parti

Above: The single was offered with either 26- or 28-inch (66 or 71.1cm) wheels, and battery or magneto ignition.

Above: The growing motorcycle industry was attracting more tire manufacturers each year. Goodyear, Firestone, U.S. and Empire competed for factory contracts.

Jerry Hatfield quotes records that put total production for 1911 as 5,625. How many were V-twins is unknown.

It is known that the new twin, designated 7D, was a considerable improvement over the 1909 version. The motorcycle was stronger, lower, more powerful, ran smoother and handled better. But the price was daunting at $300. Buyers could choose from a number of established twins with more displacement for less money, or from several four-cylinder marques. Competition in the marketplace was stiff.

Then, at mid-year, Indian stunned the sporting motorcycle world with a 1-2-3 victory sweep at the prestigious Isle of Man race. At Harley-Davidson the pressure, from within and without, to build a high performance machine grew apace. Feedback from dealers and racing privateers pointed the way. More horsepower! they pleaded, and chain drive to put the power to the ground. And for 1912, Milwaukee would make it so.

1911 7D
Owner – Dave Bettencourt
Gilroy, California
Restored by Brad Wilmarth

Above: The rear fender on both twins and singles was skirted on the left side to keep water and road debris off the drive belt. The belt tensioner had grown simpler yet, and the control wheel was closer to the drive pulley.

Above: A straight front downtube added strength to the frame. Weight distribution between the wheels remained the same, but the new frame positioned the rider several inches farther forward.

1912 MODEL X8D AND E

SPECIFICATIONS
ENGINE/DRIVETRAIN
Engine: IOE 45° V-twin
Displacement: 60.32ci (989cc)
Bore & stroke: 3.5 x 3.3125in (89 x 84mm)
Horsepower: 8
Carburetion: Schebler
Transmission: Direct drive
Clutch: Rear hub
Final drive: Belt (X8D) or chain (X8E)
Brake: Rear coaster
Ignition: Bosch magneto

CHASSIS/SUSPENSION
Frame: Steel, single downtube
Suspension: Dual spring fork
Wheelbase: 56.5in (143.5cm)
Weight: 312lb (141.5kg)
Fuel capacity: 2.5gal (9.5lit)
Oil capacity: 1gal (3.8lit)
Tires: 28 x 2.5in (71 x 6.35cm)
Top speed: 65mph (105km/h)
Color: Renault gray
Number built: 1,616
Price: $285

1912 MODEL X8A

SPECIFICATIONS
ENGINE/DRIVETRAIN
Engine: IOE single
Displacement: 30.16ci (494.28cc)
Bore & stroke: 3.5 x 3.3125in (89 x 84mm)
Horsepower: 4.3
Carburetion: Schebler
Transmission: Direct drive
Clutch: Rear hub
Final drive: Belt
Brake: Rear coaster
Ignition: Bosch magneto

CHASSIS/SUSPENSION
Frame: Steel, single downtube
Suspension: Dual spring fork
Wheelbase: 56.5in (143.5cm)
Weight: 245lb (111kg)
Fuel capacity: 2.5gal (9.5lit)
Oil capacity: 1gal (3.8lit)
Tires: 28 x 2.5in (71.1 x 6.35cm)
Top speed: 50mph (80km/h)
Color: Renault gray
Number built: 545
Price: $225

Right: "Our claims that the Harley-Davidson is the cleanest, most silent, most comfortable, and the most economical motorcycle made, are rather broad, but can easily be verified. Its extreme cleanliness is due to the fact that all moving parts requiring oil are enclosed."

MODELS 8 AND X8 (1912)

The events of 1911 worked to make the following year a biggie in the motorcycle industry. Not necessarily in terms of production numbers, but in significant changes that would firmly set patterns for the future.

The racing push had actually begun in 1910, when Milwaukee began touting wins of privateers throughout the country. One flyer cited the Harley-Davidson singles that had finished 1-2 in the Denver to Greeley Road race, "Defeating the Time of the Fastest Double Cylinder Entry by Nearly Ten Minutes." The tagline was, "The Harley-Davidson Makes Good Because It Is Made Good". The road from Denver to Greeley was surely no stretch of smooth pavement in 1910, and top speed only counted if the engine didn't blow or the rider wasn't thrown off. So steady, reliable power and sturdy construction could win the day, which Milwaukee was proud to proclaim.

Prompted by Indian's success, the factory made numerous improvements to the motorcycles for 1912. (Note should be taken that Indian held technical superiority over its 1911 competitors at The Island. Most machines were still direct belt drive, while the 1,000cc Indian V-twin was a two-speed with chain drive,

Above: The lever adjacent to the tank operated Harley-Davidson's first clutch, located in the rear wheel hub.

1912 X8E
Owner – Jeff Gilbert
Los Angeles, California
Restored by Mike Parti

Above: A nine-inch (23cm) spring in the rear downtube helped isolate the rider from bumps. It was known variously as the original Ful-Floeting, or Floeting, seat, or spring suspension seat post.

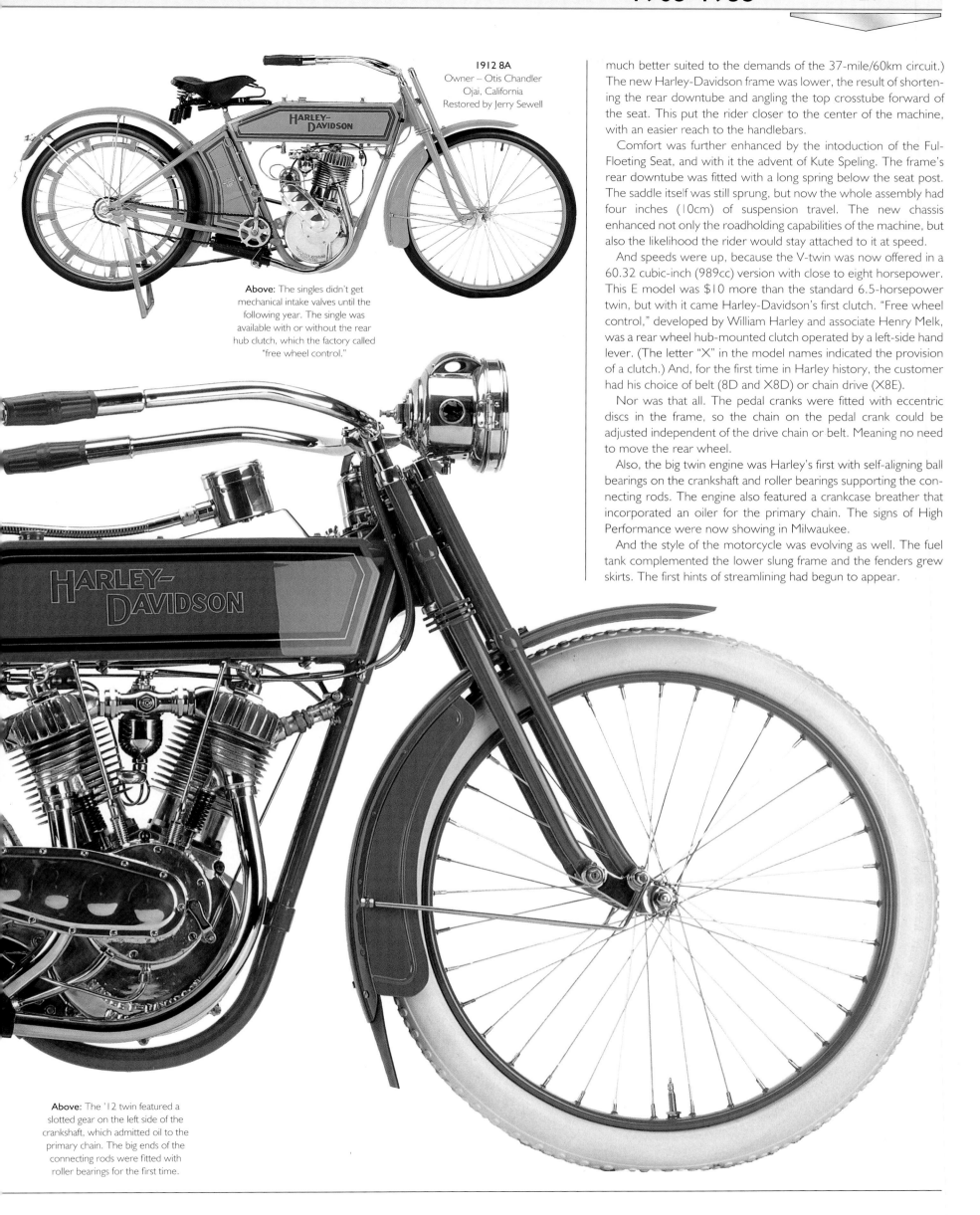

1912 8A
Owner – Otis Chandler
Ojai, California
Restored by Jerry Sewell

Above: The singles didn't get mechanical intake valves until the following year. The single was available with or without the rear hub clutch, which the factory called "free wheel control."

Above: The '12 twin featured a slotted gear on the left side of the crankshaft, which admitted oil to the primary chain. The big ends of the connecting rods were fitted with roller bearings for the first time.

much better suited to the demands of the 37-mile/60km circuit.) The new Harley-Davidson frame was lower, the result of shortening the rear downtube and angling the top crosstube forward of the seat. This put the rider closer to the center of the machine, with an easier reach to the handlebars.

Comfort was further enhanced by the intoduction of the Ful-Floeting Seat, and with it the advent of Kute Speling. The frame's rear downtube was fitted with a long spring below the seat post. The saddle itself was still sprung, but now the whole assembly had four inches (10cm) of suspension travel. The new chassis enhanced not only the roadholding capabilities of the machine, but also the likelihood the rider would stay attached to it at speed.

And speeds were up, because the V-twin was now offered in a 60.32 cubic-inch (989cc) version with close to eight horsepower. This E model was $10 more than the standard 6.5-horsepower twin, but with it came Harley-Davidson's first clutch. "Free wheel control," developed by William Harley and associate Henry Melk, was a rear wheel hub-mounted clutch operated by a left-side hand lever. (The letter "X" in the model names indicated the provision of a clutch.) And, for the first time in Harley history, the customer had his choice of belt (8D and X8D) or chain drive (X8E).

Nor was that all. The pedal cranks were fitted with eccentric discs in the frame, so the chain on the pedal crank could be adjusted independent of the drive chain or belt. Meaning no need to move the rear wheel.

Also, the big twin engine was Harley's first with self-aligning ball bearings on the crankshaft and roller bearings supporting the connecting rods. The engine also featured a crankcase breather that incorporated an oiler for the primary chain. The signs of High Performance were now showing in Milwaukee.

And the style of the motorcycle was evolving as well. The fuel tank complemented the lower slung frame and the fenders grew skirts. The first hints of streamlining had begun to appear.

1913 MODEL 9A

SPECIFICATIONS
ENGINE/DRIVETRAIN
Engine: IOE single
Displacement: 34.47ci
(564.89cc)
Bore & stroke: 3.31 x 4in
(84 x 102mm)
Horsepower: 4.5
Carburetion: Schebler
Transmission: Direct drive
Final drive: Belt (9A) or chain
(9B)
Brake: Rear coaster
Ignition: Bosch magneto

CHASSIS/SUSPENSION
Frame: Steel, single downtube
Suspension: Dual spring fork
Wheelbase: 56.5in (143.5cm)
Weight: 316lb (143kg)
Fuel capacity: 1.5gal (5.68lit)
Oil capacity: 3.5qts (3.3lit)
Tires: 28 x 2.75in (71.1 x 7cm)
Top speed: 50mph (80km/h)
Color: Renault gray
Number built: 1,510
Price: $290

Right: The 9A was the only
model with belt drive in 1913.
Tires (U.S., Empire or
Goodyear) on both the singles
and twins were still 28 inches
(71.1cm) in outside diameter,
but the width had grown to
2.75 inches (7cm).

MODEL 9 (1913)

Although the new V-twin outsold the single in 1912, the less expensive thumper still figured strongly in the motoring mix. Prosperity or not, not everyone could afford the big bike, and the single remained trustworthy and serviceable.

And it was larger. For 1913 Harley-Davidson announced what would come to be called the "5-35" motor; 5 horsepower and 35 cubic inches (565cc). The price was up to $290, for belt (9A) or chain drive (9B), which was $60 less than the V-twin (9E). Its instant popularity had bumped the price of the big-inch twin from $285 to $350.

Of course the single had benefited from the development work devoted to its big brother. Mechanically operated intake valve, lighter alloy piston and improved carburetion were included in the package. And the factory now balanced the flywheel, rod and piston as an assembly, gaining smoother engine operation.

The color choice remained gray, and all models were fitted with 28 x 2.75-inch (71.1 x 7cm) tires. The single still carried its oil supply in a compartment within the fuel tank. The bicycle pedals also remained, but the single now featured the rear hub clutch. Starting was still a matter of pedaling while on the centerstand, or pushing and running alongside.

The 5-35 soon proved itself on the road and in amateur racing around the country, and the 61-inch (1000cc) V-twin had also been posting winning results in major events in 1912. Harley riders won the Bakersfield and San Jose roadraces, and were 1-2-3 in a 1913 race from Harrisburg to Philadelphia and back. In Milwaukee, Bill Harley was finishing up his plans for the creation of a factory racing team.

Phase One of the plan was to hire Bill Ottaway as manager of the racing department and, ultimately, the racing team. Ottaway had worked as a development engineer for Thor Motorcycles, built by the Aurora Automatic Machine Tool Company of Aurora, Illinois. He had worked on Thor's 61-inch (1000cc) V-twin racer, which was outgunned by the Indian twin introduced in 1912, featuring four overhead valves per cylinder. The racing game was heating up nicely.

Milwaukee's official racing department wouldn't be announced until the following year, but work was obviously underway in advance. That included plans for Milwaukee's own 8-valve V-twin, which would become far and away the most expensive motorcycle Harley-Davidson had yet offered for sale.

In its first ten years, Harley-Davidson advanced with deliberate caution in developing new motorcycles. Nearly 100 other domestic manufacturers had come and gone in that time, and the founders were determined that if only a few builders were to survive in the business, they would be among them. Other companies might choose to experiment with new designs and materials, or invest in expensive tooling for limited production racers, and Milwaukee would take note of the results. And respond only if and when they considered it necessary.

Production and profits were up in 1913, with 12,966 motorcycles built. Two items headed the development list: more horsepower and more gears. Both were forthcoming.

1913 9A
Owner – Armando Magri
H-D of Sacramento, California

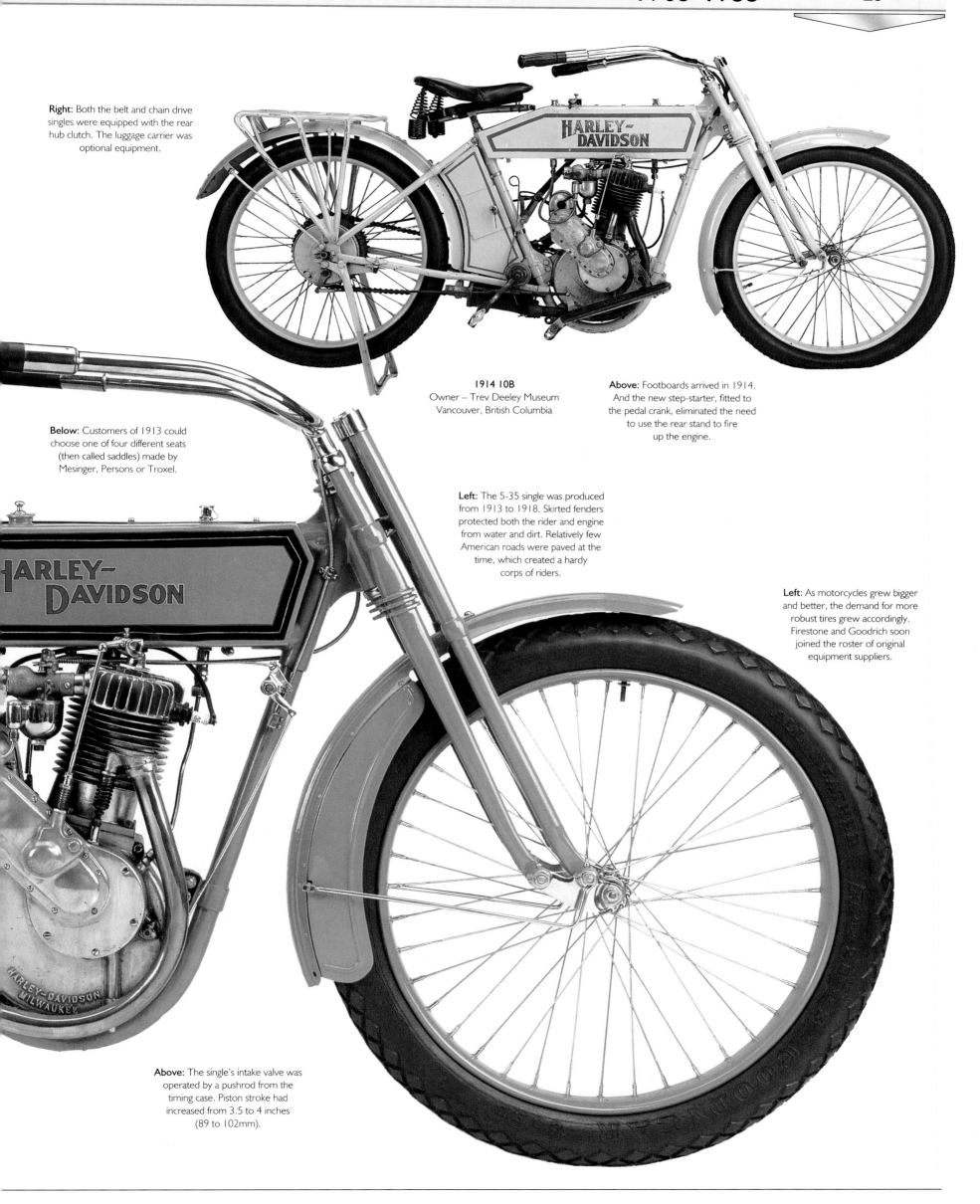

Right: Both the belt and chain drive singles were equipped with the rear hub clutch. The luggage carrier was optional equipment.

1914 10B
Owner – Trev Deeley Museum
Vancouver, British Columbia

Above: Footboards arrived in 1914. And the new step-starter, fitted to the pedal crank, eliminated the need to use the rear stand to fire up the engine.

Below: Customers of 1913 could choose one of four different seats (then called saddles) made by Mesinger, Persons or Troxel.

Left: The 5-35 single was produced from 1913 to 1918. Skirted fenders protected both the rider and engine from water and dirt. Relatively few American roads were paved at the time, which created a hardy corps of riders.

Left: As motorcycles grew bigger and better, the demand for more robust tires grew accordingly. Firestone and Goodrich soon joined the roster of original equipment suppliers.

Above: The single's intake valve was operated by a pushrod from the timing case. Piston stroke had increased from 3.5 to 4 inches (89 to 102mm).

MODEL 10F (1914) AND 11K RACER (1915)

1914 MODEL 10F

SPECIFICATIONS
ENGINE/DRIVETRAIN
Engine: F-head 45° V-twin
Displacement: 49.48ci (810.83cc)
Bore & stroke: 3.0 x 3.5in (76.2 x 89mm)
Compression ratio: n/a
Horsepower: 6.5
Transmission: 2-speed
Primary drive: Chain
Final drive: Chain
Brake: Rear coaster
Ignition: Magneto

CHASSIS/SUSPENSION
Frame: Steel, single downtube
Suspension: F. Dual spring fork
Wheelbase: 56.5in (143.5cm)
Weight: 310lb (140.6kg)
Fuel capacity: 2.5gal (9.46lit)
Oil capacity: 4qts (3.79lit)
Tires: 28 x 3.0in (71.1 x 7.62cm)
Top speed: 65mph (105km/h)
Color: Harley-Davidson gray
Number built: 7,956
Price: $285

Motorcycle technology Milwaukee-style took several more leaps in 1914. Two-speed transmissions, step-starters, footboards, enclosed valve springs and primary chains, and sidecars all debuted as the popularity of motorcycling boomed.

Harley-Davidson enjoyed a considerable measure of this mushrooming market, but was forced to share it with at least three other entrepreneurs of the age. They were George Hendee at Indian, Ignatz Schwinn of Excelesior, and the Henderson brothers, who built Ace Motorcycles. And there was one other motoring mogul in rapid rise at the time, Henry Ford.

Automobiles, like motorcycles, were still hand-made, but the advent of moving assembly lines boosted car production enormously. The mass production of motorcycles would be forever limited by the affordability of cars, and two-wheelers began the shift to sport and recreational machines rather than primary transportation. The competition for a market share of the smaller pie had grown intense.

Despite its well-deserved reputation for sturdy equipment and reliable performance, Harley-Davidson was losing the public popularity contest generated by motorcycle racing. If the machines were to be cast forever in the sporting mode, then the successful builder was obliged to meet the requirements of the sporting

rider. At the same time, the Milwaukee faction knew that the touring and Sunday-putt riders would always outnumber the young daredevils. So the task was to provide motorcycles for both.

The combined appeals of horsepower and operating ease were addressed differently by the industry leaders. The contest pitted the V-twins of Indian and Harley-Davidson against the inline fours from Henderson. The four was smooth and powerful, but more expensive to manufacture and maintain. The V-twins were less smooth but reliable, and acquitted themselves well in uses where top speed mattered little. Economics would eventually decide in the twins' favor, but the fours remained an option into the late 1920s.

Both Milwaukee and Springfield were banking on the V-twin's popularity. And Indian was forcing Harley's hand by providing sport racers to the public at low prices, and by sponsoring talented riders in closed circuit and cross country competitions. The biggest, literally, thorn in Milwaukee's side was the formidable Irwin G. "Cannonball" Baker. A large and powerful man, Baker was the dominant long-distance rider of the era. And he generated headlines for the sport and the builders of his winning machines.

Harley-Davidson had decided to first challenge the Indian team on the racetrack. The racer, designated the K model, was based

Below: Production models were all equipped with luggage carrier and Free Wheel Control. The two-speed rear hub was developed by Bill Harley and racing manager William Ottaway.

Below: The Ful-Floeting seat was also standard on all models.

By 1914 the U.S. Postal Service had nearly 5,000 Harley-Davidsons for mail delivery. Milwaukee supplied the British military with 350 motorcycles at the advent of World War I.

Above: The new internal expanding band rear brake could be applied either by the forward brake pedal or by reverse pressure on the bicycle pedals. Footboards were standard equipment.

on the model 10E, a direct chain drive, 61-inch (1000cc) V-twin. The race motors were marked by an M preceding the engine number. A handful were built for 1914, and by the following year Milwaukee had a brace of eight racing models in the catalog – six twins and two singles. Of the 16,427 production machines built for 1914, more than 13,000 were twins.

The showdown for racing supremacy was at hand. Although the first factory team bikes could match the Indians for top speed, reliability was not so high on the scale. These were long races, 200 to 300 miles (320 to 480km), and the Harleys suffered engine and driveline failures. However, the team did win one national championship race at Birmingham, Alabama in 1914, and the Harley Wrecking Crew would be in full battle trim for the 1915 season.

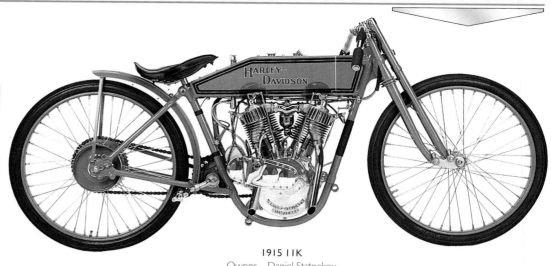

1915 11K
Owner – Daniel Statnekov
Tesuque, New Mexico

Right: The headlight's gas cannister was mounted between the handlebars.

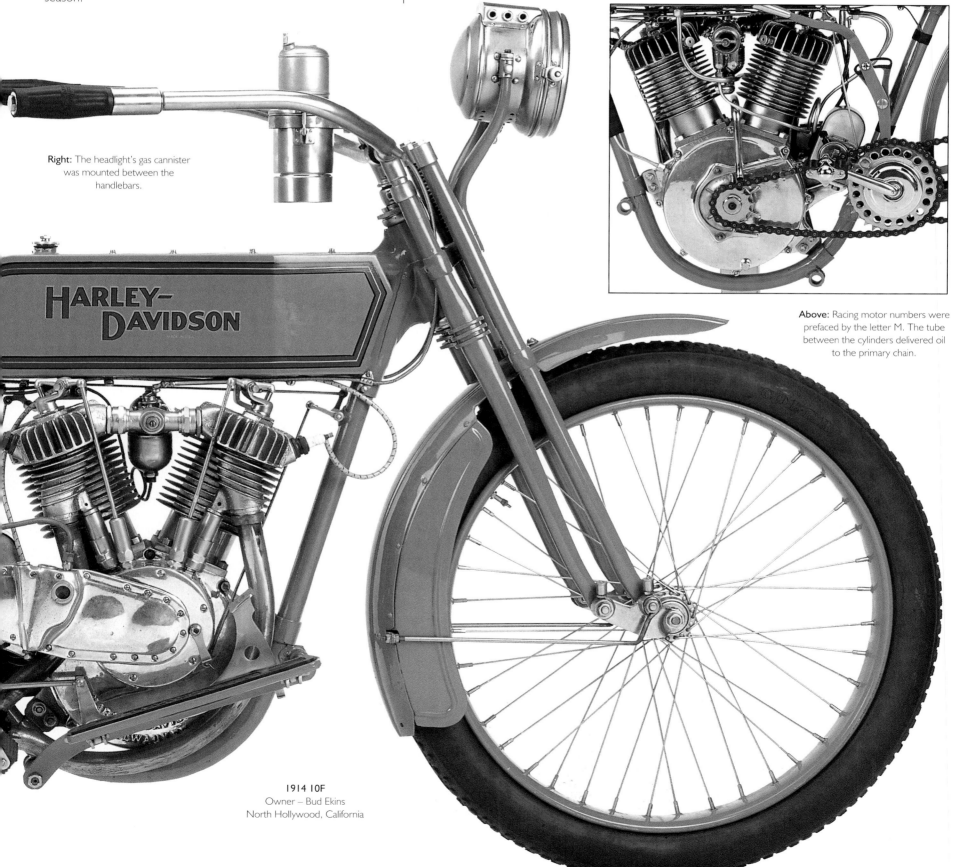

Above: Racing motor numbers were prefaced by the letter M. The tube between the cylinders delivered oil to the primary chain.

1914 10F
Owner – Bud Ekins
North Hollywood, California

MODEL 11J (1915), MODEL 16J (1916) AND SIDECAR

MODEL 16J (1916)

SPECIFICATIONS
ENGINE/DRIVETRAIN
Engine: F-head 45° V-twin
Displacement: 60.33ci
(987.67cc)
Bore & stroke: 3 .31 x 3.5in
(84 x 89mm)
Horsepower: 11 @ 3,000 rpm
Carburetion: Schebler
Transmission: 3-speed
Primary drive: Chain
Final drive: Chain
Brake: Rear drum
Battery: 6-volt
Ignition: Coil/points

CHASSIS/SUSPENSION
Frame: Steel, single downtube
Suspension: F. Leading link
spring fork
Wheelbase: 59.5in (151.1cm)
Weight: 325lb (147.4kg)
Fuel capacity: 2.75gal (10.4lit)
Oil capacity: 5pts (2.4lit)
Tires: 28 x 3in (71.1 x 7.62cm)
Top speed: 60mph (97km/h)
Color: Harley-Davidson gray
Number built: 5,898
Price: $295

Harley-Davidson had a roster
of five models in 1914, three
singles and two twins. For
1915 the selection had grown
to 16 machines, with the
options of battery or
magneto. Eight of the
motorcycles were racing
bikes.

Milwaukee had shown in 1914 that it was ready and able to build modern motorcycles. In 1915 Harley-Davidson not only quickened the pace of improvement, but also displayed its new commitment to professional racing.

The most significant advance for road and track was the introduction of a 3-speed transmission. The sliding-gear mechanism provided attachment of the step starter to the gearbox. With transmission and clutch fitted amidships, the 11J certified Harley's position in the mainstream of American motorcycle manufacturing. It was also the first model equipped with an electric headlight.

At $310, the J model carried a hefty price tag. The 60-inch twin (989cc) with magneto was offered at $240 for the single-speed version (11E) and $275 for the three-speed (11F). Two singles remained in the catalog, the one-speed B and two-speed C models at $200 and $230 respectively. The racing K model ("stripped stock") was priced at $250.

Racing would provide Milwaukee with substantial bragging rights in 1915. Following the factory team's marginal success the preceding season, Bill Harley and William Ottaway brought new determination, and equipment, to the line for the following year. Of the 17 models now offered in the catalog, eight were racing bikes.

The sidecar also took on new stature in 1915. A new chassis and longer body replaced the original model, and advertising emphasized the economic benefits of sidecar travel. The chairs or sidehacks as they came to be called, also found wide application in the postal and military services. The early sidecar bodies were built by the Seaman Company in Milwaukee. Right-side chairs were designed for the U.S. and Europe, while left-side rigs were fitted for the British market.

Most of the military motorcycles Harley-Davidson built for use in World War I were equipped with sidecars. Though employed mostly for reconnaissance and courier duty, the sidecars could be fitted with armor and machine-gun mounts. The same chassis was utilized for commercial civilian use to mount a sidevan.

One requirement shared by racers and sidecarists was the need for more power. Harley-Davidson advertised a guaranteed 11 horsepower from the 61-inch (1000cc) V-twin, noting that dynamometer readings had been as high as 16 horsepower. The racing engines were said to be making nearly 20.

These increases were largely the result of better intake and exhaust design, with larger ports, valves and carburetors. Beefier rod bearings, flywheels and crankpins were designed to handle the higher horsepower. And as we have noted, the engineering efforts were certified on the race track.

But despite the improvements and convincing victories in racing, the sales figures failed to rise accordingly. The impact of Henry Ford's manufacturing and marketing techniques had seriously constricted the U.S. motorcycle market. And even though the number of prospective buyers remained more or less static, the competition for market share was ever more rigorous.

In 1916 Harley-Davidson introduced its step-starter and dispensed with the last major bicycle component. The pedals were gone, at least on the twins with gearboxes. The model numbering system was also changed, brought up to date by using the current year as the prefix. And this would be the last year for gray paint.

Engineering changes included stronger frames that were common to singles and twins. Both were available with either direct drive or the 3-speed transmission. The basic twin with magneto sold for $240, while the gear-selecting version with battery and lights went for $295. The single-speed single was $200 and another $30 was added for the 3-speed.

Functional development resulted in styling shifts as well. The larger fuel tank and fenders featured more rounded shapes, as the first hints of streamlining appeared from Milwaukee.

As it turned out, Harley-Davidson's characteristic prudence in product development was to serve the company well in this circumscribed marketplace.

Below: The fuel tank on the '16 was more rounded than its counterpart of a year earlier (upper right). The left side now held compartments for oil and fuel, rather than oil only as before.

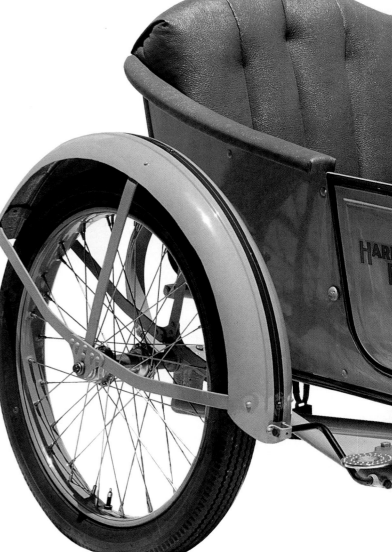

1916 16F
Owner/restorer – Mike Parti
North Hollywood, California

Left: Twentieth century or not, electric lighting was not immediately popular among motorcyclists. Gas illumination may have been marginal, but gave some warning before failing completely.

1915 11J
Owner/restorer – Bud Ekins
North Hollywood, California

Right: The kick-starter was new for 1916. The bulge in the timing cover housed the oil pump; the brass collar held a sight glass for checking oil flow. Note ratchet mechanism on brake pedal, used for parking brake on sidecar models.

Above: The tank-mounted hand shift operated the 3-speed transmission. The lower lever engaged the clutch when the left foot was in use for uphill starts. Note absence of pedals.

Left: In 1916 the frame was reinforced for sidecar use, and the steering head bearings were enlarged. The front fork was wider and the larger fender more curved.

Left: The Prest-O-Lite acetylene tank was mounted at the bottom rear of the sidecar. The chair was suspended by leaf springs on both sides, offering the passenger the most comfortable ride.

8 VALVE RACER

SPECIFICATIONS
ENGINE/DRIVETRAIN
Engine: OHV 45° V-twin
Displacement: 60.33ci (987.67cc)
Bore & stroke: 3.31 x 3.5in (84 x 89mm)
Compression ratio: Approx 6:1
Horsepower: Approx 14-16
Carburetion: Schebler
Transmission: Direct drive
Primary drive: Chain
Final drive: Chain
Brake: None
Battery: None
Ignition: Magneto

CHASSIS/SUSPENSION
Frame: Steel, single downtube
Suspension: F. Leading link spring fork
Wheelbase: 51.5in (130.8cm)
Weight: 275lb (124.7kg)
Fuel capacity: 1.43gal (5.4lit)
Oil capacity: 5pts (2.4lit)
Tires: 28 x 3in (71 x 7.62cm)
Top speed: 105-115mph (170-185km/h)
Color: Olive green
Number built: Approx 30-50
Price: $1,500

Right: The 8-valve racer was the result of another collaboration between Bill Harley and racing manger William Ottaway. The $1,500 price, more than four times its Indian counterpart, intentionally discouraged privateers.

8-VALVE RACER (1916-1928)

The Indian Motocycle Company of Springfield, Massachusetts dominated the first two decades of American motorcycling. Owner George Hendee and engineer Oscar Hedstrom were innovators in early technology, and also committed the company to a strong program of factory-supported racing.

Indian had presented its first factory racers in 1908, and quickly established a reputation as tough competitors. With their resounding 1-2-3 placing at the Isle of Man in 1911, the Springfield bunch initiated a string of racing victories that produced growing publicity and sales. Milwaukee soon realized that Something Had To Be Done.

William Harley was convinced early on that factory support for racing had tangible promotional value. It took him several years to convince Walter and Arthur Davidson that winning races would mean selling more machines to the general public. And Indian was busy proving his point.

By this time it was generally accepted that more horsepower required the movement of more air-fuel mixture in and out of the engine. The vague concepts of motorcycle handling had barely reached the drawing board. Top speed was the issue at hand, and overhead valves were one way to get it.

So Milwaukee reached corporate consensus, more or less, on a factory team in 1913. William Ottaway, a development engineer for Thor Motorcycles of Aurora, Illinois was hired to build racing engines based on the 61-inch (1000cc) twin. When the season opened in 1915, the first and last great racing battle between American motorcycle companies was joined.

Indian had introduced its 8-valve racing machine in 1912, and offered it for public sale at little more than the conventional road model. The Federation of American Motorcyclists (F.A.M.), in the interest of ensuring a level playing field, stipulated that manufacturers must offer their racers for public sale. But they said nothing about price. So Milwaukee priced the new 8-valve at $1,500 to discourage privateers, and it worked. No record has been turned up showing civilian ownership of a Harley 8-valve until after the factory team was dissolved.

Just how many of the 8-valves were built is unknown. Even among expert historians and restorers there is wide disagreement; some say as few as ten were built, others say it was more like 50. A number of engines were sent to England, Europe and Australia, and some machines were converted to singles. Since the 8-valve was still available as late as 1928, an educated guess puts the total somewhere between 30 and 50 bikes.

According to the company history, the first three OHV racers were built in 1916. One had a manual oil pump, one a mechanical pump and the third was fitted with one each. The machines

Below: The racer featured the least of everything but motor. Pedals were strapped to the frame, serving only as footrests. Starting was by tow rope.

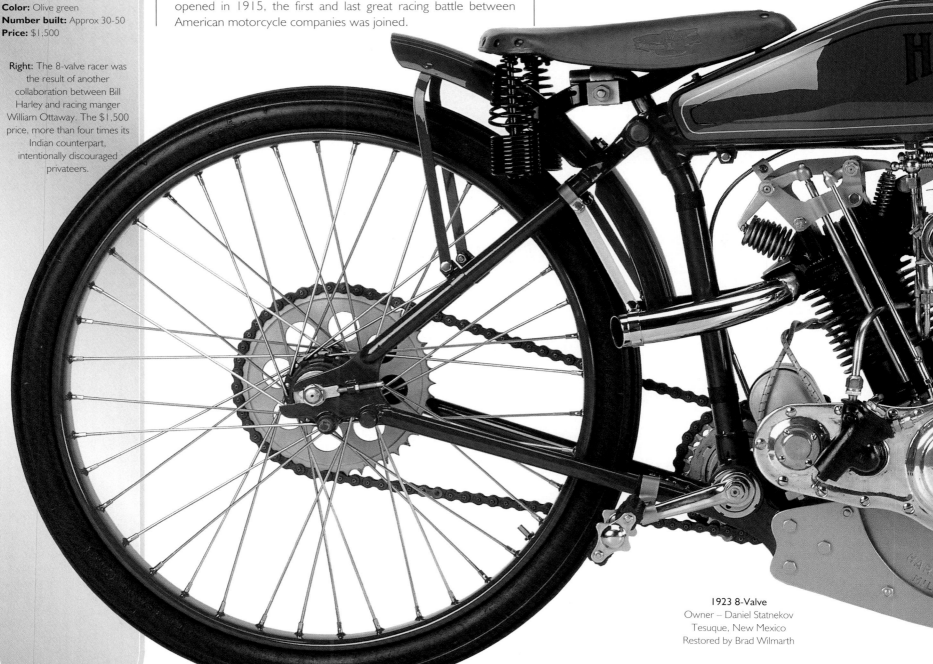

1923 8-Valve
Owner – Daniel Statnekov
Tesuque, New Mexico
Restored by Brad Wilmarth

were relatively short-coupled, with wheelbase at about 50 inches (127cm). The bikes had a keystone frame, with front and rear downtubes bolted to plates attached to the engine, making it a stressed member.

These engines made good power, probably close to 20 when the weather was right. Compression ratios were elevated considerably, and starting procedures usually required a tow rope and a car. It wasn't long before these machines were averaging over 100mph (161km/h) on the board tracks. By then the pocket-valve engines were only a few ticks slower, and often carried the day when the 8-valves expired from fried valves, seizures or fractured engine components.

Harley-Davidson advertised the 8-valve ($1,500) and the 4-valve single ($1,400) as a gesture of compliance with the F.A.M. edict. The motor was "air-cooled, piston displacement not exceeding 61cu.in. Mechanical construction to meet any requirements." The lubrication – "Hand pump or mechanical pump, either or both, or any oiling system deemed advisable for the safety or convenience of the rider."

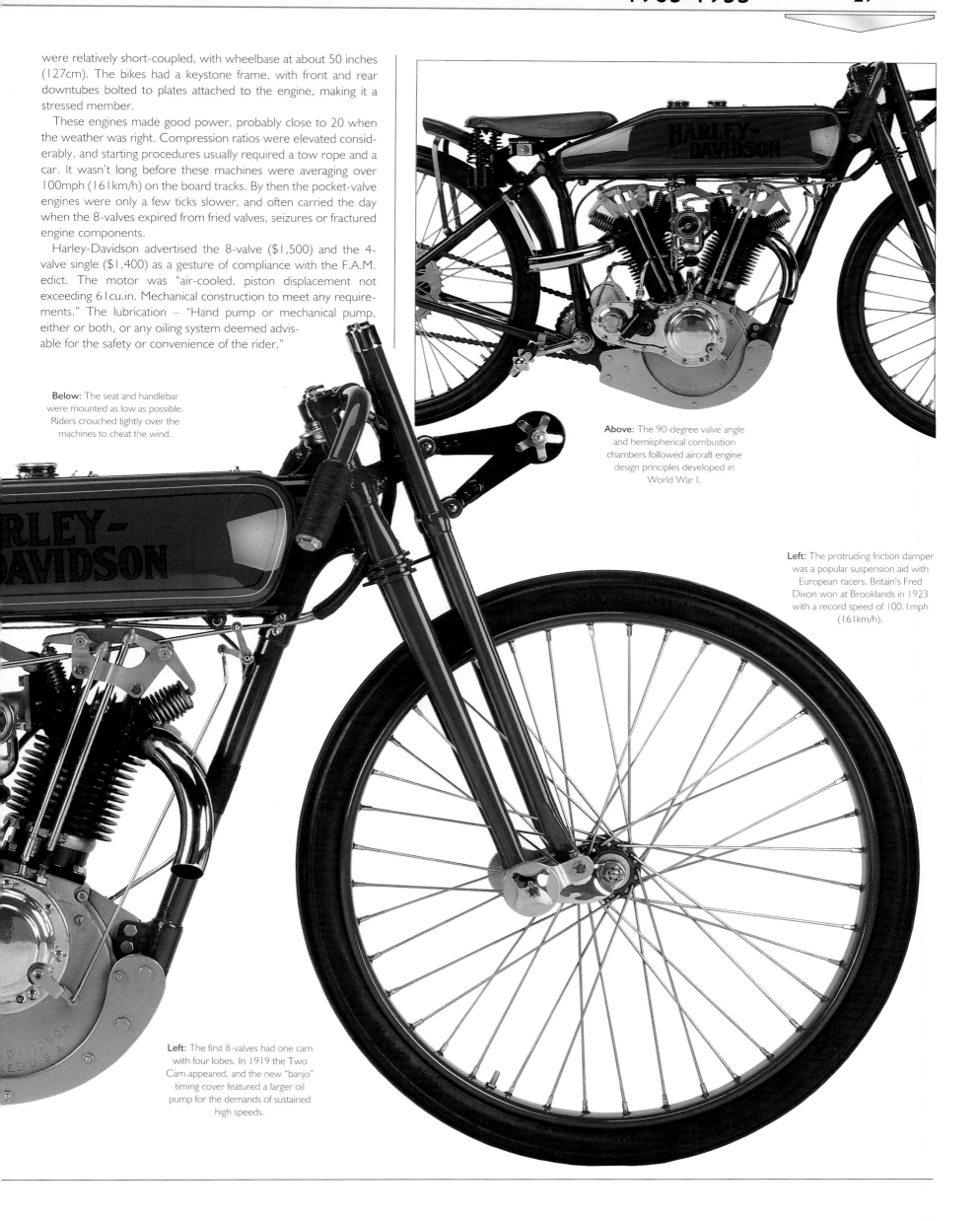

Below: The seat and handlebar were mounted as low as possible. Riders crouched tightly over the machines to cheat the wind.

Above: The 90-degree valve angle and hemispherical combustion chambers followed aircraft engine design principles developed in World War I.

Left: The protruding friction damper was a popular suspension aid with European racers. Britain's Fred Dixon won at Brooklands in 1923 with a record speed of 100.1mph (161km/h).

Left: The first 8-valves had one cam with four lobes. In 1919 the Two Cam appeared, and the new "banjo" timing cover featured a larger oil pump for the demands of sustained high speeds.

1917 MODEL J

SPECIFICATIONS
ENGINE/DRIVETRAIN
Engine: F-head 45° V-twin
Displacement: 60.33ci
(987.67cc)
Bore & stroke: 3.31 x 3.5
(84 x 89mm)
Horsepower: 16 @ 3,000 rpm
Carburetion: Schebler
Transmission: 3-speed
Primary drive: Chain
Final drive: Chain
Brake: Rear expanding band
Battery: 6-volt
Ignition: Coil/points

CHASSIS/SUSPENSION
Frame: Steel, single downtube
Suspension: F. Leading link
spring fork
Wheelbase: 59.5in (151cm)
Weight: 325lb (147.4kg)
Fuel capacity: 2.75gal (10.4lit)
Oil capacity: 5pts (2.36lit)
Tires: 28 x 3in (71.1 x 7.62cm)
Top speed: 65mph (105km/h)
Color: Olive green
Number built: 9,180
Price: $310

In 1917 Milwaukee switched
from gray to olive green paint,
apparently in over-supply
during the war years.
Although the factory referred
to the color as "military drab,"
the paint actually had a high-
gloss finish.

MODEL 17J (1917)

The early '17 models were the last of the Silent Gray Fellows as World War I brought the advent of the Silent Green Soldiers, or the Olive Drab Doughboys.

From the Harley-Davidson brochure: "It is a really strange co-incidence that within recent years various governments of the world have selected this color as the most serviceable for government equipment such as motorcycles, automobiles and motor trucks. The new military drab color furnishes a most delightful contrast with the handsome satin nickel finish used on many of the motor parts."

Serviceable indeed. Olive green would become Milwaukee's standard color for years beyond the military conflict. But for a brief interlude of darker brewster green in the early 1920s, Harley-Davidson stretched its supply of olive green paint until the 1932 model year.

In 1917 the V-twin inherited the four-lobe cam designed for the 8-valve racer. Valve lift and timing were revised for the demands of increased performance. The gear-driven oil pump, introduced in 1915, ensured that lubrication was delivered in proper amounts to the critical moving parts. The earlier hand pump and drip-feed oiling systems often created either a shortage or surplus of oil in the engine, both of which meant problems.

For sidecar use, Milwaukee recommended the 14-tooth countershaft sprocket for a higher gear ratio. The order blank noted: "This motor develops slightly less speed but gives maximum efficiency where power is needed. This motor can also be used satisfactorily for solo riding."

The sidecar enjoyed its highest popularity in this heady era that created rural mail delivery and mechanized warfare. Although Indian was the primary supplier of military motorcycles during World War I, Milwaukee provided its share of motorcycles with

Above: Two-piece spark plugs could be disassembled for cleaning.

Above: The sight-glass on the oil pump remained for many years. Recirculation of oil was 20 years away.

Below: The speedometer cable took power from the rear wheel to the instrument on the fuel tank. Driving ring gear is missing on this example.

Right: The Ful-Floeting seat received covers for its external springs. Thus began the shift toward the modern age, in which mechanical bits were enclosed.

1917 17J
Owner – Harold Mathews
Mathews Harley-Davidson
Fresno, California

sidecars rigged for combat. The "standard pleasure sidecar" for civilian use sold for $80.

According to the advertising copy, "the sidecar in the new color is a real beauty. Finished as it is in the new military drab, the strikingly handsome lines of the body are set off better than ever by near brewster green striping." Genuine brewster green was probably unavailable during the war. That was the case with German Bosch magnetos, which were replaced by American-made units.

By this point the V-twin's popularity had limited the single to mostly commercial and racing applications. Of the 18,522 motorcycles built by Harley-Davidson for 1917, only about 730 were singles. But Milwaukee had taken note of the demand for a lightweight sporting machine, and concluded that a smaller twin would be the logical choice. So work began on the Sport Model W, a 36 cubic-inch (584cc) opposed twin that would appear in 1919.

Right: A speedometer was an extra-cost accessory. The top needle remained on highest speed gained; 79mph (127km/h) indicates long downhill, strong tailwind or both.

Below: Firestone Tires put their advertising where the rubber meets the road. To motorcyclists, few words are more reassuring than Non-Skid.

Below: This restoration is un-striped. The tanks were outlined with a stripe of Pullman green with gold borders and centerline.

Above: The intake valve springs were enclosed in 1917, and valve timing on the intake side revised for more power. The war eliminated Bosch magnetos, which were replaced by Dixie units.

SPECIFICATIONS
ENGINE/DRIVETRAIN
Engine: Flathead opposed twin
Displacement: 35.64ci
(584.03cc)
Bore & stroke: 2.75 x 3in
(70 x 76.2mm)
Compression ratio: 3.75:1
Horsepower: 6
Carburetion: Schebler
Transmission: Unit 3-speed
Primary drive: Helical gears
Final drive: Enclosed chain
Brake: Rear contracting band
Ignition: Magneto

CHASSIS/SUSPENSION
Frame: Steel, single downtube
Suspension: Trailing link single
spring fork
Wheelbase: 57in (144.8cm)
Weight: 265lb (120kg)
Fuel capacity: 2.75gal (10.4lit)
Oil capacity: 2qts (1.9lit)
Tires: 26 x 3in (66 x 7.62cm)
Top speed: 50mph (80.5km/h)
Color: Olive green
Number built: 753 in 1919
(Total production: 9,883)
Price: $335

MODEL W SPORT TWIN (1919)

As American motorcycling shifted focus after the war from transportation to recreation mode, the interest in lightweight sport bikes rose accordingly. Harley-Davidson responded with the Model W Sport Twin, a 36ci (584cc) horizontally opposed twin featuring an integral 3-speed transmission.

Set lengthwise and low in the frame, the flathead boxer engine had a large external flywheel and an enclosed drive chain. Given the nearly perfect primary balance factor of this engine design, the Sport Twin was by far the smoothest running Harley-Davidson ever built, past or present. The motor, rated at a meager 6 horsepower, was comfortably understressed and the motorcycle weighed only 265 pounds (120kg).

Patterned after the British Douglas, the W model was a radical departure for Harley-Davidson in terms of design and engineering. The chassis incorporated a keystone frame, utilizing the engine as a stressed member. While that feature was familiar on the 8-valve racer, everything else about the Sport Model was different from the V-twins.

The intake and exhaust manifolds were long, siamesed tubes along the right side of the engine. The prevailing notion held that preheating the intake charge enhanced the combustion process. A single camshaft operated all four valves. The screw-in valve guides were easily accessible for replacement, and the valves could be removed without pulling the engine. The cylinders and heads were still a single casting, but they could also be detached without removing the engine. Ease of maintenance and the accessibility of components had played a role in the motorcycle's design.

Roller bearings supported both the crankshaft and connecting rods, and the geared primary drove the wet clutch and magneto mounted atop the engine. The early models came with magnetos and with or without acetylene lights. From 1921 through its final year in 1923, the Sport Twin was offered with either magneto ignition (WF) or battery (WJ).

The sporty twin also incorporated a fork unlike other Harley models. The trailing lower links connected by rods to upper links acting on a central spring. The fender, attached to the Merkel-style truss fork, was stationary as the front wheel moved up and down. Rear suspension was absent save the enclosed springs beneath the solo saddle. The fuel tank, which carried 2.75 gallons (10.4lit) of gas and two quarts (1.9lit) of oil, was situated between the upper frame tubes. The rear luggage rack was standard equipment.

Despite its shortage of both horsepower and ground clearance, the Sport Twin was a record-setting machine. Rider Hap Scherer set a winning time in the 3-Flags run from Canada to Mexico, and the WJ was the first motorcycle to ascend California's Mt. Baldy.

Unfortunately these victories had little effect on the Sport's popularity. The V-twin had been firmly established as the American motorcycle engine of choice, whether in medium, large or extra large. Utilitarian twins of non-V configuration were met with general disinterest in the United States. It was Milwaukee's good fortune that such was not the case in Europe.

The Douglas brothers of Bristol, England had developed a popular opposed twin, with the aid of Freddy Dixon. With the British motorcycle industry hobbled by the war, the market was ripe for overseas manufacturers. Thus Milwaukee's lightweights sold well in Great Britain and Europe.

Below: Luggage carrier was standard equipment on the Model W. Tires fitted to this 1919 version are larger than the original rubber.

Right: The horizontally opposed Sport Twin engine was unlike any Harley-Davidson before or since. Though advanced in many respects, the lightweight sport model achieved little success in the U.S., trailing behind Indian's Scout.

Above: The single-casting intake/exhaust manifold was something of a curiosity. Preheating the charge was thought to improve combustion. The mixture took a long trip from the carburetor.

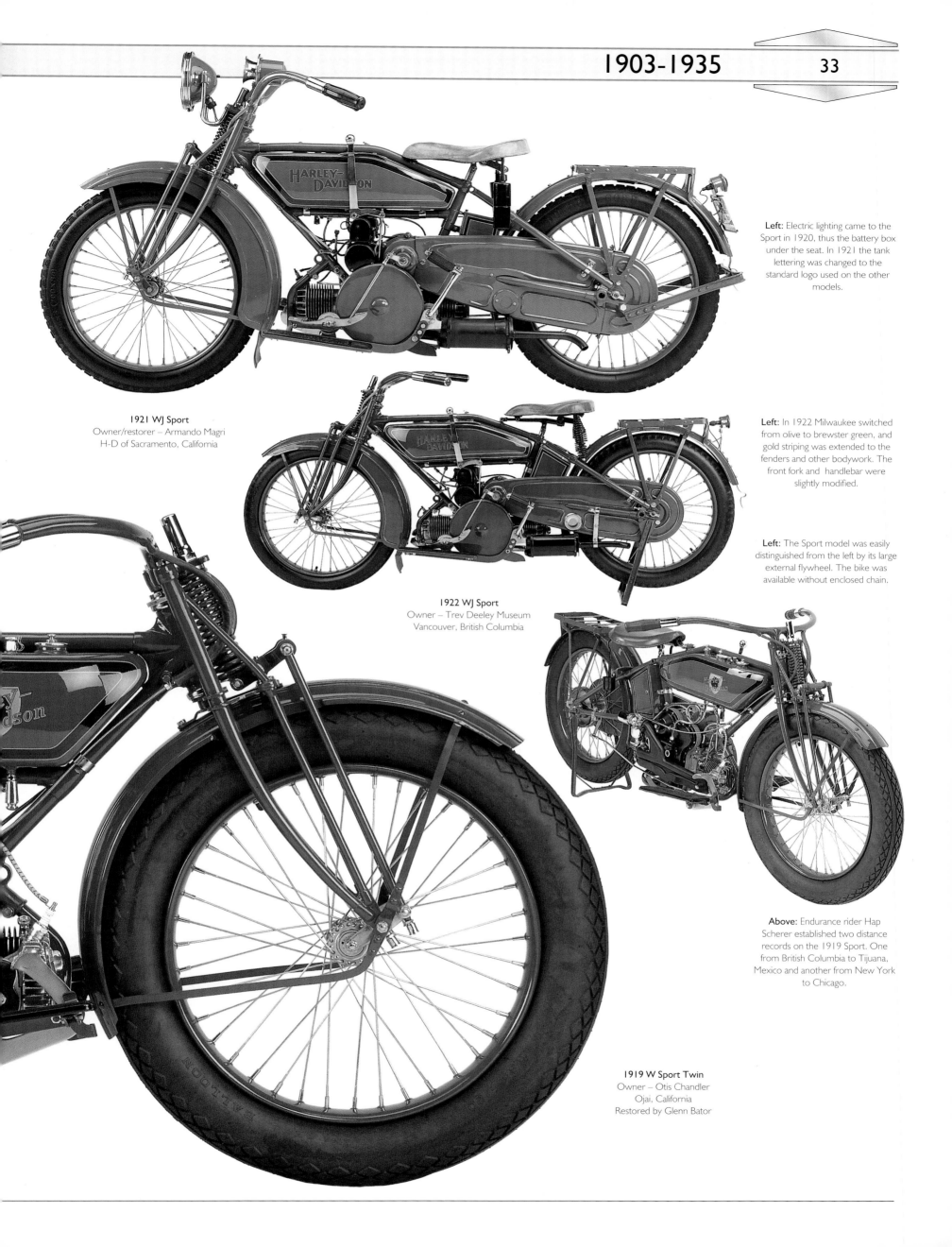

Left: Electric lighting came to the Sport in 1920, thus the battery box under the seat. In 1921 the tank lettering was changed to the standard logo used on the other models.

1921 WJ Sport
Owner/restorer – Armando Magri
H-D of Sacramento, California

Left: In 1922 Milwaukee switched from olive to brewster green, and gold striping was extended to the fenders and other bodywork. The front fork and handlebar were slightly modified.

Left: The Sport model was easily distinguished from the left by its large external flywheel. The bike was available without enclosed chain.

1922 WJ Sport
Owner – Trev Deeley Museum
Vancouver, British Columbia

Above: Endurance rider Hap Scherer established two distance records on the 1919 Sport. One from British Columbia to Tijuana, Mexico and another from New York to Chicago.

1919 W Sport Twin
Owner – Otis Chandler
Ojai, California
Restored by Glenn Bator

MODEL J (1921) AND MODEL CA (1920)

1921 MODEL J

SPECIFICATIONS
ENGINE/DRIVETRAIN
Engine: F-head 45° V-twin
Displacement: 74.66ci
(1207.11cc)
Bore & stroke: 3.42 x 4in
(87 x 101.6mm)
Horsepower: 18 @ 3,000 rpm
Carburetion: 1.25in (32mm)
Schebler
Transmission: 3-speed
Primary drive: Chain
Final drive: Chain
Brake: Rear drum
Battery: 6-volt
Ignition: Coil/points

CHASSIS/SUSPENSION
Frame: Steel, single downtube
Suspension: F. Leading link
spring fork
Wheelbase: 59.5in (151cm)
Weight: 365lb (165.6kg)
Fuel capacity: 2.75gal (10.4lit)
Oil capacity: 4pts (1.9lit)
Tires: 28 x 3in (71.1 x 7.62cm)
Top speed: 70mph (113km/h)
Color: Olive green
Numbers built: 4,526 (V-twin
total: 9,477)
Price: $485

The first Harley-Davidson J model was sold in 1915. The letter designation was applied to both the first 3-speed twin and the premier model with "complete electrical equipment." Proven on road and track, in peace and war, the J model became Milwaukee's top-of-the-line motorcycle.

In 1921 the 61-inch twin (1000cc) was joined by a bigger brother, the 74-inch (1200cc) JD (battery) and FD (magneto). Rated by the factory at 18 horsepower, the big twin was touted as the ideal mate to the new 2-passenger sidecar. The sidecar motor

(JDS) was fitted with compression shims for the lower rpm chores imposed by the chair. It also had a 16-tooth countershaft sprocket, two teeth fewer than the solo motor.

Development of the JD was prompted by the growing popularity of four-cylinder engines from Indian, Henderson and Cleveland. Smoother, more powerful fours threatened to dilute the dominance of V-twins in the sporting, commercial and police markets. Milwaukee had considered building a four, but eventually rejected the idea in favor of upgrading the V-twin. And the decision proved out.

Of course the record doesn't show whether or not the co-

Below: The Two Cam pocket-valve was dominant in 1920. Jim Davis won the Dodge City race; Ray Weishaar won the 200-miler (322km) at Marion, Indiana.

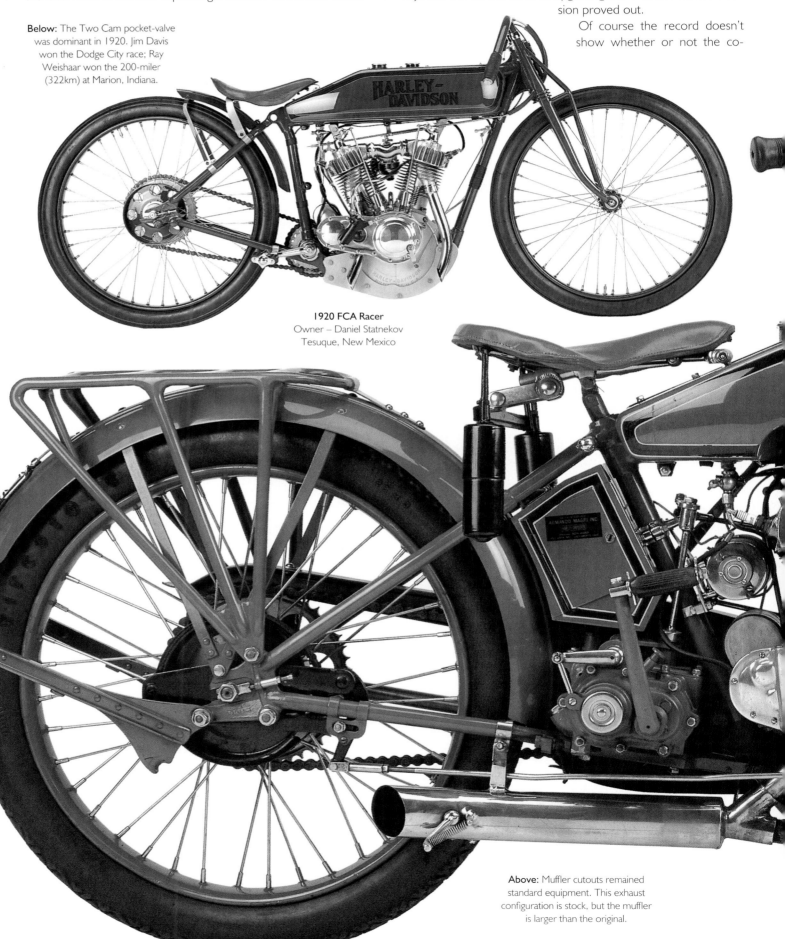

1920 FCA Racer
Owner – Daniel Statnekov
Tesuque, New Mexico

Some accessories for the Big Twins (the term now used to distinguish the V-twins from the Sport model) cost extra. The luggage carrier was $6.00. Tires were Firestone, Goodyear or Goodrich.

Above: Muffler cutouts remained standard equipment. This exhaust configuration is stock, but the muffler is larger than the original.

founders could predict the future. But 1921, as it turned out, was a disastrous year for motorcycle sales. Government contracts during the war had accelerated production, and Harley-Davidson registered a record year of more than 27,000 machines in 1920. With surplus inventory on hand, production for 1921 dropped to 11,460. Not until 1926 would the figures again top 20,000.

But the war had stimulated engineering and production improvements, due largely to research and development on aircraft engines. As these advances filtered down to automobile and motorcycle production lines, the engines showed gains in efficiency, power and durability. So even as engine technology made significant strides, the overall market was in decline. And not only

was the flat economy to blame; two other factors put motorcycles at a disadvantage. Henry Ford had again lowered the prices on his cars, and motorcycling was once more facing a public image problem.

They became known as the Roaring Twenties only in retrospect, but two-wheeled hooligans contributed their share of noise at the time. Walter Davidson urged dealers to become more aware of public relations in their communities. Advertising campaigns were drawn up to distinguish between responsible motorcyclists and hell-raising hot rodders. In the meantime, professional motorcycle racing was withering away.

Harley-Davidson was now the world's largest motorcycle manufacturer. There were dealerships in 67 countries around the globe and the advertising budget was $250,000. But a 40 percent drop in sales convinced Milwaukee that a factory racing team had become an unnecessary extravagance. And, as the story goes, Walter Davidson was more than a little miffed that after four successive wins in the Dodge City 300-mile (480km) race, the police department there was still buying Indians.

Not that Milwaukee abandoned racers altogether. Special racing frames were provided to dealers, and competition engines were built with looser tolerances and tested before delivery. So while Harley-Davidson had chosen no longer to field a factory team, they also committed the resources to ensure that privateers could buy competitive equipment.

So the first Golden Age of American professional racing was drawing to a close, yielding to an era of amateur competition. Likewise, the motorcycles would evolve in piecemeal fashion, thwarted first by a sluggish economy and later by the Great Depression of the 1930s. And the contest for supremacy would boil down to a scrap between the two surviving builders, Indian and Harley-Davidson.

Below left: Harley-Davidson extended its racing supremacy in 1921 by winning every national championship event on the calendar. D. H. Davidson (no relation) became the first rider to break the 100mph (161km/h) mark in England. On the Harley pocket-valve racer, he set the 100.76mph (162.2km/h) record at Brooklands.

Below: The horn and headlight had swapped positions in 1920. A new front fender was introduced in 1921, with skirts extending to the forward edge.

Below: The toolbox (and/or glove box, lunch box, etc.) had moved to the top of the fuel tank.

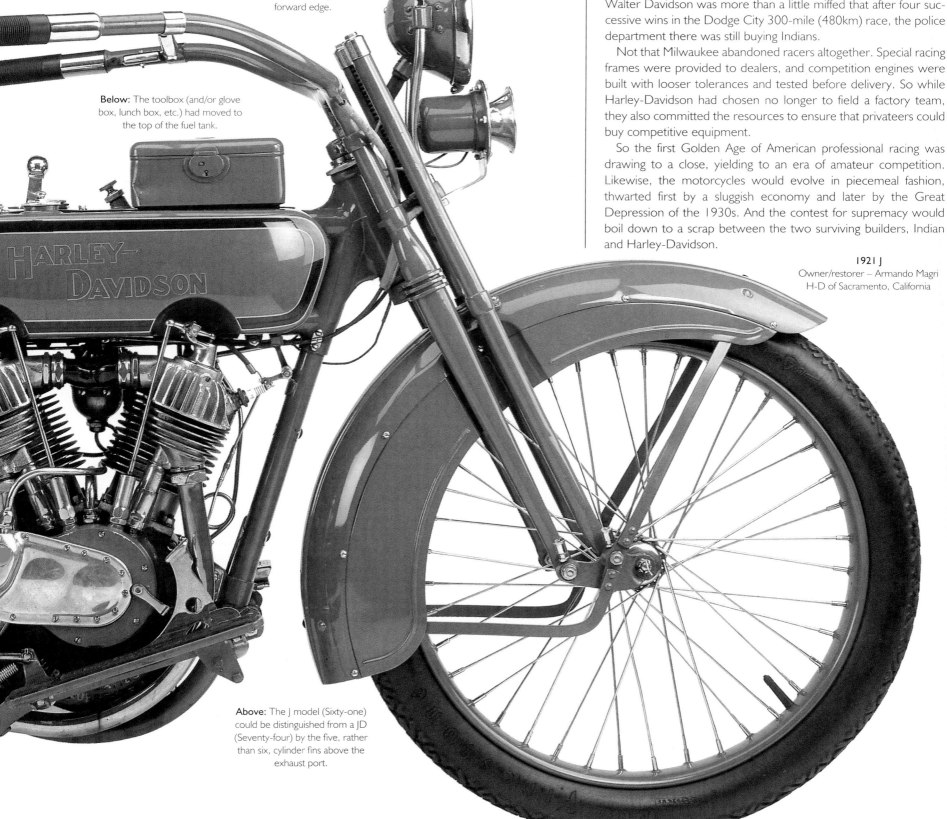

1921 J
Owner/restorer – Armando Magri
H-D of Sacramento, California

Above: The J model (Sixty-one) could be distinguished from a JD (Seventy-four) by the five, rather than six, cylinder fins above the exhaust port.

MODEL JD TWIN, MODELS A AND B SINGLES (1926)

1926 MODEL JD

SPECIFICATIONS
ENGINE/DRIVETRAIN
Engine: F-head 45° V-twin
Displacement: 74.66ci
(1207.11cc)
Bore & stroke: 3.44 x 4in
(87 x 102mm)
Horsepower: 24
Carburetion: 1.25in (32mm)
Schebler
Transmission: 3-speed
Primary drive: Chain
Final drive: Chain
Brake: Rear drum
Battery: 6-volt
Ignition: Coil/points

CHASSIS/SUSPENSION
Frame: Steel, single downtube
Suspension: F. Leading link
spring fork
Wheelbase: 59.5in (151.1cm)
Weight: 405lb (184kg)
Fuel capacity: 11.5pts (5.44lit)
Oil capacity: 5pts (2.36lit)
Tires: 27 x 3.85in (68.6 x
9.78cm)
Top speed: 60mph (97km/h)
Colors: Olive green (options:
white; cream)
Number built: 9,544
Price: $335

1926 MODEL A

SPECIFICATIONS
ENGINE/DRIVETRAIN
Engine: Flathead single
Displacement: 21.10ci
(345.73cc)
Bore & stroke: 2.875 x 3.25in
(73 x 82mm)
Horsepower: 8 @ 4,000 rpm
Carburetion: Schebler
Transmission: 3-speed
Primary drive: Chain
Final drive: Chain
Brake: Rear contracting band
Ignition: Magneto

CHASSIS/SUSPENSION
Frame: Steel, single downtube
Suspension: Leading link spring
fork
Wheelbase: 56.5in (143.6cm)
Weight: 251lb (113.9kg)
Fuel capacity: 3gal (11.36lit)
Oil capacity: 3qts (2.84lit)
Tires: 26 x 3.30in (66 x 8.38cm)
Top speed: 55mph (88.5km/h)
Color: Olive green
Number built: 1,128
Price: $210

For the first 20 years in Harley-Davidson's existence, engineering had the dominant role in motorcycle design. With the mid-1920s came a new emphasis on styling. The Silent Gray Fellow was yielding to the stylish Speedy Green Hornet.

For 1922 and '23, the traditional olive green paint was replaced by darker brewster green with gold striping. Olive remained available as an optional color, and returned as the standard hue in 1924. In 1926 Milwaukee offered white and cream as color options.

The flagging motorcycle market had stimulated action on several fronts in Milwaukee. Advertising and public relations efforts were stepped up, the designers and engineers made advances in engine efficiency, suspension and ease of maintenance for the rider. For 1924 the twins featured grease fittings on the running gear, stronger front forks, iron-alloy pistons, new exhaust pipes, larger batteries and generators. Late in the year the two-cam got a new valve train design that brought increased power.

While streamlined styling and direct mail campaigns were employed to attract new buyers, the design and construction of these new models were intended to impress riders by offering higher standards of performance and reliability. In 1925 the cradle frame was replaced by a lower unit using an engine plate between the front and rear downtubes. Seat height was reduced by three inches (7.62cm), which provided a lower center of gravity and easier handling.

Smaller diameter wheel rims also contributed to the lower overall stance, and wider tires provided better grip on the roadway. With softer front suspension, and shorter handlebars with a slight downward bend, the new twins handled significantly better than their predecessors. The more forward seat position put the rider in better control of the machine, and the seat-post spring had been lengthened from 9 to 14 inches (22.9 to 35.6cm). The ads boasted:

"Never a mount like this before – so powerful, so speedy, so perfectly balanced, so roadworthy. From every standpoint of performance, good looks and economy, the 'Stream-Line' sets a new standard. **And yet the price is reduced!**"

Indeed, Milwaukee had dropped the price of the Sixty-ones by five dollars. And the Seventy-fours were offered at the previous year's prices, despite the fact that the new models represented considerable investment in design, engineering, tooling and parts.

So despite the slow market, Harley-Davidson was obviously intent on maintaining its hard-won position of leadership in the industry. And each time Indian tried a new machine, Milwaukee responded in short order. The challenges were usually first met on the racetrack.

Board-track racing was on its way to history in 1925. The dangers invoked by the increasingly fast V-twins led to the creation of classes for slower machines – which naturally meant singles. The Thirty-fifty (500cc) engines had been used for national championship events since 1922, and by 1926 the schedule was a mixed bag of displacement classes for twins and singles.

Milwaukee had gone without a road model single for three years, but with the advent of Indian's 21-inch (350cc) Prince in 1925, Harley-Davidson reacted quickly with two singles the following year. The 350s marked Harley's first side-valve engine since the Sport Twin, and the first overhead-valve powerplant offered to the public (in the form of the AA and BA models). The ohv version actually debuted in 1925 at a Milwaukee race, and was soon dubbed the Peashooter for its staccato exhaust note. The overhead valve engine was built in limited numbers and primarily for racing.

The A (magneto) and B (battery) side-valve models accounted for more than 7,000 machines, most of which were exported to Great Britain, Europe and Australia. The single had a three-speed transmission, "ful-floeting" seat and external contracting rear brake. And it sold for $210, $50 less than its pocket-valve predecessor of 1918.

Right: The first "Stream-Line" models from Harley-Davidson appeared in 1925. The teardrop shape of the fuel tank followed contemporary styling and allowed lower seat height.

Right: The original paint scheme featured a maroon stripe with the fine gold stripe in the center.

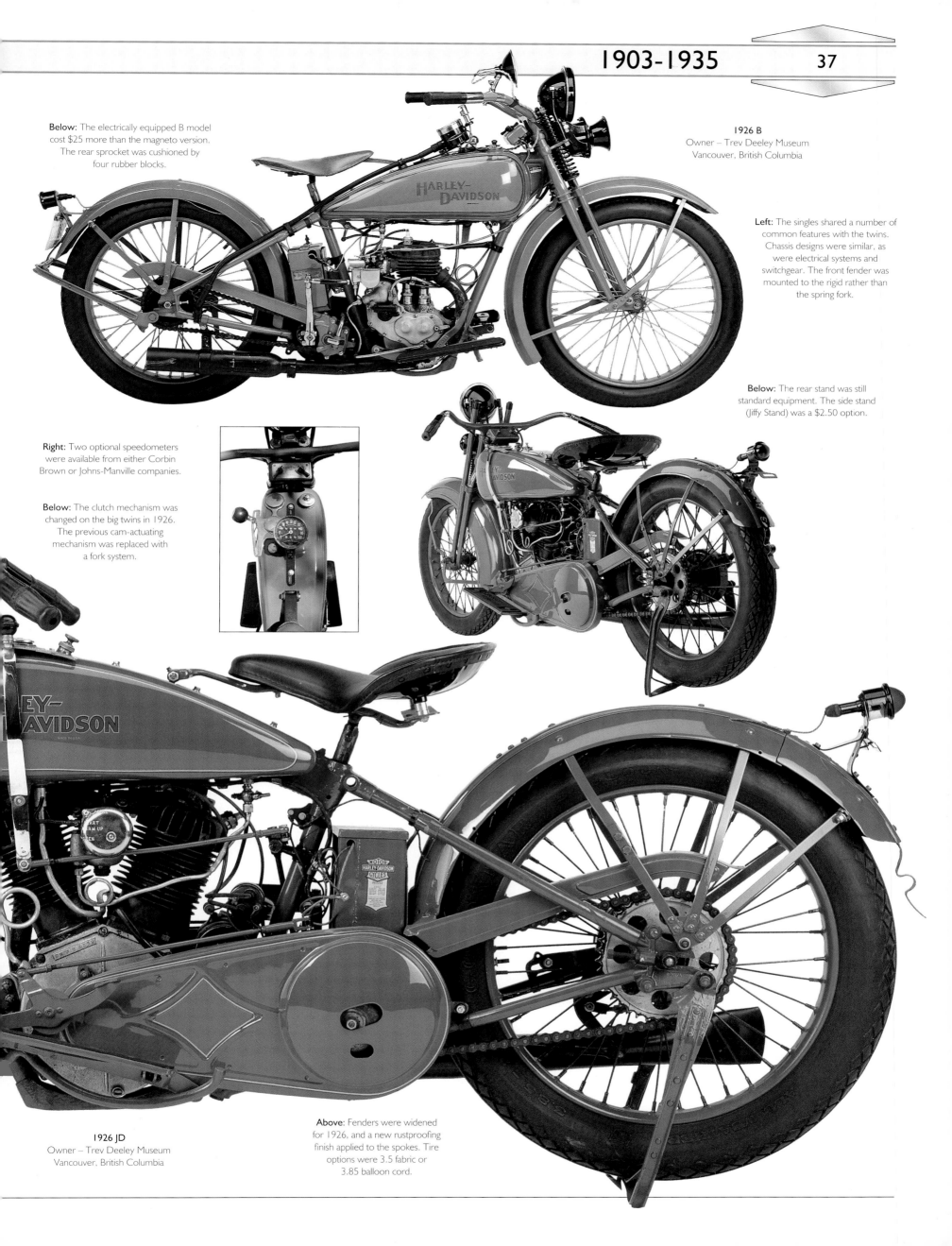

Below: The electrically equipped B model cost $25 more than the magneto version. The rear sprocket was cushioned by four rubber blocks.

1926 B
Owner – Trev Deeley Museum
Vancouver, British Columbia

Left: The singles shared a number of common features with the twins. Chassis designs were similar, as were electrical systems and switchgear. The front fender was mounted to the rigid rather than the spring fork.

Below: The rear stand was still standard equipment. The side stand (Jiffy Stand) was a $2.50 option.

Right: Two optional speedometers were available from either Corbin Brown or Johns-Manville companies.

Below: The clutch mechanism was changed on the big twins in 1926. The previous cam-actuating mechanism was replaced with a fork system.

1926 JD
Owner – Trev Deeley Museum
Vancouver, British Columbia

Above: Fenders were widened for 1926, and a new rustproofing finish applied to the spokes. Tire options were 3.5 fabric or 3.85 balloon cord.

1926 MODEL BA

SPECIFICATIONS
ENGINE/DRIVETRAIN
Engine: Overhead valve single
Displacement: 21.10ci
(345.73cc)
Bore & stroke: 2.875 x 3.25in
(73 x 82.5mm)
Horsepower: 12 @ 4,000 rpm
Carburetion: Schebler
Transmission: 3-speed
Primary drive: Chain
Final drive: Chain
Brake: Rear contracting band
Ignition: Battery/coil

CHASSIS/SUSPENSION
Frame: Steel, single downtube
Suspension: Leading link spring
fork
Wheelbase: 56.5in (146.3cm)
Weight: 263lb (119.3kg)
Fuel capacity: 3gal (11.36lit)
Oil capacity: 3qts (2.84lit)
Tires: 26 x 3.30in (66 x 8.38cm)
Top speed: 60mph (97km/h)
Color: Olive green
Number built: 524
Price: $275

Above: The simple control
panel featured an ignition
switch on the left and
light switch on the right.
The three speed
gearbox was
operated by a
shift lever on the left
side of the tank.

Right: The overhead-valve
singles were produced in far
fewer numbers than the
flatheads. More than 4,000
side-valves were built for
1927, but only 722 of the ohv
models. Included in that
number were export models
and racing bikes.

MODELS AA, BA AND FHAC (1926)

Harley-Davidson's first experience with side-valve engines, more commonly known as flatheads, was not hugely successful. The Sport Twin did not sell well in the U.S.A., losing out to the popular Indian Sport Scout, a 45-inch (750cc) V-twin. But Milwaukee hadn't lost interest in the design.

In 1924 Harley executives visited Europe and Australia, conducting their own research on the international market. The Sport Twin had sold well overseas, where light weight and fuel economy figured more strongly in buying decisions. But the opposed twin was relatively expensive to build, and the Europeans had embraced single-cylinder motorcycles as the sensible combination of sport and economy. So Milwaukee returned to singles.

Not that the one-lungers had ever been completely abandoned. Economic realities, in both commercial and sporting contexts, had perpetuated the market for less expensive mounts. Harley and Indian both built and maintained a brace of racing thumpers in the 1920s, as the big-inch twins slowly dissolved into racing history. Highly-paid factory racers had been demoted to semi-pro status, and the prospects for the growth of amateur competition began to look appealing. As did that growing population of riders who couldn't afford the twins. Yet.

Thus it was decided that two singles would be developed simultaneously; a side-valve model for economical transportation and an overhead-valve version for sport riders and racers. Naturally the flatheads, models A (magneto) and B (battery), were produced in far greater numbers. Rated at 8 horsepower, the side-valves sold for $210 and $235 respectively. The 12-horsepower overheads (AA and BA) were $250 and $275. The magneto racing model (S) was priced at $300.

Unlike the twins, the new singles featured detachable cylinder heads. The combustion chambers, pioneered and patented by British engineer Harry Ricardo, incorporated what came to be called a "squish band." The design created turbulence in the fuel charge, which translated as more complete combustion and higher horsepower. In racing trim, the Peashooter weighed about 235 pounds (106.6kg) and could reach upwards of 70mph (113km/h). Harley-Davidson won six of the 14 national championship 350cc races in 1926, with Indian victorious in the remaining eight.

So the singles appealed to that steadfast, but more or less static segment of the motorcycling fraternity that prized lightweight sport bikes, and their budget-minded counterparts who simply couldn't afford a twin. And while their numbers, at least in the U.S., were relatively small, the complementary considerations of sport riding and economic utility ensured them some choice of equipment.

And the commercial sense of producing side-valve engines would soon extend to the V-twins, as Milwaukee noted the proliferation of Excelsior and Indian 45ci (750cc) V-twin sport bikes on the road. The pocket-valve twins had served Milwaukee well for more than 20 years, but the future obviously lay in more efficient and powerful engines. Indian had demonstrated, with the aid of Irish tuning wizard Charley Franklin, that four-valve flatheads could beat eight-valve overheads on the race track, and so pointed the way to the next generation of engine design.

Right: The Ful-Floeting seat
remained standard equipment on
the singles as well as the twins.

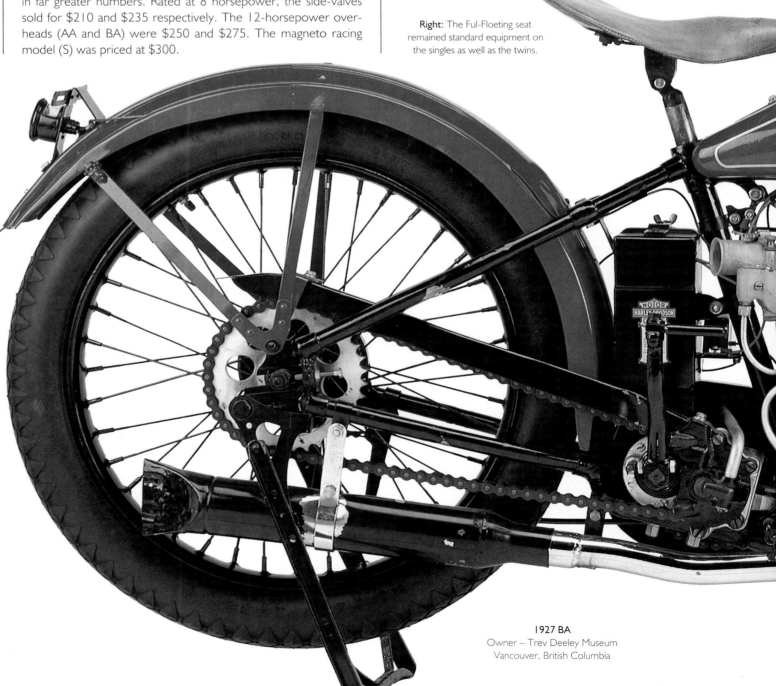

1927 BA
Owner – Trev Deeley Museum
Vancouver, British Columbia

1926 FHAC
Owner – Daniel Statnekov
Tesuque, New Mexico
Restored by Brad Wilmarth

Above: Development of the Two Cam pocket-valve racer led to the production of the Sixty-one and Seventy-four twin cam road models a few years later.

Below: Although it was well received by the motoring press, the ohv single proved more popular overseas than it did in the United States.

Right: Standard handlebar (shown) could be replaced by the shorter, flatter "speedster" bar.

Above: The 1927 singles got stronger frames, fuel tanks and engine mounts. The front fender was mounted to the rigid fork struts.

1929 JDH

SPECIFICATIONS
ENGINE/DRIVETRAIN
Engine: IOE 45° V-twin
Displacement: 74ci (1200cc)
Bore & stroke: 3.4 x 4.0in
(87 x 101.6mm)
Compression ratio: 6.5:1
Horsepower: 29 @ 4,000rpm
Carburetion: Schebler
Transmission: 3-speed
Primary drive: Chain
Final drive: Chain
Brakes: F. & R. Drum
Battery: 6-volt
Ignition: Coil/points

CHASSIS/SUSPENSION
Frame: Steel, single downtube
Suspension: F. Double spring
fork
Wheelbase: 59.5in (151.1cm)
Weight: 408lb (185kg)
Fuel capacity: 4.75gal (18lit)
Oil capacity: 4qts (3.79lit)
Tires: 18 x 3.85in (45.7 x
9.78cm)
Top speed: 85mph (137km/h)
Colors: Olive green (options:
azure blue; police blue; fawn
gray; cream; maroon; orange)
Number built: 10,182 (JD);
JDH: unknown
Price: $370

MODEL JDH (1929)

The JDH made its first appearance in 1928, and was known as the Two-Cam. Offered in both JH and JDH models, respectively 61 and 74-inch (1000cc and 1200cc) versions, this engine was derived from Milwaukee's racing experience gleaned throughout the 1920s.

Prompted by the improving performance figures of the Indian Powerplus and the four-cylinder Excelsior, Harley needed a faster machine. The factory had built many twin-cam competition bikes, and simply decided to apply that knowledge to the production of a road model. So the JDH got the racer's direct valve gear, with tappets replacing the standard roller arms. Adding dual intake valve springs, the Two-Cam was capable of higher rpm. Larger cooling fins on the head helped dissipate the heat inevitably created by more power, and a new throttle-controlled oil pump improved engine lubrication.

The Two-Cam was equipped with domed Dow metal pistons, optional on the J and JD, manufactured with magnesium alloy. This meant higher compression.

The JDH had a smaller and lighter fuel tank than the standard road machines, with capacity reduced from 5.3 to 4.75 gallons (20 to 18lit). Smaller diameter wheels lowered the center of gravity, and heavy duty spokes in the rear wheel helped handle the additional power. With the capability of more speed, the addition of a front brake was welcomed by sport riders.

More color options were also available, as more riders complained about the unrelieved flow of green from Milwaukee.

Though not touted in the general sales literature, the new colors were listed in dealer bulletins. Many two-tone combinations were available to customers willing to ask questions.

The first Golden Age of American motorcycle racing (1915-25, give or take, with time out for World War I) had now passed to history. Expensive racing budgets were no longer deemed necessary. Harley had been drawn to the track wars by Indian and Excelsior; the gauntlet thrown, challenge accepted and the battles engaged. On July 4, 1925, young Joe Petrali achieved the first 100mph (161km/h) average, riding a two-cam Harley at the Altoona, Pennsylvania board track.

That period of testing, tuning and racing accelerated Harley-Davidson's development as a builder of sporting machines, specifically in the big twin idiom. The smaller, lighter (and less powerful) 37ci (600cc) Sport Twin had achieved little success, and it lasted only five years. That failure effectively consigned American motorcycles to the heavyweight V-twin configuration they have maintained ever since. Big, powerful and, by God, American.

But 1929, at the edge of the Great Depression, would be the final year for the J series. Some 75,000 of the bikes had been built in its nine-year run, and it had evolved as the ultimate logical extension of its progenitor, the 1911 V-twin. In that time the horsepower had risen, the electrics acquired dependability, the styling had achieved acceptance and the motorcycle ranked well for overall performance and reliability. But other forces were at play in the market, and the pocket-valve engine would soon be consigned to the back pages. Which, of course, are now the front pages.

Above: The seat of the redesigned JD sat some 3 inches (76mm) lower than its earlier counterparts.

Right: The Four-Tube Muffler was introduced in 1929. "This muffler is positively the most quiet muffler ever developed for motorcycles," claimed Milwaukee. Efficiency aside, the design was not widely admired for appearance and lasted only two years.

1929 JDH
Owner – Otis Chandler
Ojai, California
Restored by Glenn Bator

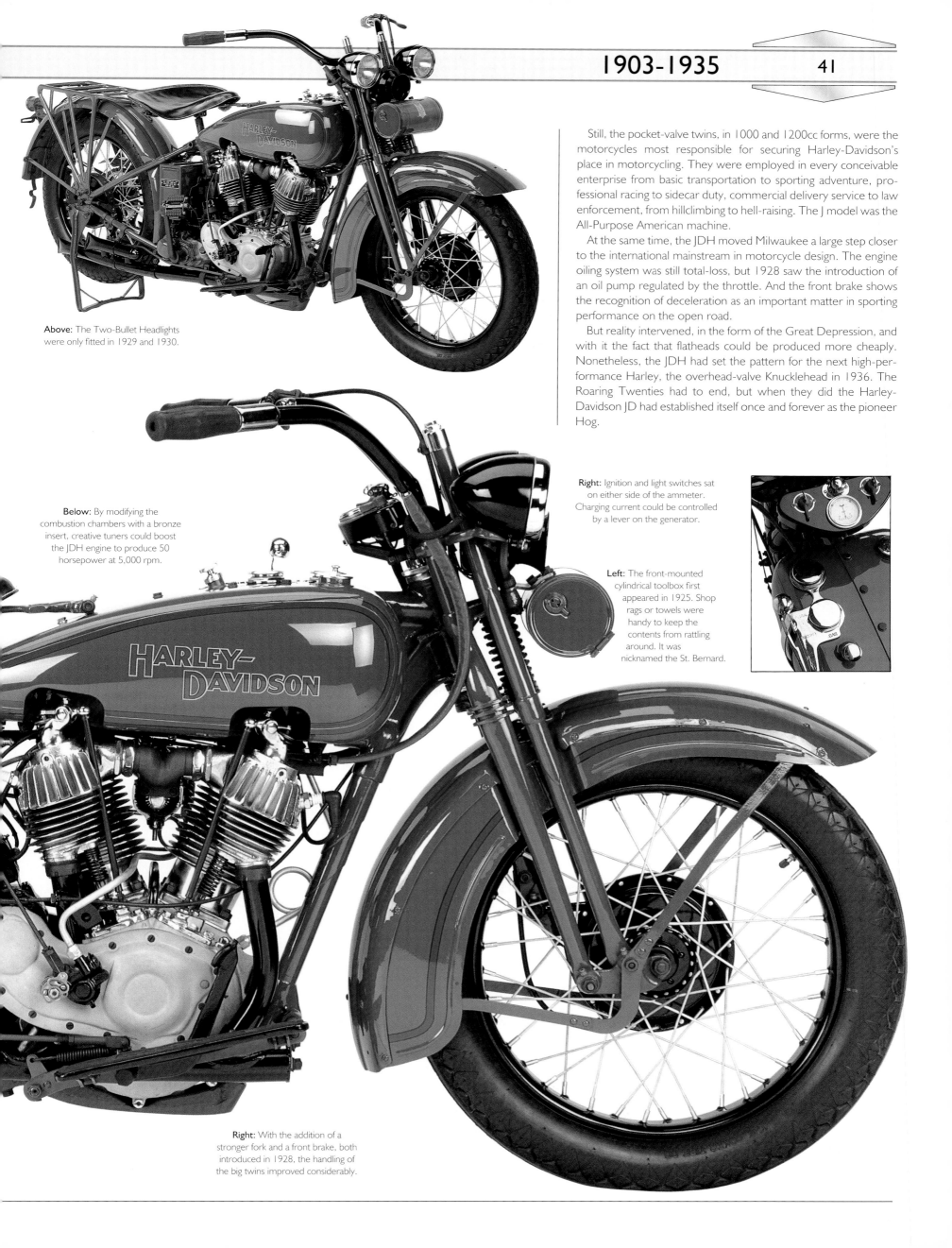

Above: The Two-Bullet Headlights were only fitted in 1929 and 1930.

Below: By modifying the combustion chambers with a bronze insert, creative tuners could boost the JDH engine to produce 50 horsepower at 5,000 rpm.

Still, the pocket-valve twins, in 1000 and 1200cc forms, were the motorcycles most responsible for securing Harley-Davidson's place in motorcycling. They were employed in every conceivable enterprise from basic transportation to sporting adventure, professional racing to sidecar duty, commercial delivery service to law enforcement, from hillclimbing to hell-raising. The J model was the All-Purpose American machine.

At the same time, the JDH moved Milwaukee a large step closer to the international mainstream in motorcycle design. The engine oiling system was still total-loss, but 1928 saw the introduction of an oil pump regulated by the throttle. And the front brake shows the recognition of deceleration as an important matter in sporting performance on the open road.

But reality intervened, in the form of the Great Depression, and with it the fact that flatheads could be produced more cheaply. Nonetheless, the JDH had set the pattern for the next high-performance Harley, the overhead-valve Knucklehead in 1936. The Roaring Twenties had to end, but when they did the Harley-Davidson JD had established itself once and forever as the pioneer Hog.

Right: Ignition and light switches sat on either side of the ammeter. Charging current could be controlled by a lever on the generator.

Left: The front-mounted cylindrical toolbox first appeared in 1925. Shop rags or towels were handy to keep the contents from rattling around. It was nicknamed the St. Bernard.

Right: With the addition of a stronger fork and a front brake, both introduced in 1928, the handling of the big twins improved considerably.

MODEL D (1929), MODEL C (1930) AND MODEL DAH (1932)

1929 MODEL DL

SPECIFICATIONS
ENGINE/DRIVETRAIN
Engine: Flathead 45° V-twin
Displacement: 45.32ci
(746.33cc)
Bore & stroke: 2.75 x 3.81in
(70 x 97mm)
Compression ratio: 5:1
Horsepower: 18.5 @
4,000 rpm
Carburetion: Schebler Deluxe
Transmission: 3-speed
Primary drive: Duplex chain
Final drive: Chain
Brakes: F. Expanding shoe. R.
Contracting band
Battery: 6-volt
Ignition: Coil/points

CHASSIS/SUSPENSION
Frame: Steel, single downtube
Suspension: F. Leading link
spring fork
Wheelbase: 57.5in (146cm)
Weight: 390lb (177kg)
Fuel capacity: 3.75gal (14.2lit)
Oil capacity: 7.5pts (3.55lit)
Tires: 4.00 x 18in (10.16 x
45.72cm)
Top speed: 70mph (113km/h)
Colors: Olive green (options:
black; maroon; gray; blue; cream)
Number built: 6,856 (D,DL) in
1929; (total production: 15,015)
Price: $290

1930 MODEL C

SPECIFICATIONS:
ENGINE/DRIVETRAIN
Engine: Flathead single
Displacement: 30.1ci
(493.28cc)
Bore & stroke: 3.09 x 4in
(78.6 x 101.6mm)
Horsepower: 10.4 @
3,600rpm
Carburetion: Schebler Deluxe
Transmission: 3-speed
Primary drive: Duplex chain
Final drive: Chain
Brakes: F. Expanding shoe.
R. Contracting band
Battery: 6-volt
Ignition: Coil/points

CHASSIS/SUSPENSION
Frame: Steel, single downtube
Suspension: F. Leading link
spring fork
Wheelbase: 57.5in (146cm)
Weight: 340lb
(154.2kg)
Fuel capacity:
3.75gal (14.2lit)
Oil capacity: 7.5pts
(3.55lit)
Tires: 4.00 x 18in (10.16 x
45.72cm)
Top speed: 60mph (97km/h)
Colors: Olive green (options:
maroon; black; blue; gray; cream)
Number built: 1,629 (C, CM,
CR)
Price: $260

Right: The quadruple
mufflers lasted several years
more on the Forty-fives
and singles.

As years go, 1929 is rarely recalled as one of America's best. But although the collapse of the stock market has become the signal event in history, the first nine months of the year looked encouraging in Milwaukee.

Two new models appeared in 1929; the 45 cubic-inch (750cc) V-twin D (standard) and DL (high compression) model and the 30.50 inch (500cc) model C single. Neither of them looked too appealing to riders accustomed to 1000 and 1200cc twins, but those models were still available. At $255, the new single was $115 cheaper than the JDH, and the 45-inch (750cc) twin only cost $290. Riders unable to afford a big twin now at least had the benefit of more economical mounts from Milwaukee.

Indian had been achieving notable performance with their flathead V-twins. Harley-Davidson was stung when Indian captured all the national championship races in 1928, a feat they repeated in 1929. Indian had proven the reliabilty and performance of flatheads in 750, 1000 and 1200cc engines. So it was obvious in Milwaukee than something more than just a mildly-tuned flathead for the road was in order.

But the smaller V-twin had never been intended as a high performance motorcycle. Practical, economical transportation was its role, and reliable service in commercial applications. Nonetheless, William Ottaway was already at work on a more powerful version of the D model (with overhead valves), and plans were well underway for big twins of the flathead persuasion. Milwaukee had faced the facts: the side-valve made

sufficient power for the open road, it was a quieter engine by design, and it was less expensive to build than its ohv counterpart. In 1930 the "small twin" got a new frame and front fork, and a sport model (DLD) was introduced that featured higher compression and a larger carburetor, producing 20 horsepower.

The singles followed a similar line of development. Even though sales of the Twenty-one had declined for several years, Milwaukee thought a bigger single was in order. Thus the C model, a 30.50 cubic inch (500cc) single which shared the same frame with the 350 single and 750 twin.

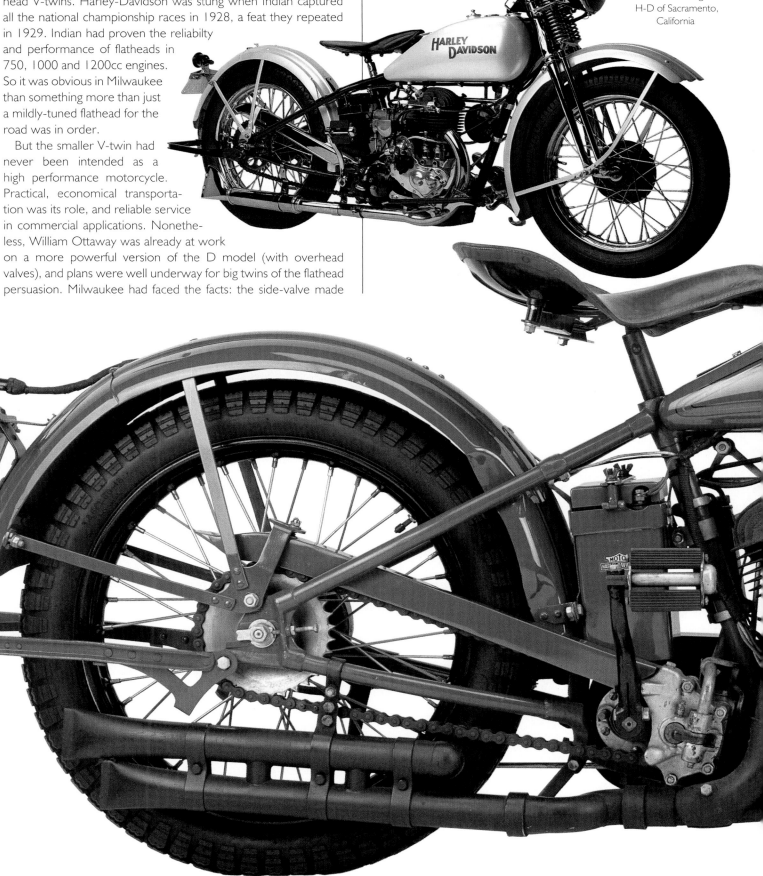

1930 C
Owner/restorer –
Armando Magri
H-D of Sacramento,
California

Below: The overhead-valve DAH 750 was built specifically for hillclimbs.

1932 DAH 750
Owner – Daniel Statnekov
Tesuque, New Mexico

1929 D
Owner/restorer – Harold Mathews
Mathews Harley-Davidson
Fresno, California

Above: The standard D model was easily changed to the high-compression DL with an optional cylinder head and a 28-tooth rear sprocket.

The 500cc single, known in the U.S. as the Thirty-fifty, became the only single in Milwaukee's lineup for 1931. Even though Joe Petrali was blitzing the race tracks on the 21-inch (350cc) Peashooter, the overwhelming effects of the depression were felt throughout the country. Most people simply couldn't afford a motorcycle. In 1932 Harley-Davidson again offered the 350 single, dropping the price to $195, the lowest tag ever on a Milwaukee machine. The 30.50in (500cc) single was reduced to $235, the price of a 350 only three years earlier.

As Europe likewise fell into economic doldrums, and protective import tariffs rose, Milwaukee's export markets shriveled up. The days of the economic and/or sporty singles were numbered, and 1934 would be their last year of production. The national championship racing class for 350s (Class A) carried on for several years, and in 1935 Harley rider Joe Petrali won every meet on the calendar. A few years later the Class C formula, for 750cc flat-heads, became the standardized format for American racing.

That both Harley-Davidson and Indian built such machines figured strongly in the formation of the competition category. The Indian Sport Scout had set the standard for the small twins, and Harley's Forty-five, following some early teething problems, became the foremost competitor on road and track. Some devotees of the big twins would deride the smaller bike for its utilitarian aspect and lack of power, but the flathead 45 would carry the longest-running production life on the Milwaukee roster.

As Harley's workhorse, the 45-inch (750cc) flathead served as police bike, commercial transporter, tow vehicle, mail carrier, combat mount and racing machine. And it was, as fate would have it, 45 years later when the last one rolled off the assembly line.

Left: The Forty-five struggled at first in the market dominated by the Indian 101 Scout. In 1930 the series was upgraded with a stronger frame, fork and clutch.

MODEL VL AND SIDECAR (1930) AND MODEL VL (1932)

1930 MODEL VL

SPECIFICATIONS
ENGINE/DRIVETRAIN
Engine: Flathead 45° V-twin
Displacement: 73.73ci
(1208.19cc)
Bore & stroke: 3.44 x 4.0in
(87.3 x 101.6mm)
Compression ratio: 4.5:1
Horsepower: 30 @ 4,000 rpm
Carburetion: 1.25in (32mm)
Schebler
Transmission: 3-speed
Primary drive: Duplex chain
Final drive: Chain
Brakes: F. and R. Drum
Battery: 6-volt/22-amp
Ignition: Coil/points

CHASSIS/SUSPENSION
Frame: Steel, single downtube
Suspension: F. Leading link
spring fork
Wheelbase: 60in (152.4cm)
Weight: 529lb (240kg)
Fuel capacity: 4gal (15.14lit)
Oil capacity: 1gal (3.79lit)
Tires: 4.00 x 18in (10.16 x
45.72cm)
Top speed: 85mph (137km/h)
Colors: Olive green (options:
black; gray; blue; maroon; coach
green; cream)
Number built: 3,246
Price: $340

Though they were still called Seventy-fours, the 1930 V (standard) and VL (high compression) models were entirely different motorcycles from the earlier FD and JD models. And at first it was not the machine Milwaukee had hoped it would be. The VL did produce a tad more horsepower than the JD, and featured a new frame and fork. But it was less than reliable.

The new 74 had appeared in mid-1929, little more than two months before the stock market disintegrated. At $340, twenty bucks more than the JD, the VL had a weak clutch, frail flywheel, poor lubrication, bad valve springs, inefficient mufflers and marginal pistons. Otherwise the motorcycle was fine.

Fans of the JD, especially high-performance adherents of the JDH, scoffed at the new flathead. To them it seemed a step backwards, a pedestrian design in a package more than 100 pounds (45kg) heavier than its predecessor. But the performance figures were nearly identical, and Milwaukee moved quickly to correct the deficiencies revealed in the early models. Moreover, the VL added features such as detachable cylinder heads, interchangeable wheels, bigger brakes and tires, lower seat height and more ground clearance. And a wider torque spread than the J motor offered.

Harley-Davidson had built the flathead big twin to contend with the

Indian Chief, which had a similar configuration. So the future, at least that foreseeable portion, was a side-valve vision. The standard V model made 28 horsepower, while the higher compression VL cranked out 30. Like the Forty-five, each valve had its own cam and the lubrication system remained total-loss. A forged I-beam front fork replaced the tube-style of the J model. New 19-inch (48.26cm) wheels came standard with 4.00-inch (10.16cm) tires and 4.40-inch (11.18cm) rubber was an extra cost option.

Four versions of the new Seventy-four were available in 1930: the V and VL with batteries and the VM and VLM each equipped with a magneto-generator. The battery was a more stout 22-amp unit and the coil was

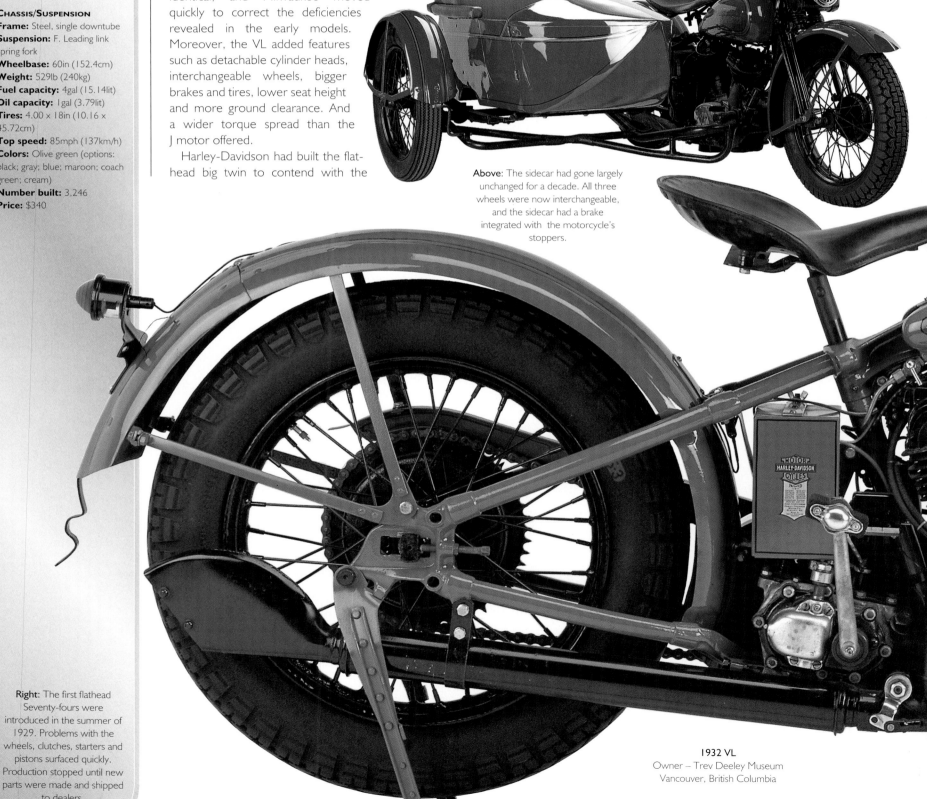

Above: The sidecar had gone largely unchanged for a decade. All three wheels were now interchangeable, and the sidecar had a brake integrated with the motorcycle's stoppers.

Right: The first flathead Seventy-fours were introduced in the summer of 1929. Problems with the wheels, clutches, starters and pistons surfaced quickly. Production stopped until new parts were made and shipped to dealers.

1932 VL
Owner – Trev Deeley Museum
Vancouver, British Columbia

1930 VL
Owner/restorer – Dave Royal
Nipomo, California

Right: Shorter solo bars were a no-cost option. A Ride Control knob (behind headlight) adjusted suspension.

better sealed against the elements. The tool box was still a cylinder fitted below the "Clear-the-way Horn" and "Two Bullet Headlights". In 1931 the tool container became an oval shape with a new disk-type horn on its front, and the dual headlights were replaced by a single unit.

The double-muffler exhaust was replaced by a single-tube pipe in 1931. A timing plug was fitted to the left crankcase to facilitate ignition adjustment, and the new Schebler carburetor was a die-cast unit. Milwaukee also offered an optional 3-speed transmission with reverse gear for sidecar and Servi-Car applications.

The factory became slightly less secretive about optional color combinations, although the information was still not included in sales brochures. Olive green remained the standard hue, but dealers could order two-tone paint schemes in black/red, maroon/cream, white/gold or blue/gray.

The flathead big twins would remain stalwarts on the Milwaukee lineup for 18 years. In 1936 the series would gain the VLH, an 80 cubic inch (1340cc) engine, and a year later would be replaced by the U series with recirculating oil system. Overhead valve engines would eventually consign the flatheads to history, but for more than a few riders, the side-valve Seventy-fours were Harley's finest machines.

Right: In 1931 the cannister toolbox was replaced by an oval unit, and the bell-mouth Klaxon horn yielded to a disc-type with a chromed grille.

Above: Cylinders for 1932 were redesigned to provide more cooling air to the exhaust ports. Both the front fork and transmission were strengthened for durability.

MODELS VLD (1934), RL (1935) AND CB SINGLE (1934)

1935 MODEL RL

SPECIFICATIONS
ENGINE/DRIVETRAIN
Engine: Flathead 45° V-twin
Displacement: 45.32ci
(746.33cc)
Bore & stroke: 2.75 x 3.81in
(70 x 97mm)
Horsepower: 18.5 @ 4,000rpm
Carburetion: Schebler Deluxe
Transmission: 3-speed
Primary drive: Duplex chain
Final drive: Chain
Brake: F. Expanding shoe.
R. Contracting band
Battery: 6-volt
Ignition: Coil/points

CHASSIS/SUSPENSION
Frame: Steel, single downtube
Suspension: F. Leading link
spring fork
Wheelbase: 57.5in (146cm)
Weight: 390lb (177kg)
Fuel capacity: 3.75gal (14.2lit)
Oil capacity: 7.5pts (3.55lit)
Tires: 4.00 x 18in (10.16 x
45.72cm)
Top speed: 70mph (113km/h)
Color: Teak red/black; venetian
blue/silver; verdant green/black;
egyptian ivory/regent brown;
olive green/black
Number built: 819
Price: $295

The VLD Special Sport Solo was introduced in 1933. The full force of the Great Depression had reached Milwaukee in 1931, and production had dropped to the lowest figure in 20 years. In the two years that followed, the picture grew even worse.

At Harley-Davidson, with management and labor working for reduced pay, technological advancement was not on the agenda. So color and graphics took on new importance. Following the lead of the automobile industry, Milwaukee introduced Art Deco styling to the motorcycles. The 1933 fuel tanks featured a stylized eagle in flight, accented by gold stripes and contrasting colors. The design, a variation on optional scrollwork on 1932 tanks, was used for only one year.

Not that the new models were simply old machines in colorful garb. Numerous improvements developed before the economic crisis had been incorporated a year earlier.

The V series had new cylinders, designed for better heat dissipation, plus an improved oil pump, new generator and stronger fork. The same upgrades appeared on the Forty-fives, now called the R series, and the Thirty-fifty singles. The small twin also carried a stronger frame, larger flywheels, better valve springs and a new 4-plate clutch.

The VLD was to the big twin flatheads what the JDH had been to the earlier 74, the factory hot rod. A new Y-shaped intake manifold gave the fuel charge a more direct shot into the cylinders, and a new Linkert die-cast brass carburetor was fitted. With aluminum alloy pistons replacing magnesium alloy, new cylinder heads and a compression ratio of 5:1, the engine made 36 horsepower at 4,500rpm. Acceleration, given the machine's weight, was robust.

In 1934 the V and R series were fitted with skirted rear fenders and upswept exhaust tips, and the 74 had a longer muffler. The decorative trend included an optional $15 chrome package that included handlebars, exhaust pipes, chain guard and generator cover. Another popular option was the Buddy Seat, an oversized saddle that would accommodate two in close proximity. The seat was also appreciated by solo riders, since it afforded space to change positions on long rides, thereby reducing the incidence of numb-butt.

For 1934 the fishtail muffler returned on the twins, and the 74 toolbox was changed to a box fitted to the frame behind the transmission. The new 80-inch (1340cc) twin appeared late the following year, and was designated VLDD. In 1936 the biggest twin was labeled the VLH. A competition version of the 74 was also listed in the 1935 catalog, with the designation VLDJ.

With the transition from professional to amateur racing, Milwaukee offered a competition-bred 45 in the RLDR. The small twin had received most of the upgrades applied to its big brother, including a constant-mesh transmission. The R series also received internal expanding rear brakes, with both drums and shoes hardened for better braking and durability. The racing bikes were set up with slightly looser piston clearances.

Five color combination were offered on the 1935 twins: teak red/black; venetian blue/silver; verdant green/black; egyptian ivory/regent brown and olive green/black.

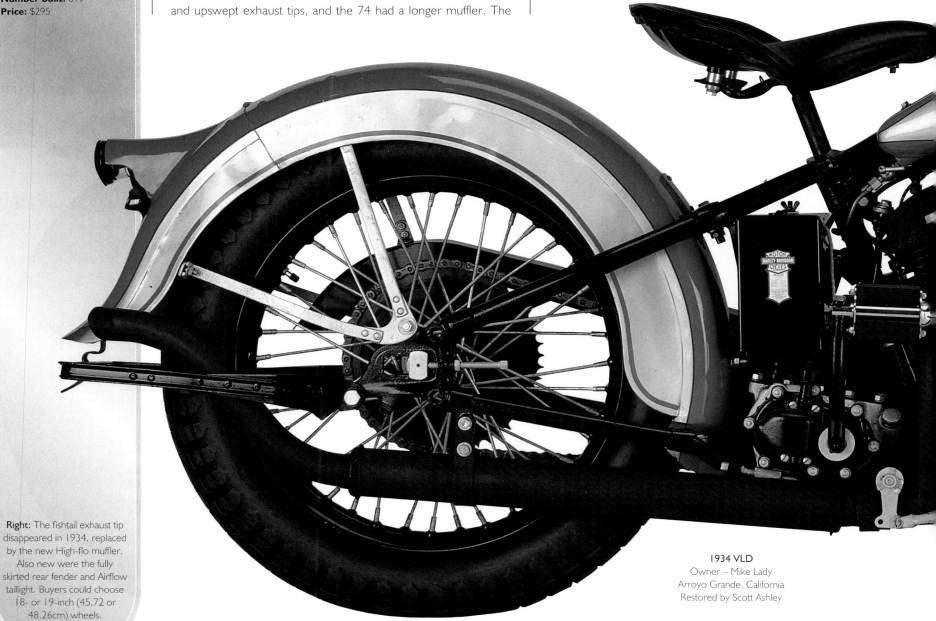

Below: The more deeply contoured saddle featured polished studs and a black enamel bar. The larger Buddy seat was a $6.75 option.

Right: The fishtail exhaust tip disappeared in 1934, replaced by the new High-flo muffler. Also new were the fully skirted rear fender and Airflow taillight. Buyers could choose 18- or 19-inch (45.72 or 48.26cm) wheels.

1934 VLD
Owner – Mike Lady
Arroyo Grande, California
Restored by Scott Ashley

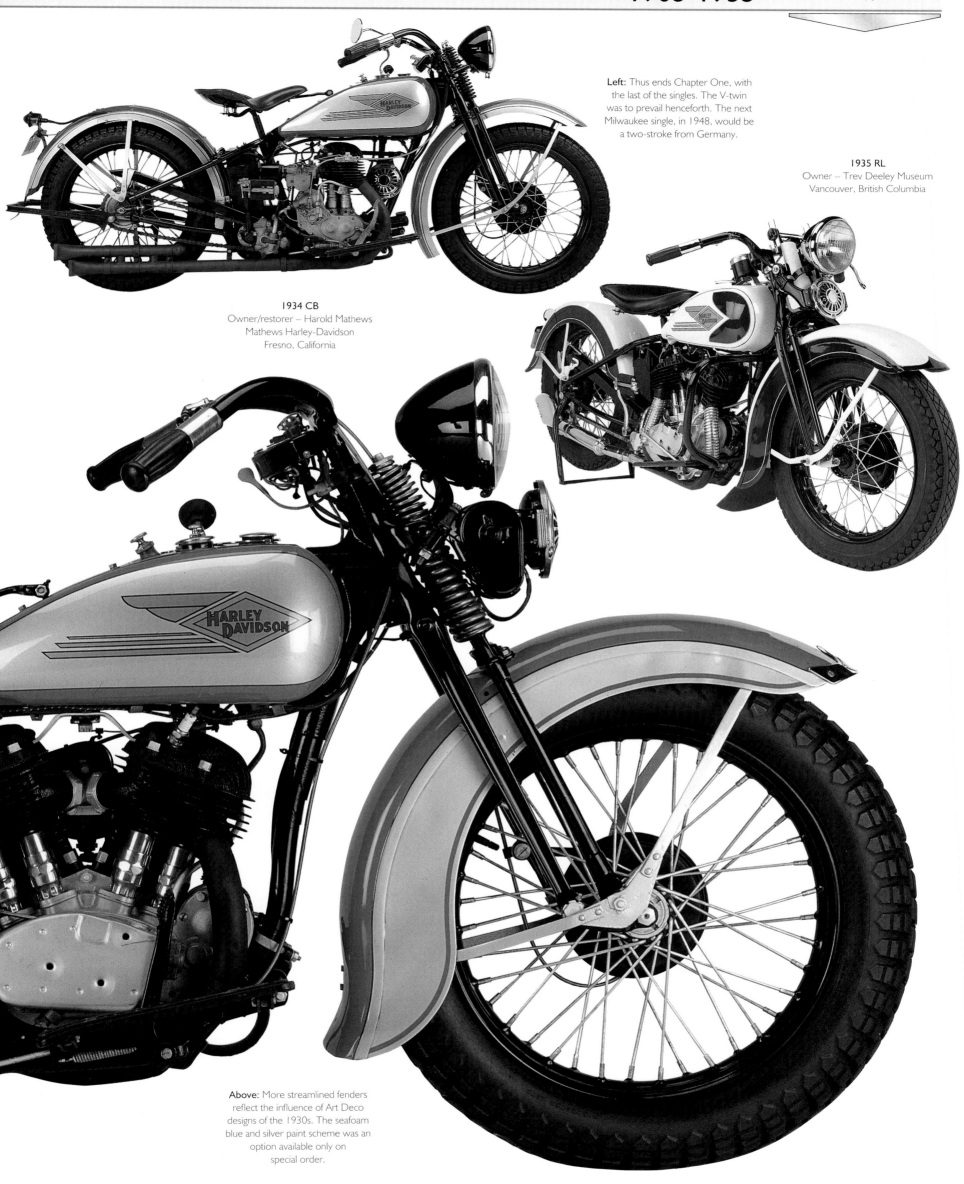

Left: Thus ends Chapter One, with the last of the singles. The V-twin was to prevail henceforth. The next Milwaukee single, in 1948, would be a two-stroke from Germany.

1935 RL
Owner – Trev Deeley Museum
Vancouver, British Columbia

1934 CB
Owner/restorer – Harold Mathews
Mathews Harley-Davidson
Fresno, California

Above: More streamlined fenders reflect the influence of Art Deco designs of the 1930s. The seafoam blue and silver paint scheme was an option available only on special order.

1936 EL

SPECIFICATIONS
ENGINE/DRIVETRAIN
Engine: OHV 45° V-twin
Displacement: 60.33ci
(988.56cc)
Bore & stroke: 3.31 x 3.5in
(84 x 89mm)
Horsepower: E 37, EL 40 @
4,800 rpm
Compression ratio: E 6.5:1,
EL 7:1
Carburetion: 1.25in (32mm)
Linkert
Transmission: 4-speed
Primary drive: Duplex chain
Final drive: Chain
Brakes: F & R. Drum
Battery: 6-volt
Ignition: Coil/points

CHASSIS/SUSPENSION
Frame: Steel, double downtube
Suspension: F. Spring fork
Wheelbase: 59.5in (151.1cm)
Weight: 565lb (256kg)
Fuel capacity: 3.75gal (14.2lit)
Oil capacity: 4qts (3.79lit)
Tires: 4.50 x 18in (11.4 x
45.7cm)
Top speed: 95mph (153km/h)
Colors: Sherwood green/silver;
teak red/black; dusk gray/buff;
venetian blue/ croydon cream;
maroon/nile green
Number built: 1,526
Price: $380

Right: The Sixty-one OHV,
which would come to be
known as the Knucklehead for
its bulging rocker boxes, was
scheduled for introduction in
1935. Minor problems, and
traditional H-D caution,
delayed intro until 1936.

EL 61 OHV (1936)

In 1931 the founders had discussed plans for a new V-twin. The motorcycle would be the logical successor to the JDH, featuring more contemporary engineering, styling and performance. Meaning faster.

That summer a mock-up was built around a proposed 65-cubic inch (1065cc) flathead. The design incorporated a twin-downtube cradle frame, reinforced fork and an integrated instrument panel on the fuel tank, featuring Milwaukee's first standard-equipment speedometer. The frame and overall styling won approval, but the flathead engine was rejected. A few months later the decision was made to design and build a 61-inch (1000cc) overhead-valve engine.

Scheduled to appear as a 1935 model, progress on the 61 OHV was slowed by the effects of the depression. Problems with oil leakage on the prototypes delayed the project further. So the debut of Milwaukee's first ohv big twin, with recirculating oil system, was postponed to 1936. Despite the delays, the stylish new machine was an instant success.

Nicknamed the Knucklehead for its bulbous rocker boxes, the 61 OHV was a new motorcycle from the bottom up. The double downtube frame was necessary to handle the added power, and the early versions were not quite up to the task. The frames were strengthed for 1937. The front fork employed oval tube struts,

more streamlined and stylish than the forged I-beam style used earlier. The 18-inch (45.7cm) wheels wore 4.50-inch (11.4cm) tires and the seat height dropped to 26 inches (66cm), lower than the Thirty-fifty singles of a few years before.

The new engine accentuated the Sixty-one's stylishly muscular profile. The polished rocker boxes and pushrod tubes added a decorative touch to the V-twin, and drew the eye to the heart of the machine. The Knucklehead engine *looked* like horsepower. And the chassis' clean, unbroken line from the rear axle to the steering head was stately and strong. The consensus among most riders in 1936: the best-looking damn motorcycle they had ever seen.

And it worked. The single camshaft was more efficent and quieter than its two- and four-shaft flathead forebears. The hemispherical combustion chambers provided by valves set at 90 degrees meant horsepower; 37 at 4,800 rpm in the standard E model, 40 from the high-compression EL. And despite the fact that a fully-fueled Knucklehead weighed in at close to 600 pounds (272kg), that was sufficient urge to propel the daring rider close to 100mph (161km/h).

Milwaukee wasn't at all shy about capitalizing on the new engine's capabilities. In March of 1937, racer Joe Petrali set a new top speed record of 136 mph (219km/h) at Daytona Beach and eclipsed the mark set earlier by Indian. Later, at California's Muroc Dry Lake, Fred Ham set a new 24-hour record on the

Below: One school of thought holds the '36 Knucklehead as the most handsome Harley ever built. Not a bad school.

Below: Rims on most models matched the secondary color. With the teak red and black paint scheme, however, the rims were painted red.

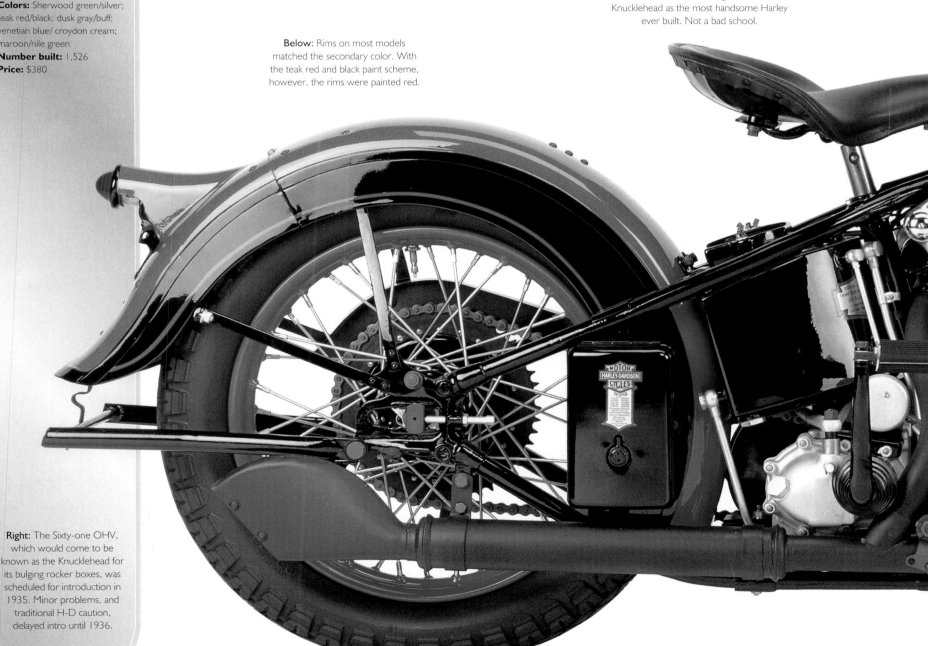

Knucklehead, over 1,825 miles (2,937km) at an average of 76 mph (122km/h). The 61 OHV had established its credentials.

Just as the economic woes of the depression began to lift, Milwaukee had come through with a modern motorcycle. They had leapfrogged Indian, their primary competitor, and captured the attention of American motorcyclists. Of course the 61 OHV was not without problems; oil leakage still plagued the early examples, and oil consumption was higher than necessary. The kick-start gearing ratio and ignition timing could make starting difficult, and the transmission required more secure mounting. But all these problems were rectified before 1937.

What the Knucklehead did was look good and run strong. It had a stout dry clutch and constant-mesh 4-speed transmission. The tank-mounted instrument panel and streamlined profile made it just about the most dashing looking machine on the road. Harley-Davidson had barely managed to stay afloat in the depression years, but they emerged with the right machine at the right time. And began a new chapter in the everlasting adventure, with a motorcycle tagged the Knucklehead.

Below: The art deco comet tank emblem was employed from 1936 through 1939. It remains one of the most popular graphics on retro bikes.

Above: The ride control knob was still on the right. Two years later it moved to the opposite side, where it could be adjusted while riding. Sensible.

Left: The first standard equipment H-D speedometer. 1936 was the only year for the 100-mph (161km/h) unit; a 120-mph (193km/h) dial came in '37. Gauges were gone in 1938.

1936 EL
Owner – Otis Chandler
Ojai, California
Restored by Carmen & Eldon Brown

1936 VLH

SPECIFICATIONS

ENGINE/DRIVETRAIN
Engine: Flathead 45° V-twin
Displacement: 80ci (1340cc)
Bore & stroke: 3.42 x 4.25in (87 x 109mm)
Horsepower: 34 @ 4,000 rpm
Compression ratio: 5.5:1
Carburetion: Linkert
Transmission: 3 or 4-speed
Primary drive: Chain
Final drive: Chain
Brakes: F. & R. Drum
Battery: 6-volt
Ignition: Coil/points

CHASSIS/SUSPENSION
Frame: Steel, double downtube
Suspension: F. Leading link spring fork
Wheelbase: 60in (152.4cm)
Weight: 545lb (247kg)
Fuel capacity: 3gal (11.36lit)
Oil capacity: 8.5pts (4.02lit)
Tires: 18 or 19 x 4.00in (45.7 or 48.3 x 10.16cm)
Top speed: 90mph (145km/h)
Colors: Sherwood green/silver; teak red/ black; dusk gray/buff; venetian blue/cream; maroon/nile green
Number built: 2,046
Price: $340

VLH (1936) AND U SERIES (1938)

The 80-inch (1340cc) flathead was introduced late in 1935 and made its official debut the following year. The big-inch twin shared with its smaller brothers new cylinder heads with larger fins and re-shaped combustion chambers. Cylinder fins were extended over the intake ports.

The Eighty shared its bore with the Seventy-four, adding displacement with a quarter-inch (6.3mm) longer stroke. The machines were otherwise identical, including the total-loss lubrication system, which would be gone the next year. Milwaukee figured the bigger twin was required for several reasons: Indian offered one, the added power would appeal to sidecarists, and the design had been proven out. Plus, it sold for $40 less than the 61 OHV, which had yet to establish its reliability.

The list of factory options had really begun growing in 1934, and a number of special equipment packages were added the next year. For 1936 the premium package included the Safety Guard (crash bars), lighted speedometer, Jiffy Stand, Ride Control, steering damper, chrome plate group, fender lamp, stop light, dice shift knob and switch keys, saddlebags and hangers. All for $49.50. And for an extra $15, the 74 or 80 could be fitted with a 4-speed transmission.

The optional speedometers were equipped with a Maximum Speed Hand, a separate indicator that remained fixed at the highest speed attained on a ride. This was to certify one's bragging rights when comparing the motorcycle's performance with other riders' machines.

In 1937 the V series were modified and became known as the U models, with the twin downtube frame, recirculating oil system and 4-speed transmission standard. The R series Forty-five was likewise revised as the W model, which also got dry-sump lubri-

cation. Most of the improvements first seen on the 61 OHV were now incorporated throughout the Harley-Davidson lineup, and all the big twins shared a strengthened frame for 1937.

The Seventy-four now had the same stroke as the Eighty, with the bore reduced to match the 61 OHV. This was done as a cost-saving move, so the two machines could use the same pistons. The big twin flatheads also had new cylinders with added finning, and improved bearings and oil seals in the transmission. For 1937 only, the oil tanks on all models were painted the same color as the tank and fenders. In succeeding years the oil tank would be painted black.

"A new high in beauty has been attained in the appearance of the 1938 models," proclaimed the brochure. Red and green lights replaced the ammeter and oil gauge on the instrument panel. Gone was the bronze brown hue, which hadn't proven popular. Teak red with black and gold striping was still available; the new color options included venetian blue with white striping, hollywood green with gold, and silver tan with sunshine blue striping. The new striping was centered on the sides of the tank and fenders. Higher handlebars were fitted to aid low-speed handling.

Once again the big twin frames were reinforced and given a larger backbone. The lower steering head cone was designed with a self-aligning feature to distribute force evenly on the bearings. Clutch assemblies were improved and the oil outlet fitting moved from the bottom to the rear of the oil tank.

The accessory groups became standard equipment in 1938. Customers could choose either the standard or deluxe group, which were $16.70 and $49.75 respectively. The latter added four-ply tires, Ride Control, colored shift knob, air cleaner, saddlebags and chrome trim package. The night rider could select either the pair of Little King spotlights ($11.50) or the Little Beauty pair at $13.25.

Right: In 1937 Harley-Davidson offered the distinctive sherwood green and silver color scheme. Standard rims were silver; cadmium plating was an extra 50 cents per wheel.

1936 VLH
Owner/restorer – Dave Royal
Nipomo, California

1938 U
Owner – Trev Deeley Museum
Vancouver, British Columbia

Above: The standard Seventy-four
U model was a popular choice for
sidecars and commercial use.
Frames, brakes, clutches and
transmissions were all strengthened
for 1938.

Left: The fork spring cover was a
one-year feature on the big twins,
but stayed on the Forty-five
for four years.

Above: The Eighty (VLH) and
Seventy-four (VLD) could be
ordered with the optional 4-speed
transmission for $15.
New cylinders had larger
cooling fins.

1938 WLDR

SPECIFICATIONS
ENGINE/DRIVETRAIN
Engine: Flathead 45° V-twin
Displacement: 45.32ci
(746.33cc)
Bore & stroke: 2.75 x 3.81in
(69 x 97mm)
Horsepower: 27
Carburetion: Linkert
Transmission: 3-speed
Primary drive: Duplex chain
Final drive: Chain
Brakes: F. Expanding shoe.
R. Contracting band
Battery: 6-volt
Ignition: Coil/points

CHASSIS/SUSPENSION
Frame: Steel, single downtube
Suspension: F. Leading link
spring fork
Wheelbase: 56.5in (143.5in)
Weight: 390lb (176.9kg)
Fuel capacity: 3.5gal (13.25lit)
Oil capacity: 7.5pts (3.55lit)
Tires: 4.00 x 18in (10.16 x
45.7cm)
Top speed: 85mph (137km/h)
Colors: Teak red/black; venetian
blue/white; hollywood
green/gold; silver tan/blue
Number built: 139
Price: $380

Above: The flathead Forty-five had become the foundation of American Class C racing. Milwaukee moved to challenge Indian's dominance.

Right: The WLDR first appeared in 1937, and cost $25 more than the standard Forty-five. The engine used roller bearings throughout, and cooling fins were added to the timing case.

WLDR (1938) AND EL (1939)

By 1938 Milwaukee had applied to the Forty-five most of the improvements made on the big twins. The baby flathead had roller bearings in the lower end and one-piece cam gears. The transmission got the new shift mechanism and stronger gears. The oil pump was upgraded and cooling fins were added to the timing case cover and the left side of the crankcase. And like the big twins, standard automotive-style grease fittings were adopted.

With the 61 OHV and flathead big twins fairly well sorted out, more attention was devoted to the small twin. The primary reason was the broad popularity of the Indian Sport Scout, which had captured numerous fans on the road and race track. Bill Harley campaigned for an overhead-valve 750, using the existing flathead bottom end. Production cost projections shelved the idea, but the decision was made to build a limited number of sportier 750 flatheads to compete with the Indian.

Class C racing became the prominent competition category in 1938. Harley-Davidson's WLDR, rated at 27 horsepower, was the closest thing Milwaukee had to a factory racer. Since Class C was formulated as amateur racing, riders were expected to ride their machines to the track, remove the lights and unnecessary equipment, and have at it. So the WLDR was configured as a standard road model, but featured higher compression and larger valves. With the addition of aluminum heads and larger intake ports in 1939, horsepower was up into the mid-thirties.

A great measure of credit for tweaking the Forty-five's performance goes to San Jose Harley dealer Tom Sifton. As a tuner, Sifton managed to solve the breathing, lubrication and overheating difficulties magnified by racing conditions. Racer Sam Arena was soon beating the Indians, and Milwaukee incorporated most of Sifton's improvements on subsequent models. The first factory version built solely for racing, the WR, would appear in 1941.

61 OHV

The mighty Knucklehead was strengthened in 1939 with splined pinion and oil pump drive gears, and a one-piece pinion gearshaft. Stronger valve springs were also fitted, and the valve train assemblies had been completely covered the year before. All big twins in the Harley roster now had upper and lower self-aligning steering head bearings.

The instrument panel was streamlined and color matched with the motorcycle, and the design came to be called the "cat's eye" panel. Painted fender stripes gave way to stainless steel strips. The available colors were airway blue/white panels, black/ivory panels and teak red/black panels. The price, for the third year running, was $435.

Development of a military motorcycle had been underway in Milwaukee for more than a year, with prototypes of both the 61 OHV and Forty-five tested. Just before the German invasion of Poland, two Forty-fives with the model designation WLA were shipped to Fort Knox, Kentucky for Army testing.

Below: There was still no evidence of rear suspension in 1938. Chromed frame was not original livery.

Below: Milwaukee's Forty-five was not so light or nimble as the flathead racer built by Indian. But it was durable, and Tom Sifton was finding more power.

Left: Painted fender stripes were replaced by stainless steel strips in 1939. The fender light was included in the standard accessory package. Airflow taillight was replaced by a larger lamp with a license plate bracket above it.

1939 EL
Owner/restorer – Harold Mathews
Mathews Harley-Davidson
Fresno, California

Above: Teak red and black remained on the color chart for '39, but fenders were not two-tone. The colors have been transposed on this example.

Above: The Knucklehead received new valve springs, pistons, intake manifold, transmission and softer fork springs.

1938 WLDR
Owner/restorer – Armando Magri
H-D of Sacramento, California

1941 GA SERVI-CAR

SPECIFICATIONS
ENGINE/DRIVETRAIN
Engine: Flathead 45° V-twin:
Displacement: 45.32ci
(742.65cc)
Bore & stroke: 2.75 x 3.81in
(70 x 97mm)
Compression ratio: 4.75:1
Horsepower: 22 @ 4,500rpm
Carburetion: Linkert
Transmission: 3-speed
w/reverse
Primary drive: Duplex chain
Final drive: Gear differential
Brakes: F & R. Drum
Battery: 6-volt
Ignition: Coil/points

CHASSIS/SUSPENSION
Frame: Steel, single downtube
Suspension: F. Leading link
spring/shock fork. R. Coil springs
Wheelbase: 61in (155cm)
Track: 42in (106.7cm)
Weight: 1,360lb (619kg)
Fuel capacity: 3.4gal (12.9lit)
Oil capacity: 3.5qts (3.31lit)
Tires: 5.00 x 16in (12.7 x
40.6cm)
Top speed: 50mph (80km/h)
Colors: Skyway blue; cruiser
green; flight red; brilliant black
Number built: 1,159 (all
models)
Price: $510

Right: The Servi-Car,
introduced in 1932, was
never produced in large
quantities. Production reached
1,159 in 1941, the highest
number Milwaukee had built.
The figures then dropped but
increased again after the war.

SERVI-CAR (1941)

Harley-Davidson recognized early on the commercial applications for motorcycles. Until 1930, most of Milwaukee's service vehicles employed the sidecar chassis. Rigs were modified to use open and closed sidevans, parcel cars and mail trucks.

The Servi-Car was spawned by the Cycle-Tow, which utilized an outrigger wheel on each side of the motorcycle's rear wheel. The device was sold to auto service shops as a tow vehicle to bring disabled cars in for service. It didn't work so well.

In 1932 the Servi-Car appeared as a genuine 3-wheeler. The following year small or large bodies were available, and the 3-speed transmission included reverse. Powered by the 45-inch (750cc) flathead, the machine was soon equipped with a towbar, bumper and spare tire mount. Final drive was by chain to a sprocket on the rear axle, which drove an automotive-type differential. The axle also carried a drum brake from the 74 VL.

The Servi-Car was widely used by car dealers and repair shops, since one man could collect and return a customer's vehicle with the 3-wheeler in tow. Small businesses used the trike as a delivery vehicle, but its most common application became the police transporter for emptying parking meters and writing traffic tickets.

Solo motorcylists generally scoffed at the 3-wheeler, which, like the sidecar, they viewed as a bastardized union of car and motorcycle. Something to be driven, not ridden. But the practical aspects of the Servi-Car were difficult to deny. Riders who, by virtue of disability or inclination, were unable to operate a two-wheeler could still travel in the wind. As motorcycle clubs gained increasing popularity, trike owners were welcomed as haulers of food and refreshments.

Commercial entrepreneurs on tight budgets utilized the Servi-Car as both delivery trucks and traveling billboards. The rear of the cargo box offered advertising space to display the company name and phone number. And to add billboards to each side, Harley-Davidson offered fender "Ad" skirts at $3.50 the pair.

The Servi-Car was continuously upgraded in the 1930s and 1940s, sharing many of the improvements made to the motorcycles. It gained two rear brakes in 1937 and an enclosed chain the following year. In 1939 the towbar was strengthened and given a permanent attachment, eliminating the need to remove it and carry it in the trunk. Larger bodies were offered and the rear suspension modified to reduce body roll.

In 1940 the axle housing was beefed up and the transmission's shifting mechanism was simplified. Cast iron brake drums replaced the stamped steel housings. A new frame was introduced in 1941, with a stronger axle in a welded rather than riveted tube. The compression ratio was upped to 4.75:1 and the front brake fitted from the Seventy-four.

Right: The Servi-Car was touted as an economical alternative to trucks for light delivery service. The 3-wheeler was widely used by the police for traffic ticket duties, and by auto repair shops to pick up and return cars.

Above: The Forty-five flathead proved to be the most durable motor in the Milwaukee roster. The Servi-Car was in production for more than 40 years.

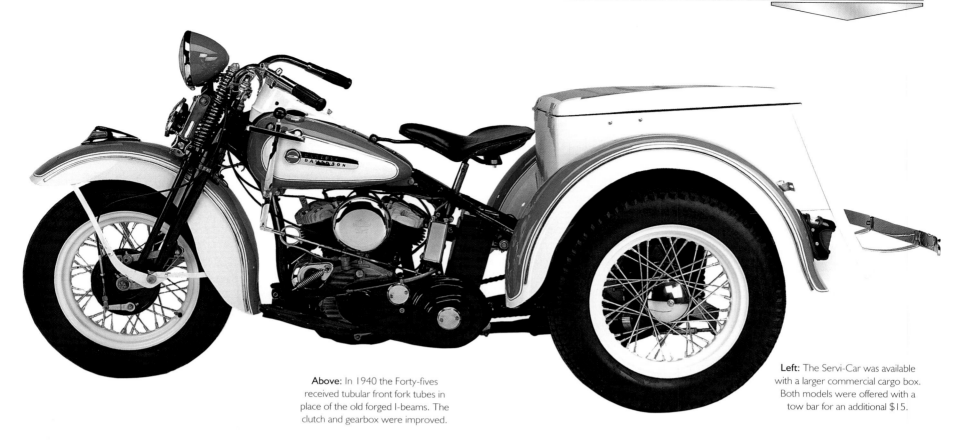

Above: In 1940 the Forty-fives received tubular front fork tubes in place of the old forged I-beams. The clutch and gearbox were improved.

Left: The Servi-Car was available with a larger commercial cargo box. Both models were offered with a tow bar for an additional $15.

1941 GA Servi-Car
Owner – Trev Deeley Museum
Vancouver, British Columbia

Left: Stronger axle housings were added in 1940, and cast iron brake drums replaced the earlier stamped steel units. Standard tire size was now 5.00 x 16 (12.7 x 40.6cm). For 1941, the compression ratio on the Forty-five was increased from 4.5 to 4.75:1.

"The great popularity of the Harley-Davidson Servi-Car with automotive establishments everywhere is based on its ability to decidedly increase business, cut costs, and produce greater profits."
(From a 1941 advertisement)

1941 WLA

SPECIFICATIONS
ENGINE/DRIVETRAIN
Engine: Flathead 45° V-twin
Displacement: 45.12ci
(739.38cc)
Bore & stroke: 2.75 x 3.81in
(70 x 97mm)
Compression ratio: 5:1
Horsepower: 23.5 @
4,600rpm
Carburetion: Linkert
Transmission: 3-speed
Primary drive: Duplex chain
Final drive: Chain
Brakes: F. & R. Drum
Battery: 6-volt
Ignition: Coil/points

CHASSIS/SUSPENSION
Frame: Steel, single downtube
Suspension: F. Leading link
spring fork
Wheelbase: 57.5in (146cm)
Weight: 540lb (250kg)
Fuel capacity: 3.375gal
(12.8lit)
Oil capacity: 7.5pts (3.55lit)
Tires: 4.00 x 18in (10.16 x
45.7cm)
Top speed: 65mph (105km/h)
Color: Olive drab
Number built: 2,282
Price: $380

1942 XA

SPECIFICATIONS
ENGINE/DRIVETRAIN
Engine: Flathead opposed twin
Displacement: 45.04ci (738cc)
Bore & stroke: 3.125 x
3.125in (78 x 78mm)
Compression ratio: 5.7:1
Horsepower: 23 @ 4,600rpm
Carburetion: 2 Linkert
Transmission: 4-speed
Primary drive: Gear
Final drive: Shaft
Brakes: F. & R. Drum
Battery: 6-volt
Ignition: Coil/points

CHASSIS/SUSPENSION
Frame: Steel, double downtube
Suspension: F. Leading link
spring fork. R. Plunger
Wheelbase: 58.75in (149.2cm)
Weight: 538lb (244kg)
Fuel capacity: 4.1gal (15.5lit)
Oil capacity: 2qts (1.89lit)
Tires: 4.00 x 18in (10.16 x
45.7cm)
Top speed: 65mph
(105km/h)
Color: Olive drab
Number built:
1,000
Price: $870.35

In 1942 Harley-Davidson's
civilian service training facility
was changed to the
Quartermaster School for
teaching military mechanics.
The maintenance and repair
of the WLA Forty-five was
given top priority.

WLA (1941-45) AND XA (1942)

Rumors of war were gaining momentum in 1938, and Harley-Davidson considered the prospect of preparing motorcycles for the military. The Army had been using Seventy-fours with side-cars, but was unhappy with them. Milwaukee prepared several Sixty-one ohv and Forty-five models for military tests.

At the time, development was underway on overhead-valve civilian versions of both the the big and small flathead twins, but the program was slowed by the military situation. In 1939 the Army conducted rigorous testing on motorcycles built by Indian, Harley-Davidson and the Delco Corporation. The latter, a BMW clone, featured shaft drive and telescopic fork. Both the Indian and Harley-Davidson were versions of each company's 750 flathead. The Army stipulated that the motorcycle must be capable of 65mph (105km/h) and not overheat at low speeds.

Despite the popularity of their Chief and Scout, Indian was not in a strong position near the end of the decade. Their four-cylinder machine had been an expensive failure, and problems with quality control created difficulties in the marketplace. Both Indian and Harley were selling motorcycles to allied military forces overseas, and the competition for the U.S. government contracts had both companies intent on becoming the major supplier.

In March of 1940 the Army ordered 745 WLAs from Milwaukee. Harley-Davidson fitted the new style tubular front fork, which was lengthened 2.375 inches (6.03cm) to provide additional ground clearance. The olive drab machines were equipped with the new aluminum heads and D-shaped footboards, crash bars, skidplates, cargo racks and saddlebags. Orders were soon forthcoming from South Africa for 2,000 machines, 5,000 for Great Britain and another 659 for the U.S. Army. Milwaukee would later furnish military motorcycles to both the Chinese and Russian armed forces.

In its final configuration the WLA had a compression ratio of 5:1, and was rated at 23.5 horsepower at 4,600rpm. An oil-bath air filter was fitted, the clutch and transmission were improved, and

engine lubrication was upgraded with the use of a bypass valve calibrated to engine speed. By the end of the war, Milwaukee had built some 88,000 motorcycles for military use.

XA

By 1941 most of Harley-Davidson's production was devoted to military machines. The new 74-inch (1200cc) overhead-valve FL was introduced, but fewer than 2,500 were built. The Army had long insisted on a prototype BMW-style, shaft-drive motorcycle. Milwaukee, though hardly convinced of the necessity for such a machine, responded with the XA.

The 45 cubic inch (750cc) flathead opposed twin was a frank copy of the BMW. It featured a foot-shift 4-speed transmission, shaft-drive, hand clutch, plunger rear suspension and a lengthened WLA fork. The Army ordered 1,000 machines at a cost of $870 each. Production ended when the military decided that the WLA would do the job at considerably less expense.

A prototype sidecar version of the boxer twin was also constructed, with a shaft driving the sidecar wheel. Development work was also underway on a shaft-drive 3-wheeler, but the creation of the Jeep canceled both projects

Below: The tubular luggage rack was replaced by a heavy-duty square-section rack to carry a radio.

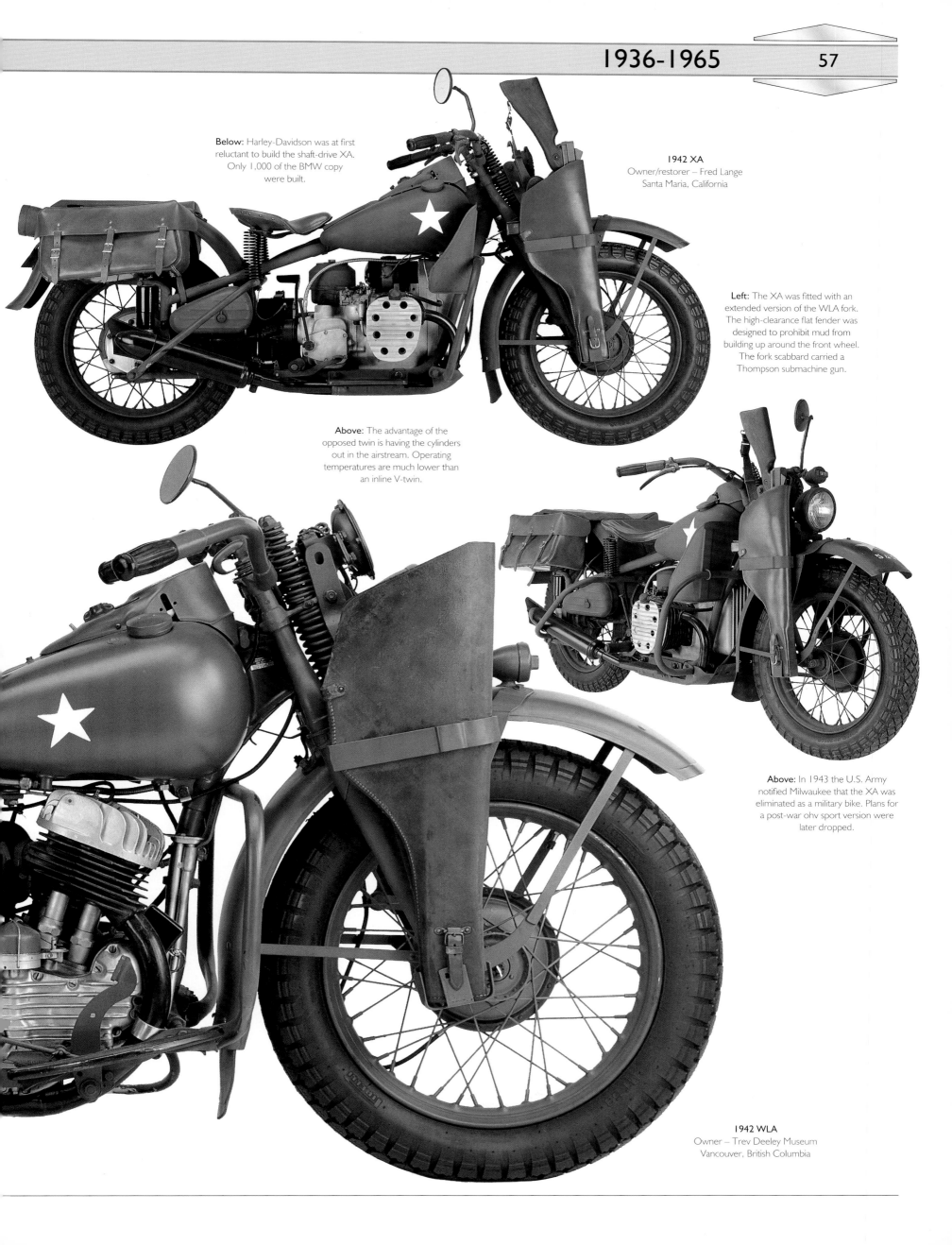

Below: Harley-Davidson was at first reluctant to build the shaft-drive XA. Only 1,000 of the BMW copy were built.

1942 XA
Owner/restorer – Fred Lange
Santa Maria, California

Left: The XA was fitted with an extended version of the WLA fork. The high-clearance flat fender was designed to prohibit mud from building up around the front wheel. The fork scabbard carried a Thompson submachine gun.

Above: The advantage of the opposed twin is having the cylinders out in the airstream. Operating temperatures are much lower than an inline V-twin.

Above: In 1943 the U.S. Army notified Milwaukee that the XA was eliminated as a military bike. Plans for a post-war ohv sport version were later dropped.

1942 WLA
Owner – Trev Deeley Museum
Vancouver, British Columbia

1941 FL

SPECIFICATIONS
ENGINE/DRIVETRAIN
Engine: OHV 45° V-twin
Displacement: 73.73ci
(1,208.19cc)
Bore & stroke: 3.43 x 3.5in
(87 x 101.6mm)
Horsepower: 48 @ 5,000rpm
Compression ratio: F, 6.6:1,
FL, 7:1
Carburetion: 1.31in (33.3mm)
Linkert
Transmission: 4-speed
Primary drive: Chain
Final drive: Chain
Brakes: F & R. Drum
Battery: 6-volt
Ignition: Coil/points

CHASSIS/SUSPENSION
Frame: Steel, double downtube
Suspension: F. Spring fork
Wheelbase: 59.5in (151.1cm)
Weight: 575lb (261kg)
Fuel capacity: 3.75gal (14.2lit)
Oil capacity: 4qts (3.79lit)
Tires: 5.00 x 16in (12.7 x
40.6cm)
Top speed: 95 mph (153km/h)
Colors: Clipper blue; flight red;
cruiser green; black; olive green
(export)
Number built: 2,452
Price: $465

FL 74 OHV (1941) AND WLDR (1941)

The 61 OHV Knucklehead was certainly a powerful motorcycle for its day, but the American notion that bigger is better would prevail. Police forces were especially keen on top speed. The J series had established in the market an affinity for the Seventy-four, so a bigger overhead-valve twin was part of the natural progression.

The big twins had been given stronger, smoother operating clutch assemblies two years earlier. The 1939 models featured a transmission combining elements of sliding-gear and constant-mesh components, with neutral between second and third gears. The design lasted only one year. Long-distance testing on the 74 ohv prototype revealed the need for stronger crankcases, and the rocker arm assemblies were also redesigned to improve top end lubrication.

Crankpins increased in diameter, and the new crankcases for the 61 and 74 ohv lacked the baffles previously employed to equalize lubrication in the cylinders. The change helped solve the persistent problem of excessive crankcase pressure, and produced an increase in power. At the top end, larger intake ports, carburetor and redesigned manifold contributed to the horsepower gain. A new vane-type oil pump assisted in ensuring the engine's overall comfort, and a change to 5.00 x 16-inch (12.7 x 40.6cm) tires provided a smoother ride. These 74-inch (1200cc) twins were designated the F and FL (higher compression) models.

Styling changed only slightly for 1941. The speedometer face changed from black numbers on white to a black background with larger silver numbers. The fuel tank featured a chrome band bisecting the sides. Four color options were still available, with cruiser green replacing squadron gray on the menu. But it wasn't long before the paint selection was subordinated by the war effort, and buyers had to take what they could get.

From the 1941 brochure: "The deluxe solo group has just about everything in it but a chrome-plated shower-bath and will decorate your new Harley-Davidson like a Christmas tree."

WLDR

Military testing had produced improvements that transferred to the civilian Forty-fives. Many big twin upgrades were applied to the little guy; the clutch assembly grew stronger and smoother in operation, and the gearbox was beefed up and given larger gears and an improved shifting mechanism.

The iron-head WL became the economy model, with compression ratio reduced to 4.75:1. The aluminum-head WLDR, on the other hand, grew even sportier with larger crankpin, stronger valve springs, hotter cams and bigger carburetor. These engines reportedly produced about 35 horsepower. It was also 1941 when the factory racing versions appeared. The WR (flat track) and WRTT (roadracing and scrambles) had flat valve lifters instead of rollers, for higher rpm.

Class C racing was achieving more popularity just as the advent of World War II put such frivolous activities on the shelf. The WLDR was discontinued during the summer, and the production of racing models was suspended with the United States' entry into the war.

But the workhorse Forty-five would continue as the motive power for Army bikes, the Servi-Car and be resuscitated once again for sport riding and racing after the war. Eventually it would develop into the K model of the 1950s, which later evolved into the Sportster. The little twin was to achieve a lasting legacy in the Milwaukee hierarchy.

Below: This was the first year for the new rocket-fin muffler. Two-tone paint was gone; teak red was one of four solid colors for 1941.

Right: The Knucklehead was first offered as a Seventy-four in 1941. Both bore and stroke increased over the Sixty-one, and the new flywheels were larger and heavier. Once again, the call was for more power.

Left: With the arrival of the racing WR, 1941 was the last year for the WLDR. The hot-rod Forty-five was rated at seven more horsepower than the WLD, the R model would pull to 5,500 rpm.

1941 WLDR
Owner/restorer – Armando Magri
H-D of Sacramento, California

Below: Stainless steel trim strips were extended to the tank. The Deluxe model had chromed rims and instrument panel.

Above: The Forty-five was granted a stronger clutch, transmission and rear brake in 1941.

1941 FL
Owner – Armando Magri
H-D of Sacramento, California
Restored by Larry Galyean

ULH (1941), EL (1941) AND WLD (1945)

Because of the war, Milwaukee made virtually no changes to the motorcycles between 1941 and 1946. Color choices dwindled to gray or silver, and in 1944 to gray only. The option of red paint returned in 1946.

As noted earlier, the big twins received numerous improvements in the years just before the war. Aluminum heads were standard on the Eighty in 1940 and optional on the Seventy-four. The alloy cylinder head weighed over five pounds (2.27kg) less than its cast iron counterpart. Bigger crankpins, stouter clutches and constant-mesh transmissions were also incorporated the same year.

Front brake drums changed from stamped steel to stronger cast iron units, and strength was also added to the fork tubes by a heat treating process. The clutch lever bracket and kickstand were redesigned, and streamlined footboards replaced the previous rectangular style. This was also the first year of the "instant reserve" fuel valve at the top left of the tank, and the larger 7-inch (17.8cm) circular air cleaner.

Buckhorn handlebars were still standard in 1941, but flatter Speedster bars remained available as a no-charge option, as they had for the previous ten years. Sixteen-inch (40.6cm) wheels were now standard and 18-inchers (45.7cm) became optional, opposite the earlier system. Chromed

rims were $2.50 apiece extra. The fishtail muffler was replaced by a longer "rocket-fin" silencer, and tail light housings were now painted black rather than the bodywork color.

The 61 ohv E series Knucklehead now shared the heavier flywheels of the Seventy-four. The change to a half-inch (1.27cm) longer intake manifold and reduction in carburetor venturi to 1.125 inches (28.6mm) aided low-speed operation. The Sixty-one also featured the clutch upgrades applied to its bigger brethren. The larger hub rode on more ball bearings, seven discs provided 65 percent more surface contact, and spring-loaded balls in the steel discs subdued clutch chatter.

1941 EL
Owner – Trev Deeley Museum
Vancouver, British Columbia
Restored by Fred Pazaski

Above: Fred Pazaski, Bellingham, Washington, put 60,000 miles (96,600km) on this Knucklehead, including racing miles. He sold it, bought it back and restored it.

Above & below:
The Sixty-one ohv and Eighty side-valve were identical but for the engines.

Right: 1941 was the last year for the flathead Eighty. The rocket-fin muffler was quieter than its predecessor, but contained no steel wool packing to eventually burn out.

1945 WLD
Owner – Trev Deeley Museum
Vancouver, British Columbia

Left: The cat's eye instrument panel
was fitted through 1946. Left
lens is the oil signal lamp; right
lens for generator.

With reductions in government orders for military bikes, Harley-Davidson began the process of converting to civilian production. Most of the 88,000 motorcycles built for the war effort were WL Forty-fives. In addition to the thousands of machines in Great Britain, Europe and the Soviet Union, a sizeable inventory remained in Milwaukee. The surplus war models were sold in large lots, at substantial discounts, to Harley-Davidson dealers and automobile dealers throughout the country.

The post-war demand for motorcycles was high, and Milwaukee resumed its emphasis on the big twins. The first model year for full-scale civilian production was 1946, and the following year Harley-Davidson manufactured more than 20,000 machines, the highest output they had reached since 1929 (excluding the years of military production).

Class C racing resumed in earnest at Daytona Beach in 1947. And although Indian, compared to Harley-Davidson, had fared poorly during the war years, the long-standing battle between the two would still be hotly contested on the race tracks. And a fair number of young men returning from war looked forward eagerly to peacetime prosperity, and the freedom of the open road.

Left: Aluminum heads were
standard on the Eighty (ULH) and
optional on the Seventy-four (UL).
The stainless steel tank trim was
used from 1941 through 1946.

1941 ULH
Owner/restorer – Harold Mathews
Mathews Harley-Davidson
Fresno, California

F AND FL (1946)

Production of the F-series Knuckleheads jumped from fewer than 1,000 for 1945 to more than 4,000 for 1946, and rose to over 7,000 the succeeding year. The Seventy-four was outselling the Sixty-one by a significant margin.

The stylish cat's-eye instrument panel made its last appearance in 1946. The speedometer face was two-tone rather than silver, with the numerals matching the color of the inner circle. The three color combinations offered were black/silver, green/cream and gray/white in a design known as the "airplane-style" speedometer. This would also be the last installment of the streamlined tail light, more evidence that the Art Deco influence was fading in favor of more squarish designs.

Wartime material shortages were still apparent early in the year. Gray and red were the only color options available until about mid-year, when skyway blue and black were offered once again. Chrome tank badges and stainless steel trim were also absent from the earlier models, and likewise for chromed shift levers and gates, headlight rims and gas caps.

Few more than 2,000 ohv models had been produced in Milwaukee during the war, and most were for military use. But testing and development continued during this period, as Harley-Davidson looked ahead to the prospects in the post-war market. Work on the first hydraulic telescope front fork was underway, and a prototype was fitted to a Knucklehead in 1945. The Hydra-Glide fork would appear on production models in 1949.

The first indication of hydraulic damping for the front wheel appeared on the big twins in 1946. A Monroe shock absorber adjoined the fork springs, replacing the rudimentary Ride-Control friction device. No corresponding cushioning occured at the rear wheel, which remained solidly bolted to the frame. Suspension advancements in Milwaukee evidently would be addressed strictly one end at a time.

The Knucklehead itself was on the road to history by 1946. Notwithstanding their reputation for caution in developing new models, Milwaukee recognized that motorcycling would soon be changing. That more riders would be demanding smoother, oil-tight engines, motors that started easily and were reliable (even for the mechanically disinclined), and transmissions that shifted without the removal of a hand from the handlebar.

These and other items were most certainly on Harley-Davidson's agenda as the United States shifted to a peacetime economy. The tussle between Springfield and Milwaukee was renewed, in the growing motorcycle marketplace and on the race track. The Daytona 200, the traditional season opener, wasn't resumed until 1947, and it went to Indian rider Johnny Spiegelhoff. And in 1948 former Harley racer Floyd Emde switched to Indian and won the prestigious beachfront competition.

In the meantime, shrewd Tom Sifton was extracting more horsepower from the venerable WR engine. And Harley-Davidson was at work on the tasks of bringing rear suspension, foot-shift and effective brakes to the racing arena. All of which would soon make their way to road machines for the public.

Above: The airplane-style speedometer was fitted from 1941 through 1946. The two-tone face was either black/silver, green/cream or gray/white.

Below: Seat options were in limited availability just after the war. The deluxe solo saddle still rode the atop the Ful-Floeting spring.

Below: The hinged rear fender remained in production for many years, making tire changes much easier.

Below: Saddlebag styles expanded after the war. The type 1 King Size version is from 1948. A fringed model arrived in 1950.

1946F
Owner/restorer – Ken Lang
Oakville, Ontario, Canada

Below: The spring fork shock absorber first appeared in 1946. The rear view mirror was included in the special solo group, which included safety guards, trip odometer and sheepskin seat cover.

Above: Chromed parts were unavailable until the middle of the year. Early model nameplates were painted.

1946 FL
Owner – Oliver Shokouh
Glendale Harley-Davidson
Glendale, California

125 MODEL S

SPECIFICATIONS
ENGINE/DRIVETRAIN
Engine: Two-stroke single
Displacement: 7.6ci (124.87cc)
Bore & stroke: 2.06 x 2.28in
(52 x 58mm)
Horsepower: 3
Compression ratio: 6.6:1
Carburetion: L & L
Transmission: 3-speed
Primary drive: Chain
Final drive: Chain
Brakes: F & R. Drum
Battery: 6-volt
Ignition: Coil/points

CHASSIS/SUSPENSION
Frame: Steel, single downtube
Suspension: F. Girder fork,
rubber band
Wheelbase: 50in (127cm)
Weight: 185lb (84kg)
Fuel capacity: 1.75gal (6.6lit)
Tires: 3.25 x 19in (8.26 x
48.26cm)
Top speed: 50mph (80km/h)
Color: Black
Number built: 10,117
Price: $325

Above: The 125cc two-stroke
was touted as both an
economical means of
transportation and
an entry-level
machine for novice
riders. The design
came from DKW.

Right: With the 1947 models,
Milwaukee returned to full
civilian production. The final
year of production for the
Knucklehead brought new
trim and accessory packages.

FL (1947) AND 125 MODEL S (1948)

The biggest change in Harley-Davidson's 1947 models was the price. The cost of the top-of-the-line 74 OHV had held steady at $465 for six years, although very few were produced from 1941-45. The price on the last of the Seventy-four Knuckleheads was $605, a 33 percent jump from the year before. Inflation was soaring, and peacetime recreation was going to be expensive.

A number of revisions were made for 1947 that distinguish the final Knucklehead from its predecessors. Streamlining was back in the form of new fuel tank nameplates, which came to be called "speed ball" badges. Stainless steel fender trim returned to production, as did the front fender lamp. A larger tail light, nicknamed the "tombstone" design, incorporated the license plate bracket.

The fuel tank was redesigned to accommodate a new instrument panel, and the speedometer face featured a two-tone black and white background with italicized silver numerals and a red pointer. The separate generator and oil lights were consolidated in a small rectangular housing with a single lens situated in the center of the tank.

The Deluxe Buddy Seat had been deleted during the war years and returned to civilian duty in 1946. The 1947 version was offered in black cowhide only, featuring a plastic skirt with a chromed star on each side.

Four color options were again offered in 1947: skyway blue, cruiser green, flight red and brilliant black. Nearly 12,000 Knuckleheads were made for the model year, over half Milwaukee's total production. In its twelve-year run the Knuckle had won a loyal following, and remains an icon in the Harley lineage as the original American superbike.

125 S

Harley-Davidson was the only U.S. motorcycle manufacturer in a strong position before, during and after the war. Among the most tangible spoils of victory was the appropriation of Germany's DKW manufacturing rights, which Milwaukee shared with BSA of Great Britain. Thus the instant lightweight.

Small two-stroke motorcycles had never achieved wide popularity in the United States, and the S model would prove no exception. But it did provide benefits for Harley-Davidson in the long term. The tiddler offered a low-cost entry into motorcycling ($5.50 per week), and surely stimulated the appetites of young novice riders for bigger and better machines. Preferably, from the Milwaukee viewpoint, bigger and better motorcycles with valves.

DKW (Dampf Kraft Wagen) had built some fast racing motorcycles, but the proletarian 125 was simply an economical utility machine. They served well as mass transportation on the congested byways of Europe, but seemed little more than a motorized bicycle to Americans weaned on big twins. Harley-Davidson dealers, by and large, didn't want to be bothered with the machine and did little to promote it.

Thousands of youngsters, on the other hand, learned to ride on the 3-horsepower machine. And racers prized the small, lightweight fuel tank, which would appear some years later on the Sportster. So while the S model never became a sales leader, it did evolve into a multi-purpose machine later tagged the Hummer, and expand to 165 and 175cc off-road variants.

The S model turned out to be a good (and inexpensive) investment in Harley-Davidson's future. It enticed a good number of young folks into the exhilarating sport of motorcycling. And, with almost perfect timing, it taught them how to clutch with the hand and shift with the foot. That process would soon accelerate with the arrival of other more substantial motorcycles from overseas.

1948 125 S
Owner/restorer – Fred Lange
Santa Maria, California

Above: The 125 S was introduced in mid-1948. Ads emphasized its economy at 90 miles per gallon (38km/lit).

Below: The red "speed-ball" nameplate made its debut in 1947, as did the off-set rubber-mounted handlebar. The instrument panel was a new design.

Above: The "tombstone" taillight first appeared in 1947. Chrome headlamp, exhaust pipe covers and fender tips came with the special solo group.

1947 FL
Owner – Trev Deeley Museum
Vancouver, British Columbia

1948 FL

SPECIFICATIONS

ENGINE/DRIVETRAIN
Engine: OHV 45° V-twin
Displacement: 73.73ci
(1208.19cc)
Bore & stroke: 3.44 x 4in
(87 x 102mm)
Compression ratio: 7:1
Horsepower: 50 @ 4,800rpm
Carburetion: 1.31in (33.3mm)
Schebler
Transmission: 4-speed
Primary drive: Chain
Final drive: Chain
Brakes: F & R. Drum
Battery: 6-volt
Ignition: Coil/points

CHASSIS/SUSPENSION
Frame: Steel, double downtube
Suspension: Leading link
spring/shock fork
Wheelbase: 59.5in (151.1cm)
Weight: 565lb (256kg)
Fuel capacity: 3.75gal (14.2lit)
Oil capacity: 1gal (3.78lit)
Tires: 5.00 x 16in (12.7 x
40.6cm)
Top speed: 100mph (161km/h)
Colors: Azure blue; flight red;
black
Number built: 8,071
Price: $650

FL (1948)

NEW! IMPROVED! No other two words figured more strongly in American advertising after World War II. As applied to motorcycle engines they usually meant overhead valves, hydraulic lifters, aluminum heads, improved lubrication and better combustion. Enter the Panhead.

If, as H-D chronicler Allan Girdler says, "technical progress is war's only useful product," the Panhead owed much of its usefulness to military combat. The development of high-performance aircraft created a sourcebook of engineering and design lessons for builders of earthbound air-cooled engines. One result was less attention to form and more on function.

Not that the new FL was an entirely new engine, as the Knucklehead had been 12 years before. Harley-Davidson product development has always been evolutionary. The frame was stretched to accommodate the taller engine, which was lighter and carried its oil lines inside. A new oil pump did a more thorough job of sending lubricant to the required parts. But the most distinctive departure from the past was the Panhead's hydraulic valve lifters, which solved two problems. Maintaining exact valve adjustment became less critical and the engine ran cooler.

With the Panhead, Milwaukee set out to make motorcycling easier. Heretofore the sport was largely limited to those capable of maintaining, and often repairing, an unforgiving mechanical

assemblage. Motorcycles that ran better and longer without expert attention were likely to attract new riders, which was the Panhead's primary mission.

The engine's bottom end was largely unchanged. A new camshaft was designed for the new valve system, and the cases modified for the new cylinders. The frame was tagged the "wishbone" for its bowed downtubes, and incorporated a steering head lock and mounting plate for crash bars. With the advent of the Hydra-Glide front fork the following year, the '48 grew to become a prized model since it was the first Panhead and the last Springer. Like the Knuckle, the Pan's designations were E for the Sixty-one and F for the Seventy-four.

Horsepower was only marginally higher for the new engine, but it was generally more reliable power. The pan-shaped valve covers kept more oil inside the motor, and the aluminum heads reduced operating temperatures on long rides and in hot weather. Steel inserts held the new 14mm spark plugs. The new system

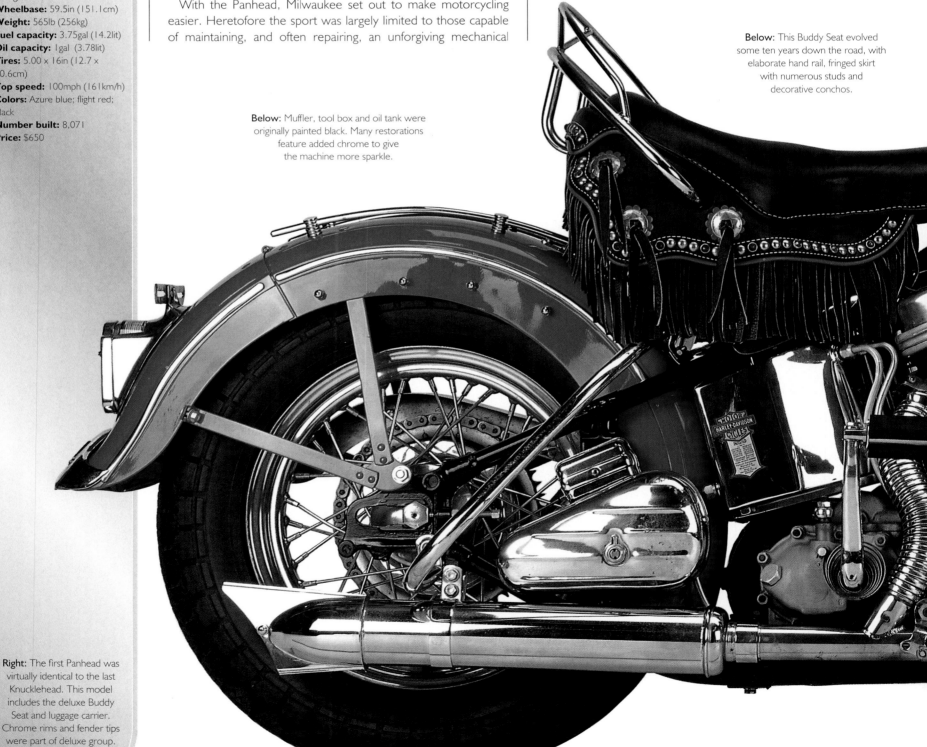

Below: Muffler, tool box and oil tank were originally painted black. Many restorations feature added chrome to give the machine more sparkle.

Below: This Buddy Seat evolved some ten years down the road, with elaborate hand rail, fringed skirt with numerous studs and decorative conchos.

Right: The first Panhead was virtually identical to the last Knucklehead. This model includes the deluxe Buddy Seat and luggage carrier. Chrome rims and fender tips were part of deluxe group.

was not trouble-free, of course. From 1948 through 1952 the hydraulic lifters rode atop the pushrods, and a low oil supply could cause them to malfunction. In 1953 the lifters were relocated to housings above the timing case.

Other changes in 1948 included the gear shift mechanism, which was reversed to put first gear at the rear and fourth in front. Speedometer faces were color matched to the motorcycle, and the debut of the relatively bright azure blue captured a measure of attention. Detractors naturally refered to it as baby blue.

The Panhead enjoyed considerable success for a first-year model. Nearly 13,000 rolled out of Milwaukee in E and F form and total Harley-Davidson production was 29,612, a new peacetime record. National advertising programs were underway once again, easy-payment plans revived, motorcycle racing had resumed and the peaceful highways of the good old U.S.A. beckoned.

And Harley-Davidson was ready with new motorcycles. Improved, too.

Right: Aluminum heads, hydraulic lifters and cake pan valve covers distinguished the Panhead from the Knucklehead. In most other respects, the engines were identical.

Right: The first Panhead was also the first big twin with the wishbone frame, featuring bowed front downtubes.

Left: The front fork assembly and springs were originally painted black. The springer front end would be gone the following year, but would magically reappear 40 years later.

1948 FL
Owner – Mike Lady
Arroyo Grande, California
Restored by Scott Ashley

EL (1950) AND FL (1951) THE HYDRA-GLIDE

1951 FL

SPECIFICATIONS
ENGINE/DRIVETRAIN
Engine: OHV 45° V-twin
Displacement: 73.73ci
(1208.19cc)
Bore & stroke: 3.44 x 4in (87 x 102mm)
Compression ratio: 7:1
Horsepower: 55 @ 4,800rpm
Carburetion: 1.31in (33.3mm)
Schebler
Transmission: 4-speed
Primary drive: Chain
Final drive: Chain
Brakes: F & R. Drum
Battery: 6-volt
Ignition: Coil/points

CHASSIS/SUSPENSION
Frame: Steel, double downtube
Suspension: Telescopic fork
Wheelbase: 59.5in (151.1cm)
Weight: 590lb (267.6kg)
Fuel capacity: 3.75gal (14.2lit)
Oil capacity: 1gal (3.78lit)
Tires: 5.00 x 16in (12.7 x 40.6cm)
Top speed: 100mph (161km)
Colors: Brilliant black; persian red; rio blue
Number built: 6,560
Price: $900

NEWER! MORE IMPROVED! Harley-Davidson leaped into the present in 1949 with the introduction of the Hydra-Glide front fork. Not long after the war, Milwaukee realized that more British and European motorcycles were headed for the U.S.A. And that the imported machines had hydraulic suspension systems. And that these motorcycles were fast.

How the foreign makes would be received by American riders, that remained uncertain in 1950. But Harley-Davidson was not so hidebound by tradition that they could wait and see. Even though Indian was in serious decline, that meant only that new competitors would arise. So development and refinement of the big twins continued, albeit with the measured pragmatism for which Milwaukee was known.

The Hydra-Glide fork served two functions. With two hydraulic/spring tubes, more compliant suspension brought a smoother ride. Secondly, it looked more contemporary. For both cars and motorcycles, the trend in the 1950s was to cover up more of the mechanical bits. Designers moved to more rounded, seamless shapes that reflected the New Modern Age.

The styling shift was also apparent in the fenders, more deeply skirted, one-piece units with contours unbroken by seams or stripes. Parking lamps adorned the upper fork cover and the horn was moved down between the frame tubes. The fuel tanks still carried the subdued nameplate, created by automotive designer Brooks Stevens, that first appeared in 1947. In 1951 the nameplates changed to a script-style logo on a bar background.

It was during this period that Milwaukee discovered what's in a name. Harley-Davidson motorcycles had always been designated only with model letters preceded by a number indicating engine displacement, as in 61 EL. The nicknames – Silent Gray Fellow, Peashooter, Knucklehead, Panhead – were monikers conferred after the fact by riders themselves. Even the Hydra-Glide was not actually a model name, but rather a label for the new front fork.

In 1952 The Motor Company (a contraction by early employees) used Hydra-Glide as a distinct model name on the order blanks. Three years later the two-stroke S model became the Hummer, and in 1957 the new XL would be christened with one of motorcycling's most winning appellations, the Sportster. And a year later, when the first big twin with shock absorbers at both ends rolled off the line, its title was prominently displayed on the front fender: Duo-Glide. Since then, but for racing models, no Harley-Davidson has gone nameless down the road.

Rewind to 1950: concurrent with the drift to less ornate motorcycles came increasing options in accessories. Milwaukee had noted the pride most riders took in outfitting the machines according to their indivuidual tastes. The term Full Dress entered the lexicon, later distilled to Dresser, meaning a motorcycle bedecked in full touring regalia. Harley-Davidson expanded both its line of add-on hardware and the selection of functional yet fashionable motorcyling apparel.

The Panhead was effectively Milwaukee's first easy rider. A big motorcycle, topping 600 pounds (272kg) fully dressed, built for comfort not for speed. Yes, it could be pushed to 100mph (161km/h) and the rubber-mounted handlebar ignored some of the vibration, but the engine was not happy. The adult portion of the 55 horsepower lived between 3,500 and 4,500rpm, plenty enough to motor smartly along. A larger front brake offered a bit more assistance in getting the big twin slowed down.

Below: This rendition of the Deluxe Solo Seat first appeared in 1955. Side trim pieces were chrome.

Right: The Speed King leather saddlebag was first offered in 1954. Milwaukee also supplied a fringed version, known appropriately as the Fringe King.

Above: The solo windshield was a $21.00 option for the 1951 FL with Hydra-Glide fork. Chrome spotlights with mounting hardware would set you back another $21.25.

1951 FL
Owner/restorer – Dave Royal
Nipomo, California

Above: DeLuxe OHV fender badges were first fitted in 1952. Two-tone paint scheme is a custom touch.

Below: Optional bumpers, available for both front and rear fenders, were known as "cheese graters." The crossover dual exhaust system was first offered as an accessory in 1954.

1950 EL
Owner – Trev Deeley Museum
Vancouver, British Columbia

FLF (1952)

Some of the veteran Harley-Davidson fraternity, now accompanied by a growing sorority, were stunned with the 1952 option of foot-shift (the designation for this version being FLF). Many riders never considered the foot-clutch/hand-shift system a major inconvenience. That's how cars operated, so what the hell. But most, after riding one and swapping the functions of hand and foot, noted the new ease of riding in traffic. In retrospect, the old method was monkey motion.

Hand-shift was still available on both the Sixty-one and Seventy-four, and would remain in the catalog until 1972 when there were too few geezers left to matter. For the second year running, only the high-compression models were offered for both the Sixty-one and Seventy-four. Now officially called Hydra-Glides. Since the hand-lever was fitted to the left handlebar, the brake lever moved to the other side and aligned Milwaukee with the rest of the world. Except Great Britain, whose motorcycles had right-side shift levers and left-side brake levers.

This was the final year for the 61-inch (1000cc) Panhead. The Seventy-four outsold the smaller twin by a greater margin each year, and Milwaukee saw no reason to offer two such similar machines. Given the stout nature of the clutch springs, the hand-clutch model was fitted with a leverage booster which came to be called a "mouse trap." (Note: According to a popular expression of the day, if you built a better mouse trap, the world would beat a path to your door. After a decade of new and improved products for the American "consumer," another possibility emerged: that what happens when you build a better mouse trap is that mother nature builds a better mouse.)

The Panhead was not entirely free of the top-end oiling

Below: For 1952 the deluxe solo group was reduced from $115 to $73.50 and included tall or short rubber-mounted handlebar. A windshield was $22.75.

Below: A buckhorn handlebar was popular on the Hydra-Glide. The tank nameplate has been replaced with the style first introduced in 1963.

Above: The first foot-shift Panhead had a clutch booster system called the "mouse trap" (just above shift lever).

problems that had nagged the Knucklehead. Difficuties with dirty oil clogging the lifters was addressed with a check valve and filter screen. This worked until the screen itself clogged up and choked the oil supply. The problem was eliminated in 1953 when the lifters moved from the tops to the bottoms of the pushrods.

Another top end modification for 1952 was the rotating exhaust valve. In an effort to reduce the likelihood of burned valves, a cap between the valve stem and rocker allowed the valve to rotate when open. This worked to equalize the wear pattern and maintain good compression. The big twin muffler looked identical to the 1951 version, but new internals made it quieter. Thus the name change from the Mellow-Tone to the Low-Tone muffler.

1951 FL
Owner/restorer – Fred Lange
Santa Maria, California

Below: In 1951 the sidecar added $240 to the cost of the Hydra-Glide, for a total of $1,140. The fork angle was adjustable on the sidecar model.

Above: The Panhead engine was rated at 55 horsepower in 1951.

Production numbers had remained about the same for three years. Motorcycling was competing with more types of recreation each year, and Milwaukee campaigned with dealers to promote the products locally. A large portion of the push for new riders focused on the new 45ci (750cc) K model, which replaced the old Forty-five. Hopes were high that a sportier middleweight would attract those riders being courted by the growing number of European motorcycle dealers in the U.S.

But despite a slipping market, the big twin still sold well. Milwaukee stuck to the development path of modifying or replacing one or two components at a time, as engineering and tooling costs were balanced with the vagaries of national economics and customer demands. And it had not gone unnoticed, by either the engineering or sales departments, that the British were coming.

1952 FL
Owner – John Tosta
Hanford, California
Restored by Jones Brothers

1952 K

SPECIFICATIONS
ENGINE/DRIVETRAIN
Engine: Flathead 45° V-twin
Displacement: 45.32ci
(742.66cc)
Bore & stroke: 2.75 x 3.81in
(70 x 97mm)
Compression ratio: 6:1
Horsepower: 30
Carburetion: Linkert
Transmission: Unit 4-speed
Primary drive: Duplex chain
Final drive: Chain
Brakes: F & R. Drum
Battery: 6-volt
Ignition: Coil/points

CHASSIS/SUSPENSION
Frame: Steel, single downtube
Suspension: F. Hydraulic spring
fork. R. Hydraulic spring shocks
Wheelbase: 56.5in (143.5cm)
Weight: 400lb (181kg)
Fuel capacity: 4.5gal (17.03lit)
Oil capacity: 3qts (2.84lit)
Tires: 3.25 x 19in (8.26 x
48.26cm)
Top speed: 80mph (129km/h)
Colors: Black; persian red; rio
blue (option: bronco bronze
metallic)
Number built: 1,970
Price: $865

WR (1950) AND K (1952)

Now it was time for something almost completely different. Almost, because it was still a 45-inch (750cc) flathead, but otherwise a workhorse of an entirely different order. As the first D model of 1929 had begat the R of '32, which sired the W in 1937, the K model became the sole surviving son in the flathead family tree.

While the engine was entirely new, improved was another matter. The K engine was a thoroughly contemporary design, incorporating the transmission in the crankcases, foot-shifter on the right side and a hand clutch. And, compared to the Panhead, it looked downright sporty. But the style went unreflected by the machine's performance, which was widely described as moderate to mediocre. Some said it was just slow.

On the other hand, the K was the first Harley-Davidson with forks in the plural. One at the front and one at the rear, commonly called a swingarm. With hydraulic suspension at both ends, the motorcycle demonstrated better handling than its springer/rigid predecessor, but with 30 horsepower hauling 400 pounds (181kg) the envelope was lightly pushed. To Milwaukee's added misfortune, the K bike arrived just as the Korean War was heating up and overall motorcycle sales were in decline.

On yet another hand, the new flathead served well in racing trim. Since racing had resumed after the war, Harley-Davidson hadn't won at Daytona Beach. Six times in a row the competition had prevailed, and for the last four years running the victor had ridden a British Norton. This caused some moodiness in Milwaukee, which had won three of the five pre-war events. Corrective measures would be taken.

The racing version, designated the KR, wasn't ready until the 1953 season. Paul Goldsmith was equipped with a 37-horsepower version and won convincingly at Daytona, upping the average speed by nearly seven mph (11.2km/h). A BSA victory interrupted Milwaukee's comeback the following year, but after that the Harley-Davidson would take first place in the next seven events in a row. Obviously there was still fight in the old flathead.

Out on the American highways it was another matter. Young hot-rodders hoping for a hopped-up Harley were getting smoked by overhead-valve 500cc Triumph and BSA twins. Milwaukee recognized the need for a sporting ohv motorcycle, and in fact had one in development, but cautionary advance was still the rule. Racing had shown that more power could be had from the flathead, and the simple route was an increase in displacement. Development work on a single-cam, overhead-valve engine designated the KL, was shelved. Work would proceed on an ohv engine called the XL, based on the K model's four-cam configuration.

So the K model, as a 750, lasted only two years. For 1953, pepper red replaced persian red as a standard color, rio blue was supplanted by glacier blue and forest green was added to the list. Cavalier brown, glamour green and white were the optional colors available at extra charge. Buyers had the option of 18- or 19-inch (45.7 or 48.26cm) tires as standard equipment, and for $2.00 extra could specify a 3.25 x 19 (8.26 x 48.26cm) or 3.50 x 18 (8.9 x 48.26cm) front and 4.00 x 18 (10.16 x 45.7cm) rear. Total production on the K model for two years was 3,693.

Right: Brand new in '52: the Sports Model Forty-five twin didn't ignite many bonfires of popularity. But it had swingarm rear suspension, hand clutch and foot shift. Good signs.

Above: The K model had its gears inside the crankcase, the term for which is unit construction. Four single-lobe cams opened and closed the valves.

Right: Riding the WR for Tom Sifton in 1950, Larry Headrick won all three national mile-track races, and the Number One plate. The dirt tracker had brace in rear frame section.

1950 WR
Owner/restorer – Mike Parti
North Hollywood, California

Below: Riders could choose either buckhorn handlebar (shown) or the lower speedster bar.

Below right: With hydraulic suspension at both ends, the K handled better than its springer antecedents.

1952 K
Owner/restorer – Fred Lange
Santa Maria, California

1955 FLH

SPECIFICATIONS
ENGINE/DRIVETRAIN
Engine: OHV 45° V-twin
Displacement: 73.73ci
(1208.19cc)
Bore & stroke: 3.44 x 4in
(87 x 102mm)
Compression ratio: 8:1
Horsepower: 60 @ 4,800rpm
Carburetion: 1.31in (33.3mm)
Schebler
Transmission: 4-speed
Primary drive: Chain
Final drive: Chain
Brakes: F & R. Drum
Battery: 6-volt
Ignition: Coil/points

CHASSIS/SUSPENSION
Frame: Steel, double downtube
Suspension: Telescopic fork
Wheelbase: 59.5in (151.1cm)
Weight: 598lb (271.3kg)
Fuel capacity: 3.75gal (14.2lit)
Oil capacity: 1gal (3.78lit)
Tires: 5.00 x 16in (12.7 x
40.6cm)
Top speed: 105mph (169km)
Colors: Pepper red; atomic
blue; anniversary yellow; aztec
brown; black (option: hollywood
green)
Number built: 1,103
Price: $1,083

Right: The Speed King
saddlebags and cheese grater
bumpers were popular
options in 1955. Bags
attached to the chromed plate
on the fender. Fishtail exhaust
tips were aftermarket items.

FLH (1955) AND SERVI-CAR (1955)

Harley-Davidson was now the only remaining manufacturer of motorcycles in the USA. A welcome but sobering thought in Milwaukee, since the tide of British and European competitors continued rising.

Milwaukee had jacked up the performance curve on the K model in 1954, and decided that the FL was also eligible for more muscle. The first of several new components was an improved intake manifold, employing O-rings to improve sealing and accommodate a measure of vibration. Intake tracts were cast into the new heads, eliminating the threaded nipples used before.

The new hot-rod heavyweight appeared in mid-1955 and was naturally designated the FLH, (H representing, as it always had, Hopped-up, a term originally coined to describe the behavior of some Milwaukee beer drinkers.) Compression ratio was up to 8.0:1 and the H was rated at 60 horsepower. The bottom end was given stoutness in the form of stronger cases and bigger bearings. The primary cases were redesigned, and for $15 could include the new optional compensating sprocket to diminish driveline lash. New aluminum rocker covers featured thick D-ring reinforcement. This hearty brew of high-performance was slightly quicker and several miles per hour faster than the standard FL.

The FL series also premiered a number of styling changes in 1955. The V-twin configuration was extended to the tank emblem, which incorporated a large V behind the Harley-Davidson script logo. A V-shaped medallion was also fitted to the front fender of the FL, FLH and KH models, a 1955-only feature. The new fork top panel was decorated with three diagonal stripes on each side, and the Hydra-Glide insignia was discontinued. The tombstone tail light was replaced by an oval unit with separate and adjustable license plate bracket.

Prices held steady in 1955 with the FL listed at $1,015. The FLH was priced $68 higher. All the big twins remained available with either hand or foot shift.

SERVI-CAR

As the post-war trends of motorcycle and automobile customizing and hot-rodding grew apace, the Servi-Car became a favored platform for all manner of outrageousness. The bodywork might be replaced by a throne, phone booth, outhouse or modified car body. The flathead V-twin was often removed in favor of a Detroit V-8, bristling with chrome and exhaust headers.

The Servi-Car evolved as Milwaukee's all-purpose, multiple-choice machine for work or play. In 1959 the factory replaced the Springer front end with the Hydra-Glide fork, and in 1964 the trike became the first Harley-Davidson ever fitted with an electric starter. The 3-wheeler extended the service life of the workhorse Forty-five all the way to 1973. When it was finally retired at the advanced age of 42 years, the Servi-Car was and remains the longest-running model ever made in Milwaukee.

The record will most likely be broken by the Sportster, which turns 43 in the year 2000. The Forty-five was, in effect, the Sportster's grandfather.

Below: The paint scheme combines
atomic blue with champion yellow
tank panels. The jubilee trumpet
horn was introduced in 1954.

Right: The Buddy Seat evolved with the
motorcycles. The auxiliary springs were
first available in 1955.

Left: The tow bar was standard equipment on the Servi-Car until 1963. Clamp adapters were offered to fit the bumpers of cars from various manufacturers.

1955 Servi-Car
Owner/restorer – Charles Holenda
H-D of El Cajon, California

Above: After 1952, the Servi-Car became the only production model powered by the Forty-five flathead. Hydraulic brakes and solid steel rear wheels appeared in 1951. Note Ad Skirts on rear fenders.

1955 FLH
Owner/restorer – Paul Wheeler
Van Nuys, California

Above: The speedometer introduced in 1956 featured clock-style italic numerals painted in day-glo green. A gold center replaced the silver background used for two years prior.

KH (1955), KHK AND KR (1956)

Following its customary letter designations, Milwaukee added an H to the K model in 1954. Fans seeking to apply some retrospective rationale to the Harley-Davidson lettering system have offered Hot, Heavy Duty and High Compression as possibilities. Hmm.

As an added letter, the H first appeared in 1915 as identification of a Fast Motor, Roadster Racer and a Track Racer. Then the letter disappeared from the roster until 1929, when the JD got an H to designate the twin-cam engine. So the mysterious H may simply be the traditional letter for the High performance version of an existing engine. Or Hero, or Hell-on-wheels.

In 1954 the H meant an additional three-quarter inch (19mm) of stroke, which upped the displacement to 54 cubic inches (883cc). This translated into a jumbo increase in torque and a tendency for the transmission gears to shred teeth. The gears were made stronger, and with its larger valves the KH cranked out a claimed 38 horsepower. Top speed was up to 95mph (153km/h), and according to a *Cycle Magazine* test, the new model was two seconds quicker in the quarter-mile. The elapsed time was 14.75 seconds.

Next came the model KHK in 1955. (Alphabet historians will note that the K also first appeared in 1915, to designate a "stripped stock" racing model.) The extra K meant that for $68 a Speed Kit was installed at the factory, which included a roller-bearing bottom end, hot rod cams and polished ports. Unlike the earlier models, the transmission in the 1954-'56 K models could be accessed without splitting the cases. The bike weighed about 440 pounds (200kg).

In 1956 the KH was fitted with slightly shorter shock absorbers, although wheel travel remained the same. The oil pump was strengthened and the rear wheel got roller bearings in place of the former double-row ball bearings. The big twin tail light replaced the old bullet-style lamp, and a bold stroke of color appeared on the fuel tank. The model shown here features the new color, champion yellow.

The K and KH models occupy a sort of curious niche in Harley-Davidson history, given their brief production runs. In its four-year span the total KH output was 2,824. Total production for the KHK was 1,163. The factory records are sketchy on the KR racing versions, but probably fewer than 500 were built over 15 years.

Although 1956 was the final year of the KH, its racing cousin the KR would carry on for more than a decade longer. Of the 15 Daytona national championship races from 1955 through 1969, the Harley-Davidson 750 KR took first place in twelve of them. Not a bad tribute to the 40 years of flathead tradition that began back in the 1920s.

Below: The KR won every Class C national race in 1956.

1956 KR
Owner – Otis Chandler
Ojai, California
Restored by Jerry Sewell

1955 KH
Owner – Harold Mathews
Mathews Harley-Davidson
Fresno, California

Below: Externally the KH and KHK were identical but for the decal on the oil tank and an extra K on the cases. KHK was the hot rod.

Left: The bold stroke of color on the '56 fuel tanks grabbed plenty of attention. The $68 speed kit brought the price of the KHK to $1,003. Standard tires were 3.50 x 18 at both ends.

Below: The Harley-Davidson logo with the V graphic was the new nameplate on the 1955 fuel tank. The new color was anniversary yellow. A new hue, hollywood green, was a $10 option.

1956 KHK
Owner – Otis Chandler
Ojai, California
Restored by Glenn Bator

Left: In 1954 the front fender carried a medallion commemorating Harley-Davidson's 50th anniversary. In 1955 the FLH, FL and KH wore a V medallion with the year, model and H-D script logo.

Above: The KH was a stroked K model. The 4.56-inch (116mm) stroke increased the displacement from 750 to 883cc.

1957 XL

SPECIFICATIONS

ENGINE/DRIVETRAIN
Engine: OHV 45° V-twin
Displacement: 53.9ci (883cc)
Bore & stroke: 3.0 x 3.81in
(76 x 97mm)
Compression ratio: 7.5:1
Horsepower: 40 @ 5,500rpm
Carburetion: Linkert
Transmission: Unit 4-speed
Primary drive: Duplex chain
Final drive: Chain
Brakes: F & R. Drum
Battery: 6-volt
Ignition: Coil/points

CHASSIS/SUSPENSION
Frame: Steel, single downtube
Suspension: F. Telescopic fork.
R. Hydraulic shocks
Wheelbase: 57in (144.8cm)
Weight: 495lb (225kg)
Fuel capacity: 4.4gal (16.7lit)
Oil capacity: 3qts (2.84lit)
Tires: 3.50 x 18in (8.9 x
45.72cm)
Colors: Pepper red/black;
skyline blue/white; birch
white/black; black/red. (Extra
charge option: metallic midnight
blue/white)
Number built: 1,983
Price: $1,103

An overhead-valve version of
the K model, designated the
KL, was built in 1952. But
Milwaukee, rushed to bring
out a more powerful sport
machine, decided on the KH
flathead. The KL became the
basis of the Sportster.

XL (1957) THE SPORTSTER

Much like the Spanish Inquisition, few people were expecting the Sportster. Insiders knew that another overhead-valve twin was in the works, and that the new cylinders would be bolted to the K model bottom end. Hopes were not exceptionally high.

But the doubters were all but dumbstruck when the XL showed up lean and mean and ready for the green. Hot rodding had become a booming national sport in 1955. When the signal came from Detroit, in the form of the square-shouldered Chevrolet coupé with a 265ci (4.3lit) V-8, the flags went up. Horsepower in the streets. By 1957 "three-quarter race" engines were rumbling at stoplights all over this land. And ka-thumping right there alongside them were Harley-Davidson Sportsters.

The Sportster perpetuated its flathead forebears' tradition of a camshaft for each valve. In addition to allowing shorter and stronger camshafts, the 4-cam design provides the pushrods more direct paths to the rocker arms and simplifies adjustments to cam timing. In stock trim the XL motor made 40 horsepower at 5,500 rpm, and the compression ratio increased to 9:1. Exhaust valves were hardened with stellite facing, and the valves were much bigger than the flathead's. The engine retained the same stroke as the K model (3.81in, 97mm), but the cylinder bore grew a quarter

inch to 3.0 (76mm). In comparative terms, the Sportster held a shorter-stroke engine that revved more quickly.

Some riders were surprised, given the Sportster's high-performance profile, that it appeared with cast iron rather than aluminum heads. Even though aluminum's superior heat dissipation was a proven factor, Milwaukee's experience with the early Panhead had been troublesome. Rather than risk similar problems with the Sportster, which had to confront the British twins from the get-go, Harley-Davidson went with the known quantity of cast iron. Heavier, yes, but durable and eminently do-able.

The first Sportster was obviously not an all-out roadburner, as indicated by the moderate state of tune. With its buckhorn bars and complement of accessories, the XL was designed as the middleweight sport-touring mount in the lineup. Only slightly more powerful, and barely faster than the KH, the 495-pound (225kg) machine reflected more of the style of high performance than the substance. The large fuel tank and full rear fender made the motorcycle look more like a shrunken Panhead than a serious backroad blaster.

And sure enough, the Sportster had barely hit the streets when sport riders and racers took up the call for a lighter and faster example. The potential was obviously there; overhead valves, unit construction transmission, hemispherical combustion chamber

Below: Standard Sportster tires were 3.50 x 18 front and rear. For off-road use, a Goodyear Grasshopper was optional for the rear wheel.

Below: The Sportster saddle was the same as the standard KH seat. The Buddy Seat was an available option.

and room for bigger valves. The throttle jockeys became so persistent that Milwaukee set to work on a high-compression rendition for 1958. More about that later.

Even though the new model didn't stun the motorcycling world with its initial appearance or performance, the Sportster was obviously Milwaukee's boldest move in a long time. And although some compromises had been made to keep production costs in line, the XL made it apparent that Harley-Davidson wasn't about to forfeit a growing portion of the market to the British and European competition.

Below: The standard Sportster handlebar was buckhorn type. Both speedster and buckhorn bar were offered in either rigid or rubber mounting.

Right: Two versions of red/black paint schemes were offered in '57: pepper red with black tank panel and red fenders (shown), or black with red tank panel and black fenders.

Below: The headlight and fork shroud with center-mounted speedometer carried over from the KH.

Above: Early Sportsters borrowed the jubilee trumpet horn from the big twin. The tank nameplate was new for 1957.

1957 XL
Owner – Otis Chandler
Ojai, California
Restored by Glenn Bator

1958 FLH

SPECIFICATIONS
ENGINE/DRIVETRAIN
Engine: OHV 45° V-twin
Displacement: 73.73ci
(1208.19cc)
Bore & stroke: 3.44 x 3.97in
(87 x 101mm)
Compression ratio: 7:1
Horsepower: 52
Carburetion: Schebler
Transmission: 4-speed
Brakes: F & R. Drum
Battery: 6-volt
Ignition: Coil/points

CHASSIS/SUSPENSION
Frame: Steel, double downtube
Suspension: F. Telescopic fork.
R. Hydraulic shocks
Wheelbase: 60in (152cm)
Weight: 648lb (294kg)
Fuel capacity: 3.75gal (14.2lit)
Oil capacity: 4qts (3.79lit)
Tires: 5.00 x 16in (12.7 x
40.64cm)
Top speed: 100mph (161km/h)
Colors: Skyline blue/white;
calypso red/white; sabre gray
metallic/white; black/white
(options: any standard solid color)
Number built: 3,178
(FL, 2,890)
Price: $1,320

FLH DUO-GLIDE (1958)

In 1958 the Hydra-Glide was re-christened the Duo-Glide, designating the arrival of suspension components at the rear wheel. The rigid frame was replaced with a swing arm and hydraulic shock absorbers, and both the FL and FLH were still offered with either hand or foot shift.

By now the foot-shifter was outselling the hand-shift model by three to one. A new marriage of convenience and necessity had been conducted in Milwaukee. Harley-Davidson was selling some 12,000 motorcycles annually for seven years running. The demise of Indian had effected the widening ripple of British dealerships in the USA. The game was on again.

Competition works implicitly to improve the product, not only in racing but at the engineer's drawing table and the designer's sketch pad. The impulse to solve the problem, whether it's higher performance, comfort, durability or style, the driving force is making it work properly. And better than the other fellow's.

The Duo-Glide had not only new shocks, but a hydraulic rear brake, new oil tank, tougher transmission and clutch, tighter exhaust manifold connectors, and optional white wall tires. Cylinder head fins were larger, the FLH got stronger valve springs, and dual exhausts with short mufflers were also available as an option. Without the rigid frame as fender mount, chromed struts extended aft of the upper shock mounts to support the mudguard, which was still hinged for tire-changing chores. The new front crash bar was a one-piece unit.

Below: The Duo-Glide emblem on the front fender distinguishes the '58 from earlier models.

Left: The windshield, still labeled the Hydra-Glide unit, remained available in clear, blue or red tinted versions.

Right: The Duo-Glide debuted in 1958, the first appearance of a hydraulic rear brake and rear suspension on the big twin. This was also the first year for optional whitewall tires.

Above: The King of the Highway group included either the Deluxe Buddy Seat or Solo Seat (shown). Dual exhausts, saddlebags, directional signals, chrome luggage rack, fender tips and bumpers were included in the package.

New bumpers for the front and rear fenders were introduced in '58. The tank nameplates were plastic, replaced a year later by metal. The color options included skyline blue/white, calypso red/white, sabre gray metallic/white and black/white.

In 1959 the circular nameplate was replaced by an oval background for a chrome arrow with Harley-Davidson inscribed. Like the previous badge, the new design was used for only two years. The foot-shift model had a neutral indicator light on the instrument panel. New metal front and rear fender tips replaced the plastic

versions, and the toolbox featured an optional chrome cover.

The motorcycle marketplace become a more crowded space in 1959. Triumph, BSA and Norton expanded their networks of dealerships, and a Japanese newcomer named Honda appeared with some miniature machines. The British challengers posed the more immediate threat to Milwaukee.

The Panhead, now in its twelfth year of production, had served Milwaukee well. The engine had remained largely unchanged as the drivetrain, suspension and accessories underwent steady revision. The engine was easy to work on, most of the important parts were interchangeable throughout the years and aftermarket accessories were multiplying.

Since the Panhead years (1948-65) coincided with the growing trends of customizing, drag racing and choppers, many bikes were seriously modified. As a result the prices of original Panheads have been leaping in recent years, and restoring these models has become something of a national cottage industry.

Right: A one-piece handrail was introduced on the Buddy Seat in 1958. After 1959 the big saddle was only offered in the accessory catalog.

Below: The nameplate and two-tone scheme changed for 1959. Saddlebags were also offered in black.

Left: Standard exhaust was two-into-one. Production for 1959: FLH – 3,344; FL – 2,423

1959 FLH
Owner – Charles Holenda
Harley-Davidson of El Cajon
El Cajon, California

Below left: Helper springs (above oil tank) swing up for attachment to the Buddy Seat. For solo riding, the springs fold down and clip to the fender.

1958 FLH
Owner – Doug Stein
Los Angeles, California
Restored by Paul Wheeler

1958 XLCH SPORTSTER

SPECIFICATIONS

ENGINE/DRIVETRAIN
Engine: OHV 45° V-twin
Displacement: 53.9ci (883cc)
Bore & stroke: 3.0 x 3.81in (76 x 97mm)
Compression ratio: 9:1
Horsepower: 45
Carburetion: Linkert
Transmission: 4-speed
Primary drive: Triplex chain
Final drive: Chain
Brakes: F & R. Drum
Battery: 6-volt
Ignition: Coil/points

CHASSIS/SUSPENSION
Frame: Steel, single downtube
Suspension: F. Telescopic fork. R. Hydraulic shocks
Wheelbase: 57in (144.8cm)
Weight: 480lb (217.7kg)
Fuel capacity: 1.9gal (7.19lit)
Oil capacity: 3qts (2.84lit)
Tires: F. 3.50 x 19in (8.9 x 48.26cm). R. 4.00 x 18in (10.16 x 45.72cm)
Top speed: 115mph (185km/h)
Colors: Skyline blue/white; calypso red/white; sabre gray metallic/white; black/white
Number built: 239
Price: $1,155

Above: The original XLCH was set up as an off-road machine, but could easily be modified for the street. Additions here include voltage regulator, horn and chromed primary cover.

Right: Straight pipes are the original configuration, but have been lengthened for top end performance. Chromed shock absorber covers were available as optional equipment.

XLCH (1958) AND XLH (1960)

Entering its second year of production, the Sportster got two burly brothers. The XL remained the standard-issue model, while the XLH featured higher compression and the XLCH was offered as a scrambler.

Horsepower was up in 1958, with bigger ports and valves, stronger gears and better oil sealing. The CH was created in response to pressure from California racers, who wanted to challenge the more nimble British twins. The original edition had twin straight exhaust pipes, painted not chromed, a bobbed rear fender, no lights and wide-ratio gearing. The fuel tank, which would come to be known as the peanut tank, was pirated from the 125cc Hummer.

The Sportster was thus destined to have two distinct identities, and generate several more hybrid versions, during the next 15 years. The XL and XLH versions were developed in Milwaukee's traditional fashion of incremental improvements from year to year. As sporting middleweights in the American idiom, the road model Sportsters were logical derivatives of the KH model. The XLH was more powerful, and became a reasonable option for riders who didn't care for the bulk and weight of the FL.

The XLCH, on the other hand, became the production prototype for all manner of snorting tire-smokers for the road and track. First, it was available with a 19-inch (48.26cm) front wheel which meant more ground clearance and stability in off-road conditions. Without the baggage of battery, lights, mufflers and chrome appointments, it weighed about 40 pounds (18kg) less than the road model. And with the proper application of throttle and clutch, the XLCH emitted an enormous roar followed by a cloud of rubber-burning smoke, until it caught traction and shot down the road in some haste.

However, for the rider positioned too far aft, or subject to attacks of panic, the CH would promptly elevate the front wheel and head quickly for vertical. Blaring through town on the back wheel tended to attract more attention than one might have wished for. But once accustomed to the Sportster's power and handling characteristics, the average rider found himself motoring smartly down the road and having a thumping good time in the bargain.

The XLCH was an instant hit with many riders who had no off-road ambitions. So in 1959 the sportier Sportster arrived in legal highway trim: muffler, lights, bigger fenders and chromium-plated accessories. Which was exactly what the hot-rod riders wanted, a street/dirt bike.

The trend in on/off-road, dual-purpose, street/trail, dual-sport motorcycles would show steady growth in the following decade, and lead to increasingly specialized motorcycles. But the Sportster remained in the street configuration from here on, while retaining the profile of the scrambler. But ten years later it would beget the XR 750, a genuine racing bike.

Below: The competition version had the fender bobbed just aft of the strut. The Sportster taillight also appeared on big twins.

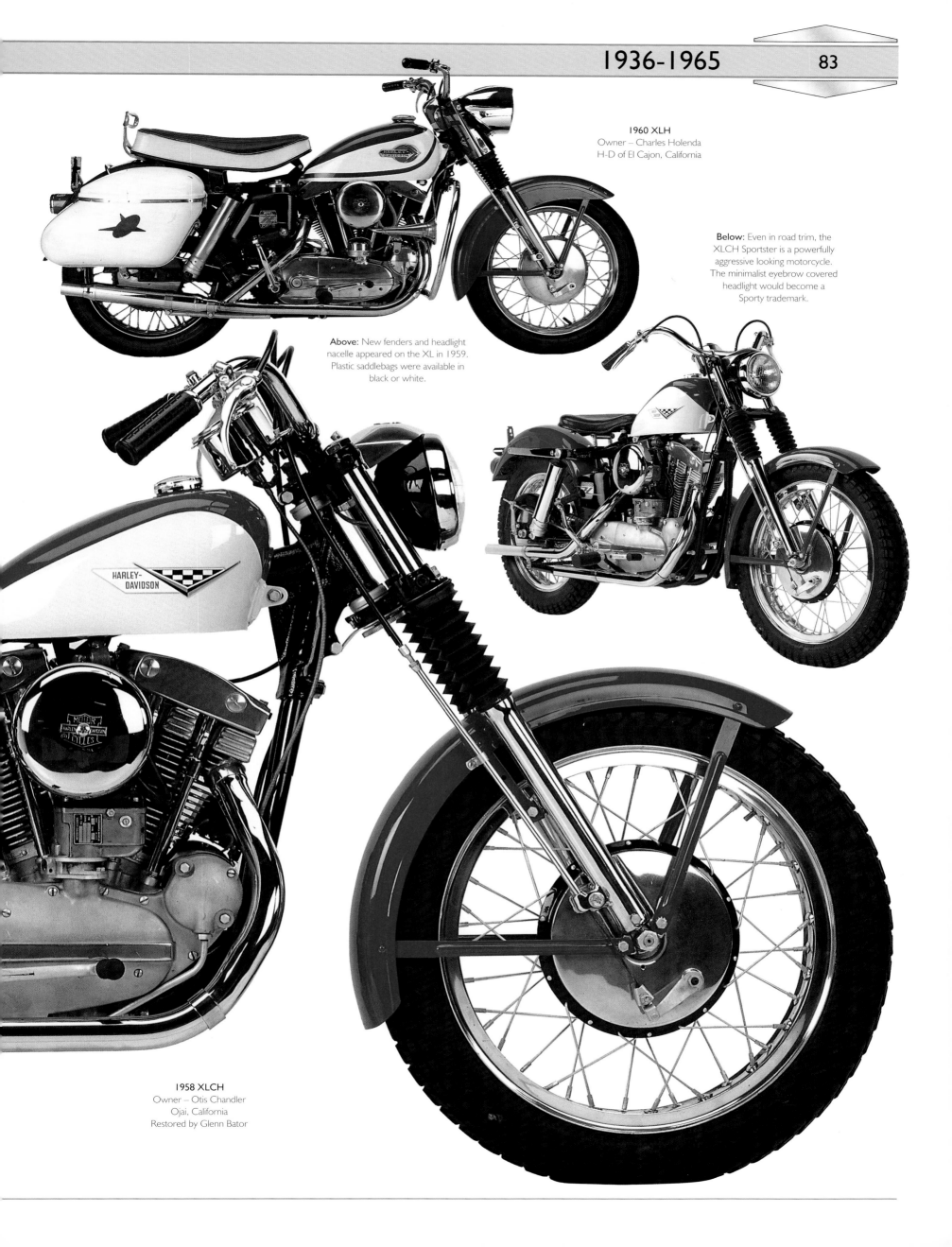

1960 XLH
Owner – Charles Holenda
H-D of El Cajon, California

Below: Even in road trim, the XLCH Sportster is a powerfully aggressive looking motorcycle. The minimalist eyebrow covered headlight would become a Sporty trademark.

Above: New fenders and headlight nacelle appeared on the XL in 1959. Plastic saddlebags were available in black or white.

1958 XLCH
Owner – Otis Chandler
Ojai, California
Restored by Glenn Bator

SPRINT (1961), KR (1960), SCAT (1963) AND TOPPER (1962)

1961 SPRINT

SPECIFICATIONS
ENGINE/DRIVETRAIN
Engine: OHV horizontal single
Displacement: 15ci (246.2cc)
Bore & stroke: 2.59 x 2.83in
(66 x 72mm)
Compression ratio: 8.5:1
Horsepower: 18 @ 6,750rpm
Carburetion: Dell'Orto
Transmission: 4-speed
Primary drive: Helical gear
Final drive: Chain
Brakes: F & R. Drum
Battery: 6-volt
Ignition: Coil/points

CHASSIS/SUSPENSION
Frame: Steel tube, single strut
Suspension: F. Telescopic fork.
R. Hydraulic shocks
Wheelbase: 52in (132cm)
Weight: 275lb (124.7kg)
Fuel capacity: 4gal (15.14lit)
Oil capacity: 2qts (1.89lit)
Tires: 3.00 x 17in (7.62 x
43.18cm)
Top speed: 75mph (121km/h)
Colors: Red/white; red/silver;
gray/black
Number built: n/a
Price: $690

In 1960 Harley-Davidson bought half-interest in the Italian firm of Aeronautica Macchi, which built single-cylinder, two-and four-stroke machines. Milwaukee knew the lightweight market was on the way up, and that the Hummer-derived two-strokes would not be competitive.

The 250cc Sprint was intoduced in 1961. The ohv single hung horizontally in a single-strut frame, which made it distinctive on American roads. The base engine had compression of 8.5:1 and produced 18 horsepower at 6,750 rpm. The styling was not an instant hit with U.S. riders.

But the Sprint had a capable engine for its displacement, and had already shown its gumption in European roadracing. Renzo Pasolini would put the 350cc version in third place for the world championship in 1966, behind Agostini and Hailwood. In 1969 Kel Carruthers was second 350 at the Isle of Man TT, with an engine making 42 horsepower at 9,000 rpm.

Once again a gaggle of Americans were keen to find out what it would do in the dirt, so the Sprint soon evolved into dual-purpose trail-bike/racer formats. The initial C model was joined in 1962 by the H rendition, a street-scrambler with smaller tank, seat, high front fender and exhaust pipe. The Sprint H later became the Scrambler and then the Sprint SS. The racing model was designated CRS.

KR

The Sprint made a fine short-track racer, but the KR 750 still ruled the mile and half-mile ovals. This reign had come at some expense in terms of good will, since the national championship rules specified 750cc flatheads (Milwaukee) ran against 500cc ohv engines (Great Britain). The deck looked stacked, but in fact there was rough parity. The results owed more to the abilities of tuners and riders than to the displacement difference. In other words, the BSA and Matchless singles, and Triumph twins, hauled ass.

Factory rider Carroll Resweber gave Milwaukee the national title four years running, from 1958 to 1961. The gifted Texan was impressive, riding a rigid-frame tracker that weighed little less than 400 pounds (181kg) and made about 60 horsepower, Resweber defined the craft. California's Brad Andres dominated the road-races on the factory KR TT, winning three of Milwaukee's six straight Daytona victories. In 1961 the beach race moved to the speedway, and Roger Reiman won it on the KR. The old flathead just kept keeping on.

Above: This is a replica of the 750 KR ridden by the remarkable young Texan Carroll Resweber, who won the national title in 1958, '59, '60 and '61.

Below: The first Sprints to be imported had white seats, no air filter and the Italian logo on the tank.

1961 Sprint
Owner – Otis Chandler
Ojai, California

Aeronautica Macchi of Varese, Italy, built its first motorcycle in 1948. The company had been an airplane manufacturer for many years. The Harley-Davidson connection was established in 1960.

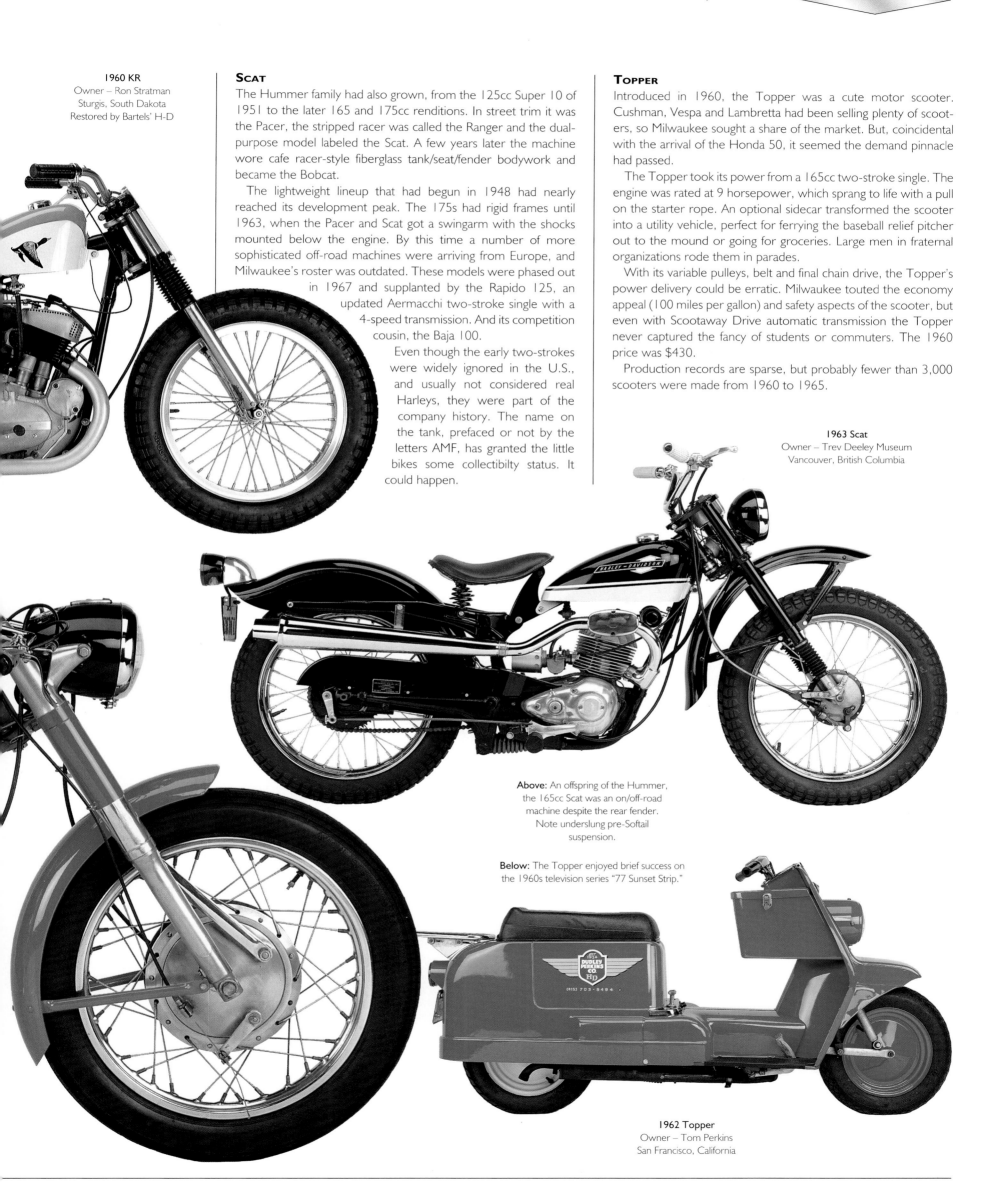

1960 KR
Owner – Ron Stratman
Sturgis, South Dakota
Restored by Bartels' H-D

SCAT

The Hummer family had also grown, from the 125cc Super 10 of 1951 to the later 165 and 175cc renditions. In street trim it was the Pacer, the stripped racer was called the Ranger and the dual-purpose model labeled the Scat. A few years later the machine wore cafe racer-style fiberglass tank/seat/fender bodywork and became the Bobcat.

The lightweight lineup that had begun in 1948 had nearly reached its development peak. The 175s had rigid frames until 1963, when the Pacer and Scat got a swingarm with the shocks mounted below the engine. By this time a number of more sophisticated off-road machines were arriving from Europe, and Milwaukee's roster was outdated. These models were phased out in 1967 and supplanted by the Rapido 125, an updated Aermacchi two-stroke single with a 4-speed transmission. And its competition cousin, the Baja 100.

Even though the early two-strokes were widely ignored in the U.S., and usually not considered real Harleys, they were part of the company history. The name on the tank, prefaced or not by the letters AMF, has granted the little bikes some collectibilty status. It could happen.

TOPPER

Introduced in 1960, the Topper was a cute motor scooter. Cushman, Vespa and Lambretta had been selling plenty of scooters, so Milwaukee sought a share of the market. But, coincidental with the arrival of the Honda 50, it seemed the demand pinnacle had passed.

The Topper took its power from a 165cc two-stroke single. The engine was rated at 9 horsepower, which sprang to life with a pull on the starter rope. An optional sidecar transformed the scooter into a utility vehicle, perfect for ferrying the baseball relief pitcher out to the mound or going for groceries. Large men in fraternal organizations rode them in parades.

With its variable pulleys, belt and final chain drive, the Topper's power delivery could be erratic. Milwaukee touted the economy appeal (100 miles per gallon) and safety aspects of the scooter, but even with Scootaway Drive automatic transmission the Topper never captured the fancy of students or commuters. The 1960 price was $430.

Production records are sparse, but probably fewer than 3,000 scooters were made from 1960 to 1965.

1963 Scat
Owner – Trev Deeley Museum
Vancouver, British Columbia

Above: An offspring of the Hummer, the 165cc Scat was an on/off-road machine despite the rear fender. Note underslung pre-Softail suspension.

Below: The Topper enjoyed brief success on the 1960s television series "77 Sunset Strip."

1962 Topper
Owner – Tom Perkins
San Francisco, California

XLR (1962), XLH AND XLCH (1964)

The Sportster continued its evolution with the XLR, which was built for TT scrambles racing. At a glance the R appeared to be simply an XLCH stripped for competition, but the engine had a number of differences. The only obvious hint was the magneto mounted ahead of the front cylinder, rather than on the right side.

The XLR ran ball bearings at the crankshaft ends and different heads, flywheels, cams, pistons and valves. In the hands of factory riders Mert Lawwill and Mark Brelsford, the machines were wicked fast on the track. With the aid of tuner Jim Belland, the motors were good for about 80 horsepower and the bike weighed little over 300 pounds (136kg). Brelsford, whose motorcycle was nicknamed Goliath, was one of the few riders to explore its limits.

The XLR engine was produced in limited numbers, probably fewer than 500 in a ten-year period. But until the rules changed and it was supplanted by the XR 750, the XLR was the horsepower king. The engine was used in many drag racing machines, and powered the Manning/Riley/Rivera streamliner that Cal Rayborn aimed to a new Bonneville record of 265mph (426.5km/h) in 1970. Strong motor.

Note: William G. Davidson joined the company in 1963 as director of styling. As the son of former president William H. and grandson of founder and works manager William A. Davidson, Willie G. had some sense of the family business. He has held the position for 34 years.

XLH

Stylistic changes were few in 1964. The Sportster received a full-width front brake hub fashioned of aluminum by the Aermacchi branch, and the company logo was redesigned to fit the fashion of the times. A center stand, officially named the Jiffy Stand, was now standard equipment on both models. In 1965 the Sportster was granted a 12-volt electrical system, and the gas tank was slightly smaller. Spark advance on the XLH became automatic, while the XLCH retained it manual advance on the left handgrip.

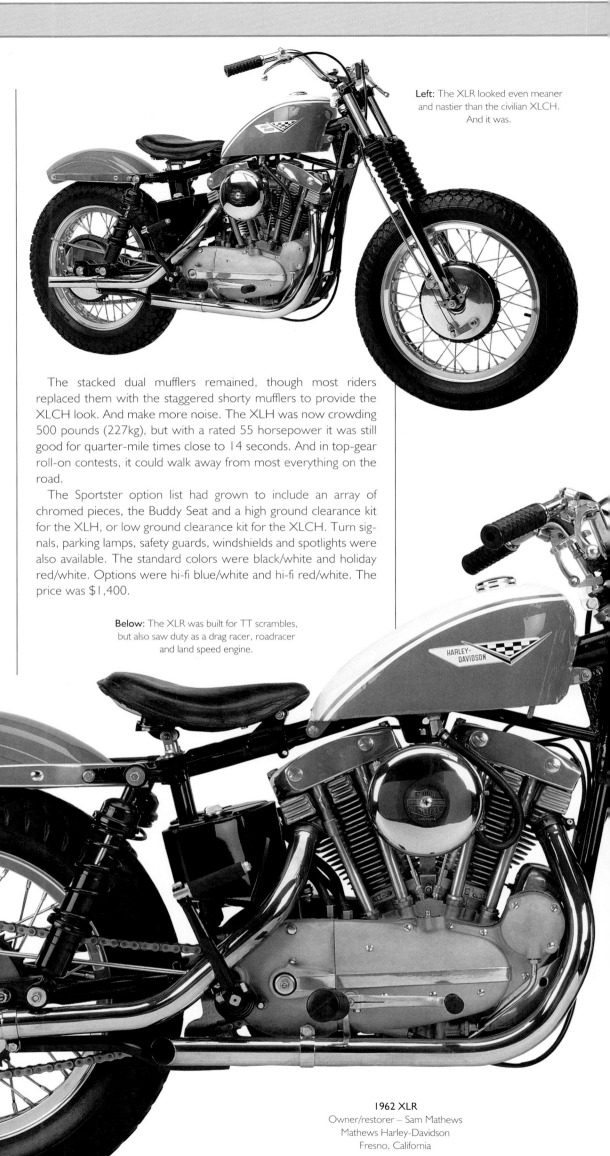

Left: The XLR looked even meaner and nastier than the civilian XLCH. And it was.

The stacked dual mufflers remained, though most riders replaced them with the staggered shorty mufflers to provide the XLCH look. And make more noise. The XLH was now crowding 500 pounds (227kg), but with a rated 55 horsepower it was still good for quarter-mile times close to 14 seconds. And in top-gear roll-on contests, it could walk away from most everything on the road.

The Sportster option list had grown to include an array of chromed pieces, the Buddy Seat and a high ground clearance kit for the XLH, or low ground clearance kit for the XLCH. Turn signals, parking lamps, safety guards, windshields and spotlights were also available. The standard colors were black/white and holiday red/white. Options were hi-fi blue/white and hi-fi red/white. The price was $1,400.

Below: The XLR was built for TT scrambles, but also saw duty as a drag racer, roadracer and land speed engine.

Right: There's nothing extra here. The XLR, overhead-valve successor to the KR, was built for the sole purpose of winning races.

1962 XLR
Owner/restorer – Sam Mathews
Mathews Harley-Davidson
Fresno, California

1964 XLCH
Owner/restorer – Randy Janson
El Cajon, California

Left: The XLCH established the Sportster Look that was to prevail to the present day. Despite the lack of amenities, it always outsold the XLH. Because it had The Look.

Left: Frame bracing above the front cylinder has been added for strength. Frames can be weakened by landings from jumps.

1965 XLH
Owner/restorer – Randy Janson
El Cajon, California

Above: Sportsters options included windshield, spotlights and Buddy Seat in white or black & white. Stacked dual mufflers weren't widely popular.

Left: The XLR was offered with a wide selection of sprockets to afford racers a range of gearing choices for various tracks.

XLCH

The lean machine saw only minor modifications until 1966 when a new carburetor and high-performance cams bumped the horsepower to about 60. This year also marked the advent of the "ham can" air cleaner cover, the result of federal emissions controls.

The larger Tillotson carburetor featured a diaphragm and accelerator pump. The new cams, designated the P profile, bumped the power in the middle and upper segments of the rev range. The CH was a certified road warrior, but for the novice it could be a bitch to kick start. Knowing the precise priming drill helped but didn't always light the engine before the operator was slumped sweating at the curb.

The problem was solved on the XLH in 1967 when an electric starter was fitted. The hard-core macho boys took this as heresy, and derided the "electric leg" crowd as sissies. But so long as the battery was charged, the sissies didn't much care. The 12-volt battery and oil tank fitted to a rubber-mounted platform, and the smaller headlight resided in a compact nacelle topped by a new indicator lamp panel.

The XLCH shared the new cases, with provision for the electric starter, but remained a kicker. In 1969 the magneto was replaced by an ignition timer/coil system which made starting easier. Two years later the ignition moved inside the timing case where it was better protected from the elements.

Approaching the 1970s, the H and CH Sportsters were losing their individual identities. Development of the racing version had shifted to the XR 750, a short-stroke version of the XLR. Honda and Kawasaki were intent on raising the stakes in the superbike game, and Milwaukee set about upgrading the Sportster in traditional fashion – more cubic inches.

1965 FLH ELECTRA-GLIDE

SPECIFICATIONS

ENGINE/SUSPENSION
Engine: OHV 45° V-twin
Displacement: 73.73ci
(1208.19cc)
Bore & stroke: 3.44 x 3.97in
(87 x 101mm)
Compression ratio: 8:1
Horsepower: 60 @ 5,400rpm
Carburetion: Linkert
Transmission: 4-speed
Primary drive: Chain
Final drive: Chain
Brakes: F & R. Drum
Battery: 12-volt
Ignition: Coil/points

CHASSIS/SUSPENSION
Frame: Steel, double downtube
Suspension: F. Telescopic fork.
R. Hydraulic shocks
Wheelbase: 60in (152.4cm)
Weight: 783lb (355kg)
Fuel capacity: 5gal (18.9lit)
Oil capacity: 4qts (3.79lit)
Tires: 5.00 x 16in (12.7 x
40.6cm)
Top speed: 100mph (161km/h)
Colors: Black/white; holiday
red/white (options: hi-fi
blue/white; hi-fi red/white)
Number built: 4,800
(FL: 2,130)
Price: $1,595 (FL: $1,530)

Right: The rocket-fin look
returned with the Super-
Quiet muffler, used on the big
twins from 1962-66.
Fiberglass saddlebags first
appeared in 1963.

FLH (1965) AND SPRINT H (1965)

The Duo- becomes Electra-, and the perennial Panhead makes its final appearance. With the addition of an electric starter, and the name Electra-Glide, the 74-inch (1200cc) Panhead meets its 18th and final year of production. Retired after mostly meritorious service.

The mantle of first thumb start/last Panhead has ensured collector status for the '65 Electra-Glide, combining as it does an end and a beginning. Premier and finale, opening act and encore, and so forth. The first electric-start big twin carries the freight of Historical Significance.

And properly so. Milwaukee was witnessing the greatest leap in motorcycle sales in U.S. history, and was determined to be more than just a spectator. Harley-Davidson's sales figures had been more or less static for ten years, and Panheads accounted for roughly half the total each year. But with the stunning ascent of Honda, soaring motorcycle sales made the old graph obsolete. And for 1965, H-D built more Panheads (6,930) than any year since its debut in 1949.

So '65 was a seminal year that came to represent Milwaukee's transition to the Modern Age of American motorcycling. With 12-volt electrics came a new frame to accommodate the large battery, the new oil tank moved to the left side and the foot-shift model got a 5-gallon (18.9lit) fuel tank. A new cast aluminum primary cover was fashioned to support the electric leg.

Below: The luggage rack with three U-section rails was first used in 1958. The fiberglass saddlebags were available in black or white. Whitewall tires were optional. Wheels were 16in (40.6cm) only

Above right: The Super Deluxe Buddy Seat was offered in white, black and white or red and white. The chrome finish group included rims, muffler, instrument panel, safety guard and timer cover.

Once again the motive was to make motorcycling easier, since it was now established that the market for user-friendly machines was larger than anyone had previously imagined. Spark advance was now handled automatically, eliminating the cable-operated mechanism. And although the Electra-Glide's engine internals were unchanged, stronger cases and clutch were also dictated by the starter. The new primary covers held the transmission in fixed position, so primary chain adjustment was done through an access hole in the cover.

1965 Sprint H
Owner – Trev Deeley
Museum
Vancouver, British
Columbia

Above: The Sprint got the H designation to give it some Sportster panache. The high-pipe street/ scrambler 250 was rated at 25 horsepower. Note cannister air filter mounted above exhaust pipe.

The Electra-Glide differed from prior Pans in several other ways. The domed caps were gone from the shock absorbers, since the upper shock mount also served to attach the rear crash bar. The trumpet horn was replaced by a disc unit fitted below the headlight, and the ribbed timing cover was supplanted by a smooth aluminum casting. Ball-end aluminum clutch and brake levers made their first appearance, and the toolbox was eliminated by the large 12-volt battery.

The only color change for 1965 was the slightly darker holiday red, which replaced the earlier fiesta red. The Electra-Glide did post two of Milwaukee's largest increases of the era; price and weight. At $1,595 and $1,530, both the FLH and FL models cost $145 more than the previous year. And with the added bulk of the starter, battery and supporting parts, the Electra-Glide weighed in at 783 pounds (355kg).

With its full complement of King Of The Highway equipment group items, including numerous chrome covers, Super Deluxe Buddy Seat, Extra Quiet dual mufflers, saddlebags, luggage carrier bumpers, fender tips, safety guards and windshield, the Electra-Glide easily topped 800 pounds (363kg). The Glides had obviously gained girth over the years, but they rolled down the road in most stately fashion.

And now they started with a push of the thumb.

Right: This speedometer was used from 1962-67. It was nicknamed the "tombstone" speedo for the center shape under the needle. The center lens is the neutral indicator, installed only on footshift models.

1965 FLH
Owner/restorer – Fred Lange
Santa Maria, California

1966 FLH

SPECIFICATIONS
ENGINE/SUSPENSION
Engine: OHV 45° V-twin
Displacement: 73.73ci
(1208.19cc)
Bore & stroke:
3.44 x 3.97in (87 x 101mm)
Compression ratio: 8:1
Horsepower: 54 @ 5,400rpm
Carburetion: Linkert
Transmission: 4-speed
Primary drive: Chain
Final drive: Chain
Brakes: F & R. Drum
Battery: 12-volt
Ignition: Coil/points

CHASSIS/SUSPENSION
Frame: Steel, double downtube
Suspension: F. Telescopic fork.
R. Hydraulic shocks
Wheelbase: 60in (152.4cm)
Weight: 783lb (355.2kg)
Fuel capacity: 5gal (18.93lit)
Oil capacity: 4qts (3.79lit)
Tires: 5.00 x 16in (12.7 x
40.64cm)
Top speed: 100mph (161km/h)
Colors: Black/white; indigo
metallic/white (options: hi-fi
blue/white; sparkling
burgundy/white)
Number built: 5,625
(FL: 2,175)
Price: $1,610

FLH (1966) AND FLH (1968)

Milwaukee wasn't entirely prepared for the motorcycle sales boom of the mid-1960s. In some quarters that might qualify as an understatement, but few prophets predicted the social or economic upheavals of the times that were "a changin". Harley-Davidson, as ever, charted its own course.

As the Electra Glide had grown in size and weight, the demands on the engine increased in proportion. Economic realities would not permit a completely new engine, so Milwaukee settled for a new top end. And although conceived in terms of functional improvement, the Shovelhead (as it came to be known) displayed a return to the forms of yesteryear. With its rocker boxes in lieu of covers, the Shovel recalled the stying cues of the mighty Knucklehead of the 1930s.

The new cylinder head was a larger aluminum version of the Sportster lid, with the same combustion chamber and valve angle. The more efficient respiration was good for an increase of five horsepower. With the power gain came a corresponding rise in vibration, but most fans of the full dressers counted it an acceptable trade-off. Properly maintained and serviced, the Shovelhead was slightly better at keeping its oil supply inside the engine.

But exploding motorcycle sales (not sales of exploding motorcycles, though there are rumors) put other forces to work. The Shovelhead would come to be widely maligned by some of the Harley faithful, for reasons often not connected to its design or engineering. The engine came to symbolize the acquisition of Harley-Davidson by American Machine and Foundry (AMF) in

1969. The Motor Company found itself in need of a substantial financial injection to produce more and better motorcycles for a growing market. Unfortunately the "better" component suffered diminishing focus in the rush to regain a bigger piece of the pie.

As friction between the corporate officers and Milwaukee's family management grew more heated, the residue of the executive chafing settled on the production force. Some of the people who built the motorcycles grew somewhat moody about breathing this boardroom grinding compound, and as a result a number of motorcycles were not properly screwed together. So the burden shifted to the dealears, who often had to shoulder extensive repairs before the motorcycles could be sold. Thus the dealers came to recognize that it was them, and the customers, who were getting screwed together.

But back in 1966, production numbers had reached a peacetime high of 36,320. Though it should be noted that 16,200 50cc "no-peds" from Aermacchi are part of the figure. Nearly 8,000 Electra Glides rolled out of Milwaukee, and Sportster production reached a new high at 4,800. For the 1967 model year, more than 9,000 Sprints were on the market.

Below: The fiberglass saddlebags were fundamentally the same from 1963 through 1980.

Below: The Buddy Seat came in white or black and white. The passenger backrest was optional.

Right: In 1966 the Electra Glide was awarded a new set of aluminum heads, for a claimed gain of ten percent more power. The Panhead's valve covers gave way to rocker boxes, which would produce the nickname Shovelhead.

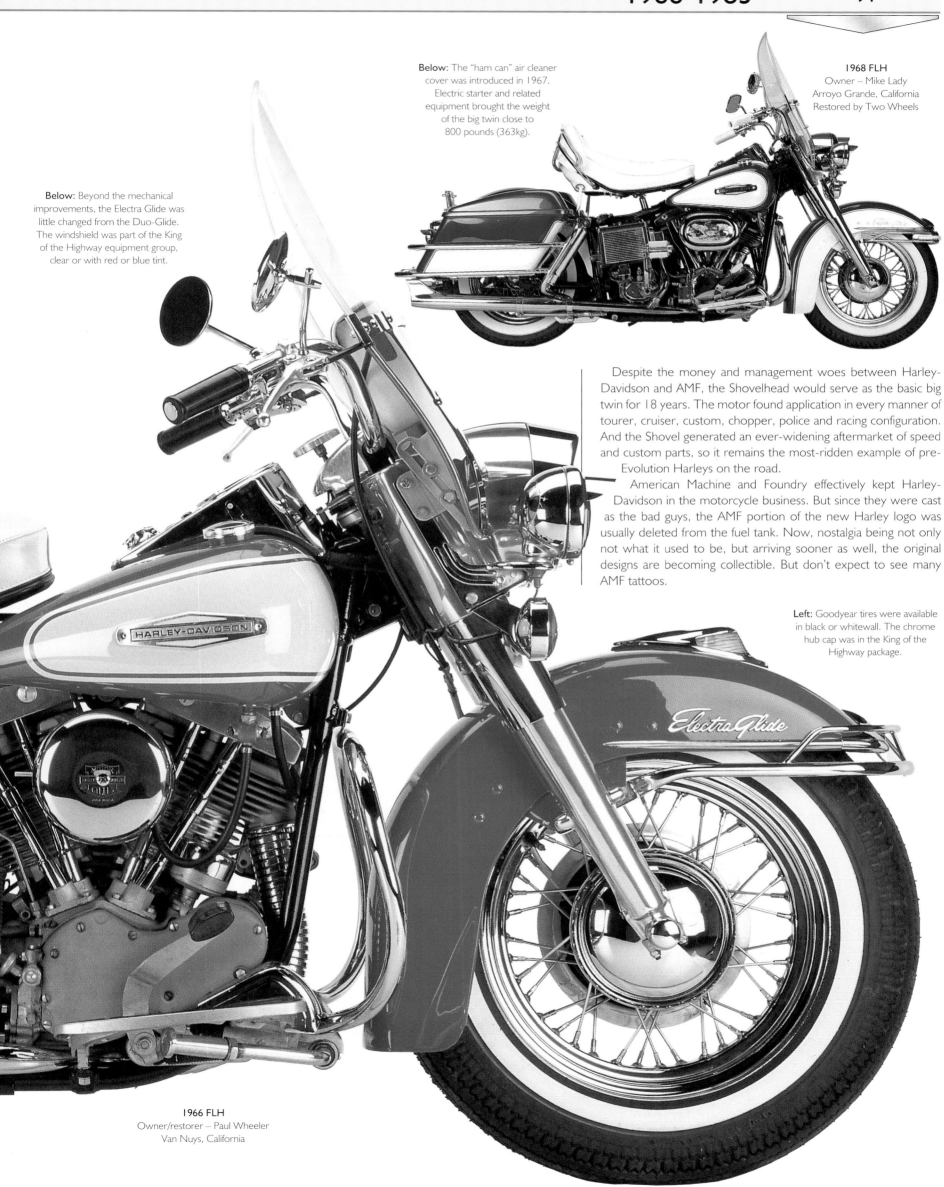

Below: The "ham can" air cleaner cover was introduced in 1967. Electric starter and related equipment brought the weight of the big twin close to 800 pounds (363kg).

1968 FLH
Owner – Mike Lady
Arroyo Grande, California
Restored by Two Wheels

Below: Beyond the mechanical improvements, the Electra Glide was little changed from the Duo-Glide. The windshield was part of the King of the Highway equipment group, clear or with red or blue tint.

Despite the money and management woes between Harley-Davidson and AMF, the Shovelhead would serve as the basic big twin for 18 years. The motor found application in every manner of tourer, cruiser, custom, chopper, police and racing configuration. And the Shovel generated an ever-widening aftermarket of speed and custom parts, so it remains the most-ridden example of pre-Evolution Harleys on the road.

American Machine and Foundry effectively kept Harley-Davidson in the motorcycle business. But since they were cast as the bad guys, the AMF portion of the new Harley logo was usually deleted from the fuel tank. Now, nostalgia being not only not what it used to be, but arriving sooner as well, the original designs are becoming collectible. But don't expect to see many AMF tattoos.

Left: Goodyear tires were available in black or whitewall. The chrome hub cap was in the King of the Highway package.

1966 FLH
Owner/restorer – Paul Wheeler
Van Nuys, California

XLH (1966), CRS (1966), M-50 (1965), AND KRTT (1968)

The overall configuration of the Sportster hadn't changed in seven years. In 1966, which would be the last chapter for kick-start only, the price of an XLH was $1,415. And although it was only $200 less than the Electra Glide, the Sporty was in great demand as a smokin' street machine.

The XLH was still chunkier than the British challengers from Triumph, BSA and Norton. But with 60 horsepower and an adult portion of torque, the V-twin held its own, especially when the engine was tweaked for a bit more urge. The factory bump in the horsepower came from new cams, pumper carburetor and better exhaust plumbing. The "ham can" air cleaner cover, fitted to meet federal emission regulations, was not generally considered an attractive addition.

In 1967 the XLH got a new battery/oil tank platform to accommodate the electric starter. As with the Electra Glide, the battery pushed the oil tank to the right side, and everything was rubber-mounted. Even with the addition of 30-some pounds (14+kg), the Sportster was still faster than it had been the previous year. The shock absorber spring adjusters were changed for a wider range of settings. The only significant styling change was the compact form of the new headlight nacelle, which included an indicator lamp panel for the oil pressure and ammeter lights The shroud also helped enclose the cables for the new "twin tach-speedo" instrumentation.

Also, as proclaimed in the magazine ads, "The Neat-Pleat All-Model Buddy Seat has California styling that says 'class' from the word go!"

CRS

The Italian Sprint from Aermacchi continued its Americanization in the mid-1960s. The generic road model had spawned a family of scramblers, flat-trackers and roadracers. The competition-only scrambler was designated CRS. The 250cc four-stroke single was now straining its legs to keep pace with the two-strokes in road-racing. But on the dirt oval short tracks the Sprint could still carry the day, as Bart Markel and Fred Nix continued to show.

In 1967 the Sprints received new aluminum barrels and heads, with shorter stroke and larger bore. The H model retained the large tank while the SS became the sportier street version with

Above: The last hurrahs of the KR roadracer were Cal Rayborn's Daytona wins in '68 and '69.

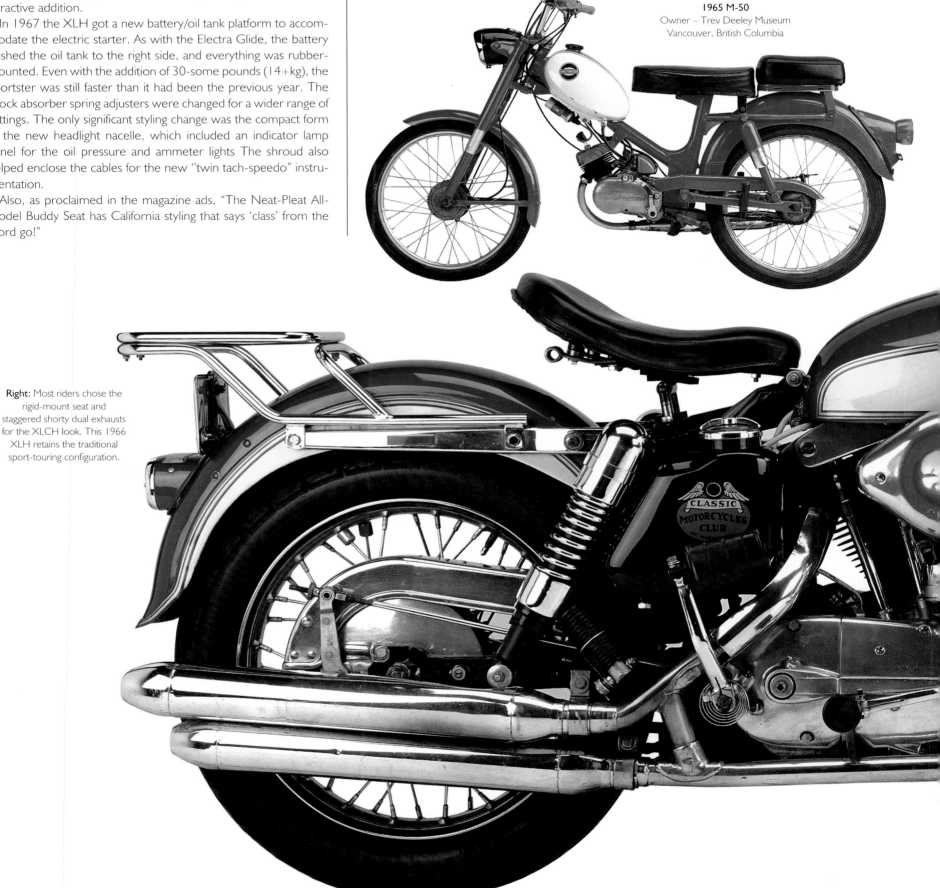

1965 M-50
Owner – Trev Deeley Museum
Vancouver, British Columbia

Right: Most riders chose the rigid-mount seat and staggered shorty dual exhausts for the XLCH look. This 1966 XLH retains the traditional sport-touring configuration.

smaller fuel tank, rear fender and detachable headlight. The CRS remained the scrambler model and the road-racing rendition, with fairing, became the CRTT. For 1969 the stroke was increased to make the Sprint a 350cc engine, with the SS serving as the street version and the scrambler re-labeled the ERS.

The total number of Aermacchi Sprints imported from 1961 to 1974 is somewhere in the neighborhood of 40,000 machines, including racing models. They received better welcome than the smaller two-strokes, but were prohibited from wide popularity by virtue of stiff competition and Italian electrics, rarely noted for their dependability. And the Sprints required more mechanical nurturing than most of their Japanese and European counterparts, not to mention the stolid V-twin.

M50

The M-50, a 50cc two-stroke motorbike from Aermacchi, and the M-50 Sport were brought in to compete with the popular Honda 50. Milwaukee's market projections turned out to be optimistic, when nearly half the 9,000 machines imported sat unordered in the warehouse. The Sport version, more motorcycle in appearance than the step-through M-50, was introduced in 1966.

The attempt to corner a share of the lightweight market came too late to provide Milwaukee any significant increase in market share. Honda had virtually secured the motorbike segment and, accompanied by the other Japanese builders, had moved strongly into the middleweight sportbike sphere. And they were joined by several Italian and Spanish contenders, as motorcycle sales in the U.S. mushroomed. In 1967 the M series went to 4 cubic inches (65cc) engines ("with 62% more horsepower"), but the numbers dropped sharply in 1968 with the arrival of a 125cc rendition called the ML 125S.

Although the M-65 and its sporty brother sold for $230 and $265 respectively, no long lines formed at the dealerships. Most dealers were not entirely happy with the small bikes, and chided Milwaukee for being less than serious about the lightweight market. Some dealers noted the obvious popularity of small-bore street machines and the booming interest in off-road riding. Leave the motorbikes to others, they suggested, and bring something with more power to the showroom.

Thus the Aermacchi era entered another chapter with the introduction of the 125cc Rapido in 1968 and the 100cc Baja scrambler in 1970.

1968 KRTT
Owner – Hayashi collection
Rick Cole Auctions

1966 Sprint CRS
Owner – Trev Deeley Museum
Vancouver, British Columbia

Above: This was the last year for the kickstarter on the XLH. The Linkert carburetor was replaced by a Tillotson. The air cleaner is aftermarket item.

1966 XLH
Owner – Trev Deeley Museum
Vancouver, British Columbia

SS 350 (1969), CRTT (1969), RAPIDO 125 (1970) AND M-65S (1968)

The Italian connection reached full-bloom in the late 1960s, when nearly half of Milwaukee's inventory was coming from Varese. The sportbike market was crowded with British, Japanese and European contenders, and the Harley-Davidson imports faced an increasingly sophisticated market that was discriminating about performance, technology and style.

As we noted earlier, Aermacchi's horizontal four-stroke single became a genuine giant-killer in Europe. In the hands of Kel Carruthers and Renzo Pasolini the rev-happy little singles humbled many of the traditional victors in continental roadracing. A small, powerful engine, hung low in a lightweight chassis, would out-perform larger and more powerful machines on a demanding road circuit. In the meantime, the Japanese were applying this knowledge to two-stroke racers.

Back stateside, Milwaukee brought the enlarged 350 to U.S. riders as the SS 350 and CRS racing models. The street version weighed 320lb (145kg) gassed up and could top 95mph

(153km/h). This Sprint reached a new statistical mark in 1969, with 4,575 machines imported. Only the Electra Glide and Sportster XLCH topped 5,000 units for the year.

The CRTT 350 remained a short-stroke racing engine, for which there was no national class in the U.S. The CRS dirt-track models remained competitive in short track against the BSA and Triumph singles, but here too the two-stroke invasion was well underway. The SS 350 remained on the Harley-Davidson roster through 1974, when the factory transferred its lightweight chores to the two-stroke Aermacchis.

1969 350 CRTT
Owner – Otis Chandler
Ojai, California

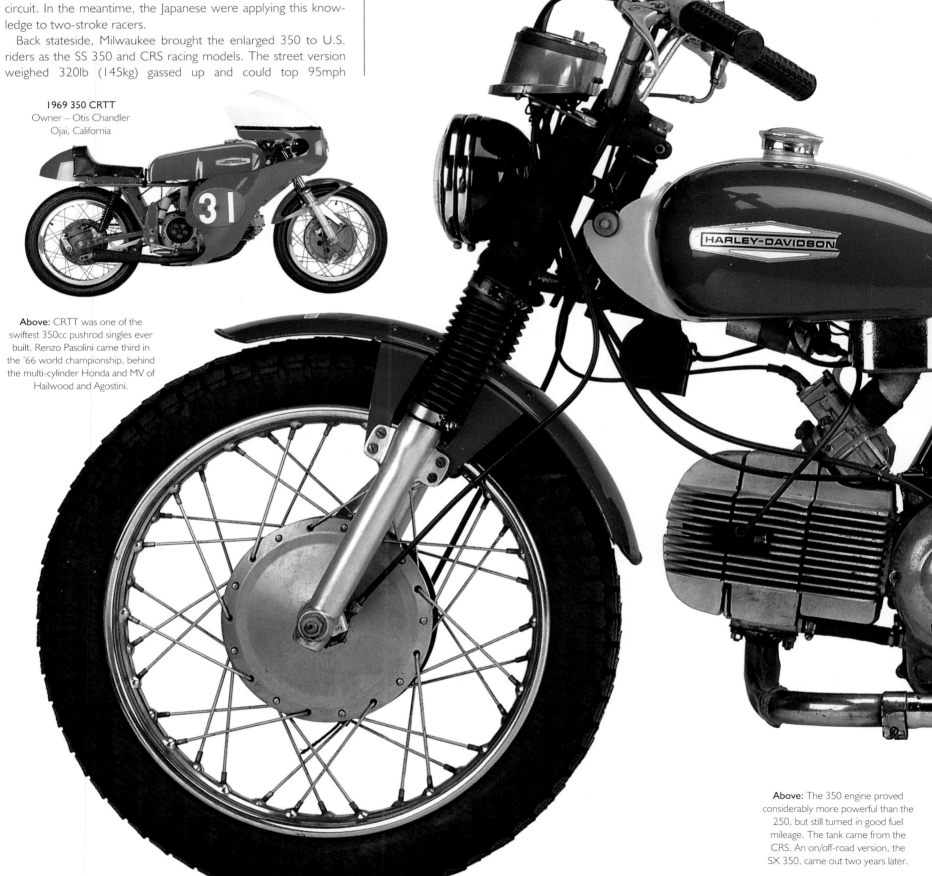

Above: CRTT was one of the swiftest 350cc pushrod singles ever built. Renzo Pasolini came third in the '66 world championship, behind the multi-cylinder Honda and MV of Hailwood and Agostini.

Below: By 1969 the Sprint showed the effects of American styling on Italian design. The attempt to cast the import as a baby Sportster was not entirely successful. The Sprint would get an electric starter in 1973.

Above: The 350 engine proved considerably more powerful than the 250, but still turned in good fuel mileage. The tank came from the CRS. An on/off-road version, the SX 350, came out two years later.

MADE IN ITALY BY
AERMACCHI HARLEY-DAVIDSON.

1968 M-65 S
Owner – Trev Deeley Museum
Vancouver, British Columbia

Below: The M-65 Leggero was
a 3-speed two-stroke machine.

1970 Rapido ML-125S
Owner – Trev Deeley Museum
Vancouver, British Columbia

RAPIDO

A larger version of the M-65 Sport, the 125cc Rapido was introduced in 1968. The following year it featured a reinforced frame,
longer seat and smaller fuel tank, and was offered in standard and
street/trail versions. The road model was discontinued in 1970
and the dual-purpose type was available through 1972.

Once again it was a matter of too little too late to make much of
a dent in the growing dirt-bike market. The Aermacchi two-
strokes were far outstripped by both the new on/off-road entries
from Japan and the purpose-built scramblers and motocrossers
from Europe.

The second upgrade of the imported single came in 1973 with
the TX-125, a full-loop frame version of the Rapido. The model
would evolve into the SS and SX 175 and 250cc singles in street,
off-road and motocross guises, which were offered from 1972
through 1978. The Italian connection ended shortly thereafter.

Left: The later model Sprints (1969-
74), in SS and SX trim, have the
advantage of added displacement
and more power. Collector status
seems ensured by the shortage
of spare parts.

1969 Sprint SS 350
Owner – Trev Deeley Museum
Vancouver, British Columbia

XR 750 (1970) AND BAJA 100 (1970)

1970-80 XR 750

SPECIFICATIONS
ENGINE/DRIVETRAIN
Engine: OHV 45° V-twin
Displacement: 45ci (750cc)
Bore & stroke: 3.125 x
2.983in (79 x 76mm)
Compression ratio: 10.5:1
Horsepower: 90
Carburetion: Two 36mm
Mikuni
Transmission: 4-speed
Primary drive: Triplex chain
Final drive: Chain
Brakes: Rear disc
Ignition: Magneto

CHASSIS/SUSPENSION
Frame: Steel, double downtube
Suspension: F. Telescopic fork.
R. Hydraulic shocks
Wheelbase: 57in (144.8cm)
Weight: 320lb (145.2kg)
Fuel capacity: 2.5gal (9.5lit)
Oil capacity: 3qts (2.84lit)
Tires: 4.00 x 19in (10.16 x
48.26cm)
Top speed: 130mph (209km/h)
Colors: Jet fire orange/black
Number built: 160 (1980);
total production, approx 530
Price: $4,000

The XR 750 began as a de-stroked Sportster, replacing the KR 750 flathead racer. Even though Cal Rayborn displayed in convincing fashion the side valve's gumption at Daytona in '68 and '69, the need for more power had arrived.

Milwaukee was assailed in dirt-track racing by BSA, Triumph and Norton, who were joined by Honda, Yamaha and Kawasaki to make the roadracing more engaging. Under the direction of racing chief Dick O'Brien, the lighter and faster Sportster drew on the KRTT and XLR for inspiration. The first XRs had iron cylinders and heads, with the exhaust pipes exiting low on the right. With the arrival of the alloy engine in 1972, the pipes curled around high on the left side and two carburetors poked out on the right.

The iron XR was about 100lb (45.4kg) lighter than a kick-start Sportster and made roughly 10 more horsepower in stock form. The ports, valves and cams got the racing treatment and the magneto went up front in place of a generator. Fuel was mixed by a Tillotson carburetor, and compression was only 8.5:1 in the interest of reliability. The motorcycle was fast but suffered serious overheating in long events, a deficiency most apparent in road races. The Harley team got spanked by Dick Mann on a Honda at Daytona in 1970, and the same Mann did it the following year on a BSA. Harley-Davidson rider and former Daytona winner Roger Reiman was fourth, a lap down on the Triumph of Gene Romero and Don Emde's BSA.

Above: Tuned exhaust pipes exit high on the left side, out of harm's way when the machine is leaned well over and sliding, at 100mph (161km/h). Dirt track tires provide the best balance between slip and grip.

Below: The XR provides only minimal accomodations for both fuel and rider. Extra weight is unnecessary.

Above: The XR-750 is fed by two 36mm Mikuni carburetors with jumbo air filters. Large volumes of air pass this way, and when properly mixed with fuel, the result is close to 100 horsepower.

Right: This is not the original XR-750, which was a de-stroked XLR engine in a KR chassis. So the early model had iron heads and barrels, one carburetor and exhaust pipes on the right side.

The alloy XR wasn't ready for Daytona in 1972, but its American road-racing career was effectively ended before it began. The impeccable Cal Rayborn took his old iron-head to England, without Milwaukee's blessing, and blistered the best of the British on tracks they knew and he didn't. The cool weather and short circuits matched perfectly the skills of Rayborn and the iron XR . He returned to the U.S. and won the Grand National road-racing events at Indianapolis and Monterey on the alloy version. But thereafter, the two-strokes consigned the XR 750 to dirt-track racing exclusively.

There it has reigned, almost uninterruped, ever since then. Now in its 27th consecutive season, the XR 750 has become the all-time durability champion among production racing machines. Well, engines at least. The factory got out of the chassis business in the 1980s because racers were choosing their own frames, wheels and suspension components.

The aluminum cylinders and heads contributed greatly to the new XR's ability to run stronger longer. The combustion chamber was improved and each was fed by a 36mm carburetor. Compression was up to 10.5:1. The rods, pistons and valves were all developed for the new engine, which had slightly less stroke and larger bore. Even though the cylinders were shorter than the iron ones, more and wider fins surrounded them.

With the technical asssistance of independent tuners C.R. Axtell and Jerry Branch, the new XR became a formidable racing engine that made about 90 horsepower. The bike was well suited to young charger Mark Brelsford, who returned the Grand National Championship title to Milwaukee in 1972. Kenny Roberts put Yamaha on top for the next two years, then Gary Scott gave Harley-Davidson another Number One ranking in 1975.

The XR 750 continues its winning ways today, several times removed from the original Class C concept of production racing, but still a traditional 45° pushrod V-twin built to go fast.

Below: Flat track racing machines have never carried front brakes. From the beginning they were considered an unnecessary hazard on machines that spent most of their time traveling sideways.

Below: The Baja 100 was developed by southern California desert racers Jack Krizman and Dave Ekins. The 5-speed, 12-horsepower racer did well.

1970 Baja 100
Owner – Trev Deeley Museum
Vancouver, British Columbia

1980 XR-750
Owner – Otis Chandler
Ojai, California

1971 FX SUPER GLIDE

SPECIFICATIONS
ENGINE/DRIVETRAIN
Engine: OHV 45° V-twin
Displacement: 73.73ci
(1208.19cc)
Bore & stroke: 3.44 x 3.97in
(87 x 101mm)
Compression ratio: 8:1
Horsepower: 65
Carburetion: Bendix
Transmission: 4-speed
Primary drive: Chain
Final drive: Chain
Brakes: F & R. Drum
Battery: 12-volt
Ignition: Coil/points

CHASSIS/SUSPENSION
Frame: Steel, double downtube
Suspension: F. Telescopic fork.
R. Hydraulic shocks
Wheelbase: 62in (157.5cm)
Weight: 560lb (254kg)
Fuel capacity: 3.5gal (13.25lit)
Oil capacity: 4qts (3.79lit)
Tires: F. 3.50 x 19in (8.9 x
48.26cm). R. 5.00 x 16in (12.7 x
40.64cm).
Top speed: 110mph (177km/h)
Colors: Black; birch white
(options: sparkling green;
burgundy; blue; turquoise; red;
copper; "sparkling America" [red,
white and blue])
Number built: 4,700
Price: $2,500

FX (1971) THE SUPER GLIDE

When Harley-Davidson was acquired by AMF in 1969, several new models were already on the drafting table. One of them, penned by design director William G. Davidson, was the first attempt at a factory customized production roadster. And it was special enough to have a name like Super Glide.

The FX 1200 represented the response of Milwaukee, Willie G. in particular, to the spreading popularity of customs, cruisers and choppers on the motorcycle scene. Numbers of aftermarket performance and accessory makers had been established around the Shovelhead's platform, which didn't harm sales of the Electra Glide. But Harley-Davidson reckoned there was a market for a moderately-styled production cruiser with a sporting flair. And they were right.

The Super Glide, as the FX designation suggests, was part Electra Glide and part Sportster. The FL series had grown larger and heavier through the years, as the Sportster was becoming lighter and leaner. Somewhere in the middle, between porky and piglet, there was ground for a big-bore sport/cruiser. Some riders would revise and reshape the Super Glide to suit their own preferences, while others would be well served by the factory styling. Something for most everybody.

The FX combined the 74ci (1200cc) Shovelhead engine and frame with the Sportster front end. The electric starter was omit-ted, so a smaller battery was mounted on the right side. A European-style fiberglass seat/tail section was fitted, and a Sportster-type two-into-one exhaust system. The red, white and blue paint scheme reflected the current swell of patriotism in reaction to the Vietnam war. The new racing logo, a block numeral 1 in stars and stripes, decorated the top of the fuel tank. Ads touted the FX as the "All-American Freedom Machine." The Super Glide weighed 560lb (254kg), only about 60 (27kg) more than a Sportster and some 150lb (68kg) less than the Electra Glide.

The concept was sound, although the boat-tail seat/fender was destined for early retirement. The prospect of European-style cafe racers achieving wide acceptance in the U.S. seemed at least a possibility in the early 1970s. But the Super Glide was hardly a backroads scratcher, and the tailpiece was over-sized to include space for a passenger. Set against the spare front end of the Sportster, the FX looked just like what it was – two different motorcycles. For 1972 the Super Glide had a standard rear fender, and sales began rising.

In 1973 the FX slimmed down even further when the wide 3.5-gallon (13.25lit) fuel tank was replaced with the slimmer tank from the Sprint. The suspension got stiffer springs and a disc brake appeared at each wheel, as the Super Glide became more performance-oriented. Not that it was becoming a Sportster. In 1974 electric start was offered as an option (FXE), and the thumb-starter sold in twice the numbers of the kick-start FX.

Below: The Euro-style seat and tail section answered a question few American riders had asked.

Right: The Super Glide attempted to combine the rear end of the Electra Glide with the front end of the Sportster. Not entirely successful from a design standpoint, the FX did forecast a new series of bikes from Milwaukee.

The Super Glide is properly considered a seminal machine in the evolution of the Harley-Davidson Motor Company. It was the catalyst for a continuing variation of FX series machines, starting in 1977 with the Low Rider. Then followed the more retro Fat Bob and the custom Wide Glide, which begat the Sturgis, the Softail, the FXR sport model and the nostalgic Springer.

The FX series became more popular with each succeeding rendition, and provided a substantial boost to Milwaukee's balance sheet as the Electra Glide slipped against the wave of Japanese touring bikes. Most of the firm's styling and engineering emphasis focused on the FX models throughout the 1970s, and introduced the belt drive system that would later be adopted across the line.

Above: The singular red, white and blue logo combined patriotism and Milwaukee's racing heritage.

1971 FX Super Glide
Owner – Trev Deeley Museum
Vancouver, British Columbia

Above: Even though the boat tail styling was rejected, the cruiser concept won wide approval. The Super Glide family continues to grow.

1971 FX Super Glide
Owner – Otis Chandler
Ojai, California
Restored by Jerry Sewell

XLH (1971), RR250 AND X-90 (1972)

By 1968 the XLCH Sportster was outselling the XLH by two to one. High performance motorcycles were in demand as more new riders moved up from lightweight machines. The race was on for top honors in the power and speed categories, and new contenders from Japan challenged the current champs from the U.S. and Britain.

But while the XLH was in the process of looking more like the CH, and producing the same power, it was still outfitted in sport/touring trim. Windshield, saddlebags, and Buddy Seat were all available options, and one could still choose the Low or High Ground Clearance style, which meant either 18- or 19-inch (45.72 or 48.26cm) front wheel. The fork received an improved damping mechanism and increased travel. In 1968 the XLH sold for $1,650.

The heads were slightly redesigned for 1969 and got bigger valves, which with more efficient exhaust plumbing produced a five horsepower increase. In 1971 the Sportster was changed from a dry to wet clutch, which solved the problem of gear lube causing slippage. The ignition points now moved inside the timing case, and featured an automatic advance mechanism. An optional boat-tail seat, a reduced version of the Super Glide tail, was offered in 1970 and 71 but roundly rejected. Of course it's now a collector's item.

The Sportster's standard colors were black or birch white. The options were sparkling burgundy, turquoise, green, blue, red or copper. The buyer could also order the bike in gray primer and have it painted to taste.

Below: The Sportster had changed little in the past ten years. Aluminum wheels were optional.

RR250

The RR250, a road-racing two-stroke twin from Aermacchi, appeared in 1971. Yamaha had begun demonstrating the speed and reliability of their two-strokes in world roadracing, but Walter Villa dominated the class from 1974-76. And in the third year he also collected the world 350cc championship.

The RR was built solely for roadracing, and neither Aermacchi nor Harley-Davidson offered a comparable road model. The engine was a short-stoke vertical twin (bore/stoke: 2.21 x 1.96in, 56 x 50mm), with a 5-speed transmission in a tidy package weighing 230lb (104kg). The early air-cooled engines made about 50 horsepower at 10,000 rpm, but as development continued and

Below: The Aermacchi RR 250 roadracers were popular mounts until Yamaha came to dominate the class. Dual disc brakes replaced original drum. AMF logos appeared on all Harley bikes by 1972.

1972 RR 250
Owner – Trev Deeley Museum
Vancouver, British Columbia

water-cooling was added, the figure rose to 58 at 12,000. The otherwise identical 350cc version was said to produce nearly 70 horsepower.

To appreciate the potential for acceleration and velocity, compare the RR250 to the Sportster, no slouch itself. The Aermacchi, stronger by 10 horsepower and with the (small) rider aboard, weighed 150lb (68kg) less than the Sportster alone.

Very few RR250 roadracers came to the U.S. Gary Scott rode one briefly for the factory, and Canadian Harley-Davidson distributor Trev Deeley fielded a team for several years. But the Aermacchi was soon outclassed by the rapid development in the world championship racing efforts of both Yamaha and Kawasaki. A few RR250s still appear in vintage races, but most are in museums.

Above: The ham can air cleaner cover was not a popular addition to the Sportster. Staggered shorty duals replaced the stacked mufflers.

Below: The X-90 was the big brother (!) of the 65cc Shortster. The 90cc 4-speed was useful as a pit bike and for teaching youngsters to ride.

1972 X-90
Owner – Armando Magri
H-D of Sacramento, California

1971 XLH
Owner – Eva Mathews
Mathews Harley-Davidson
Fresno, California

XLH (1972), XLH (1974) AND SX 350 (1973)

The Sportster's development route had taken few turns in its first 15 years. The H and CH models became more similar than different, and the Superbike market was crowded with high-performance motorcycles from Italy, Britain and Japan. Time for more horsepower.

In 1972 the Sportster engine was bored to 3.18in (81mm) while the stroke remained at 3.81in (97mm). This brought displacement into the original Knucklehead realm, 61 cubic inches or 1000 cubic centimeters. In keeping with the European and Japanese emphasis on metric designations, the new Sporty was christened the XL 1000. The factory rating was 61 horsepower, meeting the popular standard of one pony per cubic inch. In the test by *Cycle World* magazine the new Sportster ran a 13.38 quarter-mile at just under 98mph (157.7km/h). The top speed was posted at 116mph (186.7km/h).

The wet clutch got mixed reviews; engagement was good and only severe abuse would induce slippage, but lever effort was higher than before. An improved shifter drum in the transmission made gear changes more predictable, and the 530-pound (240kg) machine was easy to ride. The new seat, while stylishly thin and swoopy, had too little padding for long-ride comfort. But the Sportster wasn't in the cozy corner anymore. The new look was naked aggression, or partially clothed at best.

For 1973 both Sportsters were awarded a front disc brake, which improved stopping but required a stout squeeze. (Meaning lever pressure, not a passenger.) The new fork, from Showa of Japan, improved suspension compliance at the front, but better rear shocks remained several years distant. The federal government's safety program brought throttle return springs to the Sportster in 1974. Throttle controls had previously been simple push/pull cables. The horsepower rating remained at 61, but the XL 1000 was slightly quicker and faster than the 883.

Sprint SX 350

The Sprint closed out its Milwaukee period with an on/off-road package called the SX 350. Although the four-stroke single had proven its merit in European roadracing and American dirt track,

1974 XLH
Owner – Sam Williams
Los Angeles, California
Restored by Richard Brazas

1972 XLH

SPECIFICATIONS
ENGINE/DRIVETRAIN
Engine: OHV 45° V-twin
Displacement: 61ci (1000cc)
Bore & stroke: 3.19 x 3.81in (81 x 97mm)
Compression ratio: 9:1
Horsepower: 61
Carburetion: Bendix/Zenith
Transmission: 4-speed
Primary drive: Triplex chain
Final drive: Chain
Brakes: F & R. Drum
Battery: 12-volt
Ignition: Coil/points

CHASSIS/SUSPENSION
Frame: Steel, double downtube.
Suspension: F. Telescopic fork. R. Hydraulic shocks
Wheelbase: 58.5in (148.6cm)
Weight: 530lb (240kg)
Fuel capacity: 3.7gal (14lit)
Oil capacity: 3qts (2.84lit)
Tires: F. 3.00 x 19in (7.62 x 48.26cm). R. 4.00 x 18in (10.16 x 45.72cm)
Top speed: 116mph (187km/h)
Colors: Black; white; sparkling burgundy; green; red; blue
Number built: 7,500 (XLCH: 10,650)
Price: $2,120

Right: Most Sportsters edged toward the leaner XLCH look in the 1970s. Seats varied from the straight two-place bench style to a curved "banana" seat to a stepped buddy seat.

1972 XLH
Owner – James Kirchner
San Diego, California

Above: The SX 350 was a popular mount with on/off-road riders who preferred the power delivery of a four-stroke engine. A heat shield prevented toasted legs.

the civilian versions never captured the public fancy. As a trail bike it was greatly outclassed by purpose-built European and Japanese machines.

But it was cute, and different, and had a nice motor. Plus it was fast for a 350cc four-stroke single, and enjoyed a fair market among students, wanna-be racers and sport riders on a tight budget. All of which didn't add up to the numbers Milwaukee required to keep the Sprint in the lineup. Many of these bikes were ridden to rubble by less sensitive souls, or left to decompose behind the barn. But although parts supplies are limited, some 50,000 Sprints were brought in from Italy during the 14-year run.

Collectibility is assured for the limited production racing models, but standard versions regularly appear on the market at reasonable prices. Sprints have begun appearing in some numbers at vintage races in the U.S., which may predict renewed interest in the road models.

Below: The SX 350 fared poorly against the Japanese and other European dual-purpose motorcycles. With sales slipping, Harley-Davidson dropped the four-stroke singles following the 1974 model year.

1973 Sprint SX 350
Owner – Trev Deeley Museum
Vancouver, British Columbia

Above: A new Bendix/Zenith carburetor improved the Sporty's starting habits. A front disc brake became an option in 1973.

1973 FLH

SPECIFICATIONS
ENGINE/DRIVETRAIN
Engine: OHV 45° V-twin
Displacement: 73.73ci
(1208.19cc)
Bore & stroke: 3.44 x 3.97in
(87 x 101mm)
Compression ratio: 8:1
Horsepower: 66
Carburetion: Bendix
Transmission: 4-speed
Primary drive: Chain
Final drive: Chain
Brakes: F. Disc. R. Drum
Battery: 12-volt
Ignition: Coil/points

CHASSIS/SUSPENSION
Frame: Steel, single downtube
Suspension: F. Telescopic fork.
R. Hydraulic shocks
Wheelbase: 61.5in (156.2cm)
Weight: 738lb (355.2kg)
Fuel capacity: 5gal (18.93lit)
Oil capacity: 4qts (3.79lit)
Tires: 5.00 x 16in (12.7 x
40.64cm)
Top speed: 100mph (161km/h)
Colors: Black; sparkling purple;
sparkling burgundy; sparkling
blue; sparkling red; sparkling
turquoise; "sparkling America"
(red, white and blue)
Number built: 8,100
(FL: 1,600)
Price: $2,500

FLH (1972 AND 1973)

Harley-Davidson faced a sea of troubles in the 1970s. Added to the intense competition from overseas, a growing roster of management, economic and political concerns required attention.

As more manufacturers joined the movement to consumer-friendly motorcycling, and two-wheeled traffic increased accordingly, the federal government noted that the machines might well be made safer. Or at least have uniform operating controls, and run cleaner. And be quieter.

Milwaukee's big twins had always been left-side shifters, so no expensive modifications were required. But the Sportster had to be converted from right- to left-side operation. Noise and emission regulations affected all models, and turn signals beacame mandatory equpment.

The Electra Glide was fitted with a front disc brake in 1972, adding needed stopping power to the heavyweight. The disc brought the FL a step closer to the mechanical mainstream, into which new and better technology was flowing faster each year. Even though the sales boom of the late 1960s had peaked, the market remained relatively strong and brand competition reflected equally dedicated competition. To the extent that the British were driven from the field.

Harley-Davidson was challenged not only to build better motorcycles, but a lot more of them as well. The AMF partnership was expected to accomplish that, and production did increase dramatically in three years. But the parent company decided that the Milwaukee facility lacked the capacity for greater output. So in 1974 the original factory was responsible for building engines and transmissions, while chassis construction and final assembly shifted to AMF's plant in York, Pennsylvania. This led to problems.

Motorcycle production had risen about 30 percent in the first two years under AMF, with total output for 1971 at 37,620 machines. The biggest jump came the following year, when Milwaukee recorded output of nearly 60,000 motorcycles. In 1973 the number climbed to 70,903.

But the transfer of final assembly to York was hardly a seamless matter. A three-month strike in 1974 put a serious crimp in the production schedule, and other difficulties were at hand. Harley-Davidson was now confronted with a discontented work force, increasingly expensive modifications required by the government, the so-called Oil Crisis, conflicts between the old and new management, the arrival of the Honda Gold Wing, and quality control problems in the manufacturing and assembly processes.

Then, when it seemed things could hardly get worse, national motorcycle sales went into decline. But there was some good news.

Milwaukee management, abetted by increasingly hard-nosed road tests in the enthusiast press, convinced AMF that better motorcycles were required. And machines that looked a bit more contemporary. Approvals were issued, and the first of the next generation would arrive with the XLCR sport bike and FXS Low Rider in 1977.

Meanwhile the Electra Glide was subjected to incremental modification. The horsepower rating for the FLH was 66 in 1973, and the front disc brake extended to the Super Glide. For 1974 the smaller Glide got an electric starter (FXE), and Keihin carburetors replaced the Bendix units on the big twins.

Right: The trend to mix and match components gathered strength during the AMF period of the 1970s. This 1972 FLH features saddlebags from the 1950s, with a paint scheme and nameplate of 1965.

Below: More retro-activities have been applied to this '73 Shovel: whitewalls and nameplate from the 1950s, paint of the 1980s, aftermarket disc brakes.

1973 FLH
Owner/restorer – Steve Alamango
Hot Bikes, Venice, California

Below: The chromed panels below the seat and on both sides of the rear frame section were Harley-Davidson accessories. A tinted windshield was a popular option.

Left: The tinted windshield became one of the longest-running accessories in the Harley catalog.

Above: Front disc brakes first came available on the Electra Glide in 1972, though drum units remained an option. Fishtail mufflers also represent an earlier era.

1972 FLH
Owner – Bob Rocchio
San Francisco, California

FLH (1975), SX 250 (1975), MX 250 (1976) AND Z-90 (1975)

1975 SX & MX 250

SPECIFICATIONS
ENGINE/DRIVETRAIN
Engine: Two-stroke single
Displacement: 14.81ci
(242.6cc)
Bore & stroke: 2.83 x 2.34in
(72 x 59mm)
Compression ratio: SX,
10.3:1. MX, 11.8:1
Horsepower: SX, 18. MX, 32
Carburetion: Dell'Orto
Transmission: 5-speed
Primary drive: Chain
Final drive: Chain
Brakes: F &R. Drum
Ignition: CDI

CHASSIS/SUSPENSION
Frame: Steel, double downtube.
Suspension: F. Telescopic fork.
R. Hydraulic shocks
Wheelbase: SX, 56in
(142.2cm). MX, 57in (144.8cm)
Weight: SX, 270lb (122.5kg).
MX, 233lb (105.7kg)
Fuel capacity: SX, 2.8gal
(10.6lit). MX, 2.2gal (8.3lit)
Oil capacity: SX. 3.3pts
(1.56lit)
Tires: F. 3.00 x 21in (7.62 x
53.3cm). R. SX, 4.00 x 18in
(10.16 x 45.72cm). MX, 4.50 x
18in (11.43 x 45.72cm)
Top speed: 90 mph (145km/h)
Colors: SX, Blue; black.
MX, Orange
Number built: SX, 14,162 (75-
78). MX, 87
Price: SX, $1,142

Not much happened in 1975. Just one of those years, distinguished by its lack of distinction. Harley-Davidson was in the process of sorting out its corporate and production concerns, and struggling to bring new products to the showroom.

The racing department did provide good news when Gary Scott returned the Grand National championship to Harley-Davidson, following two successive titles by Yamaha's Kenny Roberts. Fewer road-racing events appeared on the national schedule, and Milwaukee still held the edge in dirt track. The situation was to prevail, as Jay Springsteen brought Harley three successive titles from 1976 through 1978.

The King of the Road touring accessories package, introduced in 1973, remained a popular option for the Electra Glide, and the electric-start Super Glide was winning more fans. Also in 1975, the Sportster was fitted with a circuitous shifting linkage to put the shift lever on the left side. There were few changes to any of the twins for 1975 or the following year.

SX 250 AND MX 250

The SX 250 was a large-bore version of the SX 175 introduced the year before. The Aermacchi two-strokes now represented Milwaukee's on/off-road offerings, since the four-stroke Sprints had been dropped from the roster. The 250 was created to combat the success of Yamaha's similar DT-1, but despite making reasonable horsepower, the handling and reliability were not widely praised. The two-strokes still had to battle against widespread dealer indifference, and the price/performance dominance of the Japanese machines.

In its final two years in the lineup, the 250 was offered in a

motocross version. Unfortunately the MX bike came in just as the sport had become an engineering study on long-travel suspension, and once again the dominant contenders were the Japanese manufacturers. Milwaukee did field a motocross team featuring the talented Rocket Rex Staten, but the effort was short-lived.

In 1978 Harley-Davidson made the decision to concentrate on its traditional strengths and leave the lighweight market to others. The Aermacchi interest was sold to the Cagiva group in Italy, which went on to build a broad-based motorcycle company that would later include Ducati and Husqvarna.

Below: The deluxe solo seat saw only minor revisions over the years. The tombstone taillamp is another nostalgic touch.

Right: This 1975 Electra Glide has been given a retro-look with the 1959 paint scheme and nameplate on the fuel tank. Crossbreeding between Pans and Shovelheads is traditional.

Right: A front disc brake first appeared on the big twins in 1972. It performed so much better than the old drum, some riders frightened themselves.

1976 MX 250
Owner – Oliver Shokouh
Harley-Davidson of Glendale
Glendale, California

Below: The SX 250 had few components in common with the motocross model. Here again, the dual purpose bike was outgunned by more purpose-built imports, and was discontinued in 1978.

1975 SX 250 and 1975 Z-90 (below)
Owner – Trev Deeley Museum
Vancouver, British Columbia

Above: The Rapido was replaced by the TX-125, which begat the Z-90. It also disappeared with the sale of Aermacchi to Cagiva in 1978.

1975 FLH
Owner – Bartels' Harley-Davidson
Marina Del Rey, California

XLCR (1977) THE CAFE RACER

1977 XLCR

SPECIFICATIONS
ENGINE/DRIVETRAIN
Engine: OHV 45° V-twin
Displacement: 61ci (1000cc)
Bore & stroke: 3.19 x 3.81in
(81 x 97mm)
Compression ratio: 9:1
Horsepower: 68
Carburetion: Keihin
Transmission: 4-speed
Brakes: Triple disc
Battery: 12-volt
Ignition: Coil/points

CHASSIS/SUSPENSION
Frame: Steel, double downtube.
Suspension: F. Telescopic fork.
R. Hydraulic shocks
Wheelbase: 58.5in (148.6cm)
Weight: 515lb (234kg)
Fuel capacity: 4gal (15.14lit)
Oil capacity: 3qts (2.84lit)
Tires: F. 3.00 x 19in (7.62 x
48.26cm) R. 4.00 x 18in (10.16
x 45.72cm)
Top speed: 110mph (177km/h)
Color: Black
Number built: 1,923
Price: $3,623

William G. Davidson had not been disheartened by the lukewarm reception accorded the styling of the first FX Super Glide when it appeared in 1971. He recognized that one design could hardly serve the requirements of two distinctly different sorts of motorcycle buyers. So, since the Super Glide was short on sportiness, he elected to base the next sport bike on the Sportster, and the next cruiser on the FX.

The former took form in the XLCR of 1977, a stark, Euro-style cafe racer (borrowing the British tag for a street racer) with a Sportster engine and modified chassis. The new frame took some design elements of the XR 750, with a box-section swingarm. Both upper and lower shock mounts were farther aft on the CR chassis, and allowed more room amidships for the battery and oil tank. Cast alloy wheels were fitted at both ends, with dual disc brakes in front and a single disc at the rear. The engine's black cylinders and sidecovers presented an imposing effect, and the siamesed exhaust system was, well... different. The design was said to produce an extra five horsepower.

The XLCR had the looks of a real sprinter for the twisties. The bikini fairing, low handlebars, racing-style seat, cast aluminum wheels and rear-set footpegs were all standard equipment for the civilian roadracers of the day. But in the 1970s, the real bad boys of the back roads had a sumptuous menu of street rods from which to choose. In addition to genuine cafe racers from Britain

Above: With the rear-set footpegs, both the shift lever and shifting drum were reversed, retaining the one-down, three-up pattern. Triple disc brakes appeared on Sportsters in 1978.

Below: The upswept solo saddle and low handlebar put the rider in a partial crouch. The tank held four gallons; the tach and speedometer were below the windscreen.

Right: Black-on-black was the motif for the XLCR Cafe Racer. With its cast alloy wheels and fiberglass fenders and minimal fairing, it looked the part. And the Euro-style Sportster's quarter-mile times were below 13 seconds.

Above: The siamesed exhaust system was good for a power increase, but was comparatively heavy. The ham can air cleaner covered a Keihin carburetor, made in Japan.

1977 XLCR Cafe Racer
Owner – Oliver Shokouh
Harley-Davidson of Glendale
Glendale, California

and Italy, the Japanese offered platforms with great heapings of horsepower in both four- and two-stroke engines. The XLCR was designed to appeal to this segment of the market, but once again the effort was too little too late. The CR had little performance advantage to boast over a stock Sportster, and neither the chassis nor suspension were in line with prevailing sport bike performance standards.

Most dealers showed little interest in the XLCR, and some showrooms still contain the same machine that first rolled in 20 years ago. Now, of course, they are worth considerably more

than they were then, despite the failure to generate much response among riders. The XLCR became a collector's item at the beginning.

Some have characterized the Cafe Racer as a design masterpiece that was a commercial failure, that it was unappreciated because it was ahead of its time. Fact is, although the XLCR featured new and improved engineering for the Sportster, it was primarily a design exercise. Its time had already come and gone before it reached the market, and sport bike design and performance were about to take another giant step in the 1980s.

Harley-Davidson's profit margins had reached the comfort zone that allowed some market research in the form of new models with limited production runs. Given the ability to produce new machines using mostly existing parts, Milwaukee was once again willing to test the public's response to something different. Willie G. had expected a better reaction to the XLCR, and was more than a little disappointed with the results.

But while the Cafe Racer's appearance captured few hearts among either backroads racers or traditional Sportster fans, it signaled better Sportsters for the future.

The XLCR was only in production for two years, and a total of 3,123 of them were built. Unlike most 20-year-old motorcycles, nearly all of them exist in reasonably good condition today. Most have quite low mileage and very few are ridden regularly, because the collector value is still expected to rise, which it does only slowly because so many remain. Curious.

The Cafe Racer may not have lived up to its name, but in fact it was a good motorcycle within the Sportster design parameters. In terms of pure performance – acceleration, handling, braking and overall agility – it was the best XL ever. But to the Sportster enthusiast it just didn't look right, and was thus consigned to collectibility.

Below: Morris wheels and Kelsey-Hayes brakes helped the Cafe Racer live up to its name. But it didn't "look like a Harley."

1977 XLCR Cafe Racer
Owner – Otis Chandler
Ojai, California

**1977
FXS LOW RIDER**

SPECIFICATIONS
ENGINE/DRIVETRAIN
Engine: OHV 45° V-twin
Displacement: 73.73ci
(1208.19cc)
Bore & stroke: 3.44 x 3.97in
(87 x 101mm)
Compression ratio: 8:1
Horsepower: 65
Carburetion: Bendix
Transmission: 4-speed
Primary drive: Chain
Final drive: Chain
Brakes: F & R. Drum
Battery: 12-volt
Ignition: Coil/points

CHASSIS/SUSPENSION
Frame: Steel, double downtube
Suspension: F. Telescopic fork.
R. Hydraulic shocks
Wheelbase: 63.5in (161.3cm)
Weight: 623lb (282.6kg)
Fuel capacity: 3.5gal (13.25lit)
Oil capacity: 4qts (3.79lit)
Tires: F. 3.50 x 19in (8.9 x
48.26cm). R. 5.00 x 16in (12.7 x
40.64cm)
Top speed: 100mph (161km/h)
Colors: Gunmetal gray
Number built: 3,742
Price: $3,475

FXS (1977) THE LOW RIDER

Fortunately the limited success of the XLCR was compensated for by the next member of the Super Glide family tree – the FXS Low Rider.

After a thorough survey of the custom/cruiser marketplace, Willie G. adopted the "less is more" credo of the times. The original FX had made the same gesture, but lacked the components for genuine sport-bike minimalism. The larger market for economy of design (and purpose) lived closer to the other side of the demographic chart, toward the chopper profile.

Thus the FXS. The junior Glide had produced steady 30 to 40 percent sales gains each year since 1973. The image of the back-roads rambler had been supplanted by the outline of a boulevard brawler. The low-slung riding position, kicked back and looking cool, and the low seat offered chopper-style posture within easy reach of the tarmac.

By now the cruiser-bike styling had reached popularity levels that attracted other manufacturers. In a few years the Japanese offered a series of semi-custom bikes but achieved little success. The notion of a machine with form as its primary function was difficult to grasp in cultures outside the U.S.A. The second generation of imported cruisers, provoked by the continuing popularity of Harley's FX series, has arrived only recently. Time will tell.

The AMF/Harley-Davidson team had managed to double the production of motorcycles in four years. But the rush to put machines on the market had created difficulties in form and structure, in the motorcycles, the company, its dealers and their customers. Production and assembly quality control had been poorly observed, and many machines were shipped in less than roadworthy condition. Which caused widespread moodiness.

Most of these difficulties had been solved by 1977, but the damage to reputation took some years to repair. The FXS, distilled as the Low Rider, accomplished for Milwaukee a tighter focus on the custom/cruiser style, and expanded the consumer base in substantial numbers. And the pattern was set for the next 20 years of variations on the theme.

Despite its parts-bin parenthood, the Low Rider emerged as the most coherently integrated motorcycle in the FX series to date. With its kicked-out Sportster front fork, deeply stepped dual seat and cast alloy wheels, the Low Rider looked both lean and muscular. It shared the front dual disc brakes with the XLCR, but had its own graceful two-into-one exhaust pipe, low-rise handlebars and the 3.5-gallon (13.25lit) fuel tank of the original FX. The lowered rear suspension brought seat height down to 27 inches (68.6cm). The Low Rider set the cruiser-look standard still in evidence today.

Right: The traditional fat bob dual fuel tanks were adorned with contemporary instruments, with speedometer above the tachometer. Neutral indicator and oil pressure lights are on the headlight nacelle.

Right: The Low Rider joined the Cafe Racer as the other son of Super Glide. Configured in the custom/cruiser mode, the FXS reflected the growing market for the look of long, low and laid-back.

1977 FXS Low Rider
Owner – Oliver Shokouh
Harley-Davidson of Glendale
Glendale, California

1979 FXE
Owner – Chris Lamb
Hollywood, California
Built by Richard Brazas

Left: The Super Glide was a natural candidate for customizing to the owner's individual tastes. The paint, bobbed rear fender, exhaust pipes and custom western saddle set it apart from the crowd.

Below: In its debut year, the Low Rider was offered only in gunmetal gray. The low handlebar and deeply stepped seat mirrored the chopper-style riding posture of the 1970s.

Left: The Low Rider lifted the FX series to the top of Harley-Davidson's sales charts. Milwaukee's mix 'n' match of components from cruisers, dressers, choppers and sport bikes arrived when help was truly needed.

Milwaukee was moderately conservative with the introduction of the FXS, which totaled 3,742 machines for 1977. Its success is indicated by the production run for 1978, which went to 9,787 and outsold the FXE. The Low Rider provided convincing proof that the cruiser market was alive and well, and that it would help balance the dwindling sales of the Electra Glide, which had been slipping against the Honda Gold Wing.

In 1978 Harley-Davidson also premiered the 80-cubic inch (1340cc) engine for the Electra Glide. A year later the bigger twin came available in the Low Rider, which once again set sales records. For the year, the FX-series models represented more than half of Harley-Davidson's total sales.

So the Low Rider went into the record books as benchmark machine, a thumping success in a market that had begun to decline in terms of overall sales for Milwaukee. The FXS became a beacon of hope, just as the AMF partnership was going sour and the future of the Harley-Davidson Motor Company was a dubious prospect

Above: A shorter fork, shocks and scooped saddle brought seat height down to 27 inches (69cm). Styling was a hit, and sales soared.

FLH (1977) AND FXEF (1979)

Harley-Davidson celebrated its 75th anniversary in 1978. The occasion was marked by the arrival of the 80-cubic inch (1340cc) Electra Glide, and anniverary editions of the the FL 1200 and the Sportster in black with gold striping. The Eighty featured the rocket-disc tank emblem of the late 1930s. Nostalgia returns.

Even though Milwaukee's overall sales had slipped nearly 30 percent, and the guys upstairs in suits were at odds over the company's future, work had proceeded on both new cruisers and tourers. The FLH 80 would head the effort to recoup some of the riders who had defected to Asian touring bikes. The baby Glides were expanding into more varied cruiser motifs, mixing styles of past and present. Despite the encroachment of economic recession, the game had grown more interesting.

With a slight increase in bore and larger one in stroke, the new Eighty recalled its flathead ancestor as big inch king. At a glance the engine was identical to the Seventy-four, but had one less fin on the cylinders and a huge ham-can air cleaner cover with 80 on the face. With cast alloy wheels, fairing, saddlebags and trunk the FLH-80 registered 750lb (340kg) on the scale.

Although the big incher showed no power increase over the 1200, the stroker motor did produce more torque and worked more comfortably with a large load. The sculptured, solid-mount seat was comfortable and not a long reach from the pavement. The FLH-80 went down the road in grand fashion, carried a passenger and fair amount of gear, and somehow combined the best of Milwaukee tradition, styling and unhurried performance.

The new Eighty totaled 2,525 machines in its debut year, compared to 6,881 for the Seventy-four. Production rose to 3,429 the following year, but the engine also was used in the FX series and accounted for some 15,000 motorcycles between the Low Rider and the new Fat Bob.

1979 FXEF

SPECIFICATIONS
ENGINE/DRIVETRAIN
Engine: OHV 45° V-twin
Displacement: 81.65ci (1338cc)
Bore & stroke: 3.5 x 4.25in (89 x 108mm)
Compression ratio: 8:1
Horsepower: 66
Carburetion: Bendix
Transmission: 4-speed
Primary drive: Chain
Final drive: Chain
Brakes: F. Dual discs. R. Drum
Battery: 12-volt
Ignition: Coil/points

CHASSIS/SUSPENSION
Frame: Steel, single downtube.
Suspension: F. Telescopic fork. R. Hydraulic shocks
Wheelbase: 63.5in (161.3cm)
Weight: 642lb (291kg)
Fuel capacity: 5gal (18.9lit)
Oil capacity: 4qts (3.79lit)
Tires: F. 3.5 x 19in (8.9 x 48.26cm). R. 5.00 x 16in (12.7 x 40.64cm)
Top speed: 105mph (169km/h)
Colors: Vivid black; brilliant red; concord blue; chestnut brown
Number built: 5,264 (1200: 4,678)
Price: $4,260

Left: FXEF had both tach and speedo on the console. The 150mph (241km/h) limit indicated Milwaukee's sense of humor.

Right: The view from astride the '77 FLH. This speedometer is an aftermarket accessory.

Right: The Low Rider got a more muscular-looking brother with the FXEF Fat Bob. The burly boy was offered with a choice of 74 or 80in (1200 or 1340cc) engine, and the profile of Muscle Beach machismo.

Above: Forward-mounted highway pegs and controls became mandatory for genuinely kicked-back cruising. Standard footpegs remained for city riding.

FXEF

The next model to slide into the custom/cruiser/chopper parade was the FXEF Fat Bob. The nickname came from the customizer's coinage for the first home-built cruisers with separate fuel tanks. Bobbed bikes with single tanks never got a distinctive moniker, other than choppers, and were never called Skinny Bobs.

The FXEF was a Low Rider with the choice of either 74- or 80-inch (1200 or 1340cc) engine, buckhorn handlebars, cast or spoked wheels, dual exhausts and a profile both long and lean. Once again Milwaukee had provided a motorcycle cast roughly in the styling fashion adopted by its customers years earlier, offering a taste of specialized fashion to a wider audience. And in naming the factory fat bob the Fat Bob, adjoined by a symbol of trademark registration, Harley-Davidson staked legal claim to the name. The same was true for the labels Electra Glide, Sportster, Super Glide and Harley-Davidson.

Concurrent with the arrival of retro-styling and factory folk art came the age of trademark protection. That story, which yet unfolds, has been, is and will be told elsewhere.

With Bob the FX series had grown to five models, which represented more than half of the Harley-Davidson production run. The Super Glide serial had come at just the proper time to write more chapters in the Milwaukee journal. Internal corporate strife and an ailing economy had combined to revise the plans for Harley-Davidson's return to glory.

As The Motor Company reached the end of its relationship with AMF, the sales figures remained reasonably stable. Total production for 1979 was just under 50,000, and dropped slightly in 1980. But in 1981, the year Harley-Davidson returned to private ownership, the output would fall to under 42,000, and drop to 30,000 a year later. The hard times had not yet ended.

1977 FLH
Owner – Jim Furlong
Northridge, California

Above: The big twin got a new saddle in 1977. The tank nameplate is retro (pre-AMF) as are the tailpipes. The two-tone saddlebag motif was the owner's choice.

1979 FXEF
Owner – Brad Richardson
Hemet, California

1980 FXB STURGIS

SPECIFICATIONS
ENGINE/DRIVETRAIN
Engine: OHV 45° V-twin
Displacement: 81.65ci
(1338cc)
Bore & stroke: 3.50 x 4.25in
(89 x 108mm)
Compression ratio: 8:1
Horsepower: 65
Carburetion: Bendix
Transmission: 4-speed
Primary drive: Belt
Final drive: Belt
Brakes: F. & R. Drum
Battery: 12-volt
Ignition: Electronic

CHASSIS/SUSPENSION
Frame: Steel, double downtube
Suspension: F. Telescopic fork.
R. Hydraulic shocks
Wheelbase: 64.7in (164.3cm)
Weight: 610lb (277kg)
Fuel capacity: 3.5gal (13.25lit)
Oil capacity: 4qts (3.8lit)
Tires: F. 3.50 x 19in (8.9 x
48.26cm). R. 5.00 x 16in (12.7 x
40.64cm)
Top speed: 106mph (171km/h)
Colors: Black
Number built: 1,470
Price: $5,687

FXB (1980) AND XLH (1979)

Hard times or not, Harley-Davidson had introduced new models each year during the AMF decade. Not entirely new from the ground up perhaps, but the company had demonstrated its commitment to remain a force in the motorcycle market. And from the Milwaukee perspective, that meant machines which retained the traditional Harley appeal and also met higher standards of performance and reliability.

So in 1980, classic style met contemporary technology in the form of belt drive. The newest rendition of the Super Glide was called the FXB Sturgis; B for belt and Sturgis for the South Dakota town hosting the annual summer gathering of the clans. The latest cruiser was another Wille G. creation in basic black with orange and chrome trim. The styling was immediately popular, but the rubber primary and final drive belts aroused suspicion. How durable would they be? What if they broke in the middle of nowhere? Valid questions.

But the return to belt drive proved out, because 70 years of development had produced belts that could withstand considerable abuse. Manufactured by the Gates Rubber Company using Aramid nylon fiber, the belts provided quieter operation, required no adjustment or lubrication and outlasted steel chains. But replacement, when it was necessary, of the final drive belt was no simple matter, since it required removal of the primary drive and inner cover. As it turned out, the belts exhibited longer working life than the factory expected, lasting from 30,000 to 40,000 miles (48,000-64,000km).

The new driveline also originated a new transmission with revised gear ratios. The new 4-speed gearbox offered the tallest overall ratio (3.27:1) in the Milwaukee lineup, which meant 60-mph (97km/h) highway speeds at little more than 2,500rpm. Acceleration was naturally less than brisk, but the Sturgis engine was pleasantly relaxed in the element for which the bike was designed, easy cruising.

Once again Harley-Davidson had proceeded with caution in untested waters. Only 1,470 examples of the Sturgis were made in its debut year, and production went to 3,543 the following year. The FXB accounted for only 1,833 bikes in 1982, its final year of production. But the Sturgis had met its design and performance requirements as a limited edition machine, and provided the test bed for the belt-drive system that would soon spread to other models.

Left: The drive belt was developed by Gates Rubber Company, using nylon fiber for strength. Belts proved more durable than expected.

Right: Following the Low Rider, Willie G. was on a roll. The time was at hand to take the custom/cruiser styling a step farther, and dress it in basic black once again. The eighty-inch engine was new in '78; belt drive debuted on the Sturgis.

1980 FXB Sturgis
Owner – Otis Chandler
Ojai, California

SPORTSTER

Sales of the Sportster had been relatively strong throughout the decade, but declined in 1978. The touring version (XLT) introduced in 1977 was not successful and the XLCR Cafe Racers were mostly collecting dust as they became collectibles sitting in dealerships hither and yon. Given the success of the Low Rider, Milwaukee decided to apply the same styling to the Sportster to see what happened.

Not much. The 1979 XLS had the updated XLCR frame, 16-inch (40.64cm) rear wheel, extended fork, cast wheels and siamesed two-into-one-into-two exhaust system with a muffler on each side. And no kick starter. The bike had flat handlebars and a stepped dual seat with sissy bar. Decidedly un-Sportster-like. The disparate styling cues from cafe racer, cruiser and sport bike were met with nearly universal derision. Many dealers swapped the exhaust systems and cruiser seats for standard Sportster items immediately.

The XLS got its own name, the Roadster, despite the fact that it was more cruiser in appearance. The cafe racer pipes were later discontinued and the production numbers for the Roadster dropped considerably. But it stayed in the lineup for several years and gained even more resemblance to the Super Glide, with two-tone paint and the old Sprint gas tank.

Most Sportsters, regardless of the letter designations posted by the factory, ended up looking much like the example pictured here. The Peanut tank, shorty dual exhausts and earlier air cleaner cover were simply part of The Look. The side panels covering the battery and oil tank were perceived as non-Sportster items and were discontinued two years later.

Below: The Sturgis had a three-year production run. By 1982, the FX series had expanded to include six models and accounted for nearly half of Harley's annual output.

1979 XLH
Owner – Dwight Yoakam
Malibu, California

Below: The '79 Sportster frame originated with the XLCR. A new master cylinder for the rear brake eliminated the kickstarter. Dual exhausts are aftermarket items.

Left: Cast wheels on the Sturgis sported a distinctive orange stripe. Twin front disc brakes and Showa fork remained fixtures on several FX models.

Above: The stylish two-into-one exhaust system never achieved the popularity of dual mufflers. The Sturgis was fitted with new electronic ignition. Oil cooler was standard equipment.

1980 FLT TOUR GLIDE

SPECIFICATIONS
ENGINE/DRIVETRAIN
Engine: OHV 45° V-twin
Displacement: 81.65ci
(1338cc)
Bore & stroke: 3.5 x 4.25in
(89 x 108mm)
Compression ratio: 7.4:1
Horsepower: 65
Carburetion: Bendix
Transmission: 5-speed
Primary drive: Chain
Final drive: Chain
Brakes: F. Disc. R. Drum
Battery: 12-volt
Ignition: CDI

CHASSIS/SUSPENSION
Frame: Steel, single downtube
Suspension: F. Telescopic fork.
R. Hydraulic shocks
Wheelbase: 62.5in (158.75cm)
Weight: 781lb (354kg)
Fuel capacity: 5gal (18.9lit)
Oil capacity: 4qts (3.8lit)
Tires: 5.00 x 16in (12.7 x
40.64cm)
Top speed: 95mph (153km/h)
Colors: Vivid black; rich red;
bright blue; saddle brown
Number built: 4,480
Price: $6,961

FLT (1980) AND FXWG (1980)

Although the Sturgis drew attention with its brawny appearance and belt drive, the most important news of 1980 was the arrival of the FLT Tour Glide. Milwaukee had given its competitors something to strive for in the cruiser/custom format, and turned its attention to the the touring machine. But unlike the primarily cosmetic touches applied to the FX editions, the FLT was virtually a new motorcycle.

Only the Tour Glide's engine identified it with the FLH-80. With the next generation big twin still in the design stage, the interim fix was to bring the enlarged Shovelhead to a new standard of performance. Not in terms of more power, but by reducing chassis vibration and improving the handling. The engine featured transistorized ignition and a spin-on oil filter, and was buttoned to a new 5-speed transmission.

The vibration and handling goals required a new frame and engine-mounting system. Harley engineers designed a three-point attachment system with rubber-shimmed mounts between frame and engine, which worked to absorb vibration. The swingarm bolted directly to the transmission case, so the entire engine/drivetrain assembly was effectively isolated from the rest of the machine. The nickname Rubber Glide remained unofficial and untrademarked.

The free-floating energy was directed to the rear wheel first by the new 5-speed transmission. The more compact gearbox reduced the distance to the crankshaft, which allowed a shorter primary chain. And the final drive chain was fully enclosed and sealed. With full-time lubrication it performed much longer without adjustment, and was also much cleaner.

Supporting all this jiggery-pokery was a new frame, distinguished by a protruding steering head and trailing fork. With the object of improving the heavyweight's low-speed handling, the engineers

1980 FLT
Owner – Doug Holden
Gustine, California

Right: The FLT Tour Glide was designed to combine long-distance touring comfort with sport bike handling. The new frame improved steering and the engine's rubber-mount system absorbed annoying vibration

1980 FXWG
Owner – Otis Chandler
Ojai, California

crafted an extended frameset with a steep, head-first steering stem set at 25 degrees. The set-back fork was canted at 28 degrees to offer enough trail for stability at highway speeds. The frame-mount stepped saddle fit lower in the chassis, putting the seat height at 29 inches (73.6cm).

The Tour Glide signaled that the design and engineering folks in Milwaukee had been busy. This was the first step toward building an entirely new motorcycle, engine included. The forecast for future Glides was in place; the 45-degree air-cooled V-twin would remain, in quieter and gentler form, in a contemporary chassis. All enclosed in traditional Harley-Davidson bodywork. Evolutionary.

THE WIDE GLIDE

The Fat Bob got a broad brother in the FXWG Wide Glide, a Super Glide with the Electra Glide front fork. The styling curve had swung from Electra Glide to Super Glide to Sportster and back again. Whether by accident or intent, Milwaukee had created the perpetually circular design continuum.

With three basic platforms alternating mechanical components and sheetmetal, the cross-pollination could continue indefinitely. As the identity of one model aged, it could adopt features of one or other sibling. A Möbius strip of infinite design variation.

Meanwhile, the appearance of the motorcycles notwithstanding, the task at hand was to make them work better. The Wide Glide also employed the 80-inch (1340cc) motor, which was now optional in the Low Rider and Super Glide. The Seventy-four engine was dropped from the lineup the following year and all the big twins were 1340cc engines. Once again the FX series accounted for over half the machines produced.

Above: Milwaukee grew even bolder with the introduction of the Wide Glide in 1980. The factory chopper had a 21-inch (53.3cm) wheel, flame paint job and the lowest seat in the lineup.

Left: The Tour Glide was distinguished by its frame-mount fairing and dual headlights. The cargo capacity, enclosed final drive chain and five-gallon (18.9lit) fuel tank were appreciated by touring riders.

Above: With its five-speed transmission and triple disc brakes, the Tour Glide signaled a new commitment at AMF/Harley-Davidson, a title soon to be shortened.

FLH (1981) AND XLH (1981)

The 1981 FLH became the final Electra Glide of the the AMF chapter in Harley-Davidson's biography. That may or may not confer upon it collectible status, but stranger things have happened. Much like the '65 Panhead, the final AMF/FLH represented an end and a beginning.

The signed copy in limited numbers for 1981 was titled the Heritage Edition, an appropriate term. The relationship with American Machine and Foundry had enabled Milwaukee to increase production and develop new models. But it had also created some scarred confidence among both dealers and customers, an issue the new owners were determined to address. A heritage restoration program.

New and better motorcycles were then half-way between the sketch pads and the assembly line. The new management team, thirteen former officials who had pooled their resources and borrowed lots of money, had to balance caution with daring. The sales of motorcycles had fallen in an economic recession, but new models were still arriving from Japan, meaning a smaller and tougher market.

The new Harley-Davidson Motor Company had to be a thoroughly modern example of efficient management, marketing, design, engineering and manufacturing. In order to meet those objectives, the new owners undertook a three-channel plan to control production costs and simultaneously ensure higher standards of quality control. Part of the new system gave factory workers more responsibilty in the manufacturing and assembly processes.

1981 XLH
Owner – Clay Osincup
Los Osos, California

Above: The last AMF Sportster in the traditional orange-and-black racing team colors. Front dual discs were deleted two years later.

Below: The Heritage Edition naturally received old-fashioned style saddlebags and fringe. The heritage of nostalgia, or vice-versa, had only just begun.

Against long odds, and after a four-year struggle, it worked. Harley-Davidson was back, same as it ever was but much better.

Sales of the Electra Glide had averaged better than 10,000 annually for several years. But the flagging economy combined with efficient Japanese touring bikes cut the total to under 6,000 in 1982. The FX models remained Milwaukee's top sellers, followed by the Sportster. Despite the improvements exhibited by the Tour Glide, the Shovelhead Electra Glide suffered by comparison with the newest touring machines from abroad. The pace of evolution was forced to move more quickly.

Entirely new versions of both FL and FX models had been approved for production, and were naturally the focus of attention in Milwaukee. Though little changed from the year before, the five 1981

Right: The 1981 Electra Glide was the first non-AMF motorcycle off the assembly line. The limited edition Heritage Edition (784 built) was orange and green. New officers awarded the first one a gold dipstick.

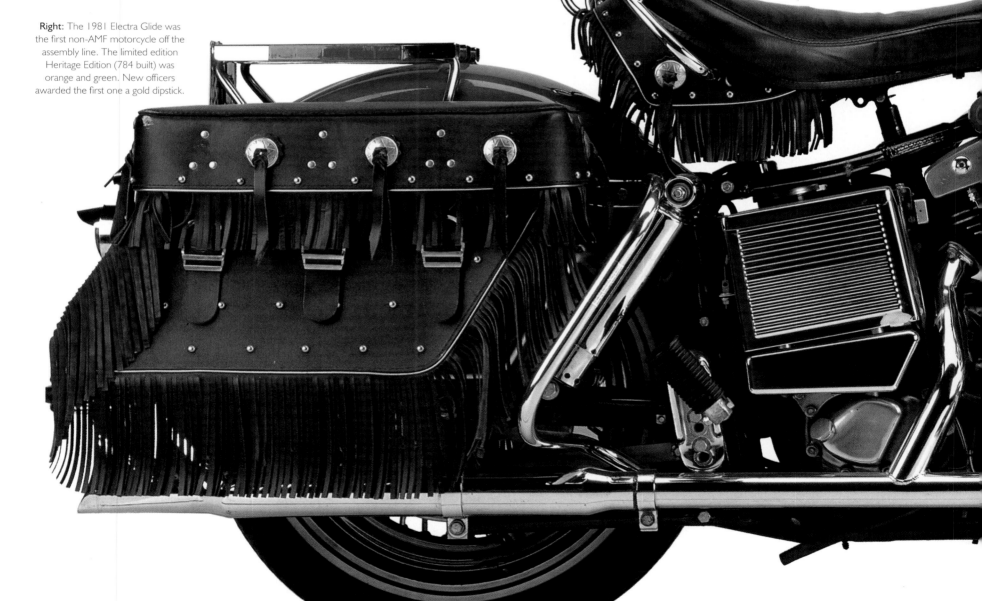

FX models accounted for some 23,000 machines. Sportster figures topped at just over 10,000. Not record-setting numbers, but enough to maintain Harley-Davidson's production force and proceed with work on the new machines. Many of the chores ran overtime.

The Sportster, in form and function, would retain most of its original components during the period of corporate transition and beyond. Always the most resistant to change, the XL fans demanded that the fundamentals not be fiddled with, unless it looked or ran better. Few of the enthusiasts could imagine how the Sportster could look any better, except for the custom touches the owners applied themselves.

The factory custom/cruisers were another matter, of course, so Milwaukee's design and engineering elements were busy preparing the next generation of Low Riders. Development ran concurrently on the new FL touring machines, which were now two years from the showroom floors.

Left: The standard traditional windshield also kept the Heritage Edition from looking too modern.

Below: The AMF heritage had produced a classic case of nostalgia, and set the stage for a new chapter of Harley evolution.

1981 FLH
Owner – Trev Deeley Museum
Vancouver, British Columbia

Above: Footboards provided a final touch of tradition. Enlarged ham can air cleaner covers were required to meet federal emissions standards.

1982 FXRS SUPER GLIDE II

SPECIFICATIONS
ENGINE/DRIVETRAIN
Engine: OHV 45° V-twin
Displacement: 81.65ci (1338cc)
Bore & stroke: 3.50 x 4.25in (89 x 108mm)
Compression ratio: 8:1
Horsepower: 65
Carburetion: Bendix
Transmission: 4-speed
Primary drive: Duplex chain
Final drive: Chain
Brakes: Dual discs. R. Disc
Battery: 12-volt
Ignition: Electronic

CHASSIS/SUSPENSION
Frame: Steel, double downtube
Suspension: F. Telescopic fork. R. Hydraulic shocks
Wheelbase: 64.7in (164.3cm)
Weight: 610lb (277kg)
Fuel capacity: 3.5gal (13.25lit)
Oil capacity: 4qts (3.8lit)
Tires: F. 3.50 x 19in (8.9 x 48.26cm). R. 5.00 x 16in (12.7 x 40.64cm)
Top speed: 115mph (185km/h)
Colors: Vivid black; candy red; metallic blue; metallic green; brown and black
Number built: 3,190 (FXR: 3,065)
Price: $6,690

FXR (1982) AND XLH (1982)

The first of the next generation middle-Glides was the FXR, which debuted in 1982 as the Super Glide II. The new chassis featured another version of the FLT frame, with a strong box-section backbone and rubber-mount system. The letter R distinguished the new model from the standard FX models, which retained solid-mount 4-speed engines.

The 5-speed 80-inch (1340cc) Shovelhead retained the lower compression first used in the FLT. The transmission was improved by revising the linkage and shift mechanism, which produced shorter lever throws and more positive gear changes and made neutral easier to select. Heim-jointed turnbuckles prevented the engine from rocking or twisting in the frame. The massive backbone and larger-diameter frame tubes provided a stiffer chassis.

The FXR was another product of established Milwaukee development paths. The engine had been upgraded first in the time-honored tradition of more displacement and more tractable power. Reliabilty was enhanced with improved lubrication delivery, better valve guides and electronic ignition. Then the new chassis came along to improve handling, comfort and overall performance. And, keeping with the circular development system, a new engine was soon forthcoming.

The FXR matched the FLT for seat height (29 inches, 73.6cm), but its 31-degree steering head extended the wheelbase to 64.7 inches (164.3cm). A long motorcycle normally suffers some clumsiness at low speeds, and the Super Glide II was no exception. But at highway speeds it was impressively stable, and the new quotient of chassis rigidity allowed the FXR to handle twisty roads with considerable composure. Most testers agreed that this was the best-handling big twin ever to come out of Milwaukee. Ground clearance didn't match the pure sport bikes, but within its limits the new model could straighten turns with new levels of speed and security. A cruiser that could scoot.

Fortunately the new handling standards were accompanied by better brakes. Two discs at the front and a dual-piston caliper disc

Below: The stepped seat and separate passenger pad reflected the Super Glide's factory chopper heritage. The sissy bar/backrest had achieved instant popularity with passengers aching for more comfort and security.

Above: The tradition of simple meters; tach and speedo side by each. This is a British model, indicated by kilometer face on the speedometer.

Right: The FXR Super Glide benefited from the development of the Tour Glide, gaining the five-speed transmission and rubber-mount engine. The standard FXE remained a solid-mount four-speed.

Above: The 80in (1340cc) Shovelhead had nearly reached the end of its lifespan in the Super Glide II. But the new gearbox and mounting system was a welcomed advance from Milwaukee.

at the rear elevated braking performance. Redesigned brake and clutch levers offered better leverage than previous controls. With form dialed in to Milwaukee's satisfaction, the function was coming up to speed. The FXR made a number of riders take another look at Harley-Davidson.

XLH

The Sportster was 25 years old in 1982. Naturally the occasion was honored with an anniversary edition, of which 932 were made in XLH trim and 778 in XLS configuration. The Roadster had lost the XLCR exhaust system in favor of dual pipes on one side, but retained the Sprint tank and sissy bar/back rest.

Sportster production was holding at about 8,000 per annum, but federal environmental regulations and low-octane fuel were not kind to high performance engines. For 1982 the Sportster's compression ratio was dropped to 8:1, with a consequent reduction in horsepower and speed. But it still weighed under 500lb (227kg) and could clip the quarter-mile under 14 seconds at 100mph (161km/h), which was about the top speed.

In terms of pure performance the Sporster had one real problem, which was designated the Honda CB900F. The four-cylinder sport bike sprinted the quarter at well under 13 seconds at 110mph (177km/h), and topped out around 130 (209km/h). And it cost about $1,000 less than a Sportster. Traditional enthusiasts were left wondering why the Sportster was getting slower and more expensive.

Even though elapsed times and speeds no longer figured strongly in the Sportster's marketing profile, price was another matter. The XLH retained its distinctive profile, featuring a lot of engine in a minimum of motorcycle, and still upheld its bad boy image after 25 years. But the job had grown more difficult, and the next year would see minimalism redefined in the XLX and a calculated drop in price.

Below: The FXR signaled Harley's intent to bring higher performance standards to the custom/cruiser category; more function for the form.

1982 XLH
Dudley Perkins Company
San Francisco, California

Left: Harley-Davidson marked the 25th anniversary of the Sportster with a special edition in silver and black.

1982 FXR
Owner – Ginger Gammon
Cranleigh, England

1983 XR-1000

SPECIFICATIONS
ENGINE/DRIVETRAIN
Engine: OHV 45° V-twin
Displacement: 61ci (1000cc)
Bore & stroke: 3.19 x 3.81in
(81 x 97mm)
Compression ratio: 9:1
Horsepower: 71 @ 5,600rpm
Carburetion: Two 36mm Dell'
Orto
Transmission: 4-speed
Brakes: Triple disc
Battery: 12-volt
Ignition: V-Fire CDI

CHASSIS/SUSPENSION
Frame: Steel, double downtube
Suspension: F. Telescopic fork.
R. Hydraulic shocks
Wheelbase: 60in (152.4cm)
Weight: 490lb (222kg)
Fuel capacity: 2.5gal (9.5lit)
Oil capacity: 2.5qts (2.36lit)
Tires: F. 110/90-19. R. 130/90-
16 (18in, 45.72cm rear wheel
optional)
Top speed: 125mph (201km/h)
Color: Slate gray (option:
orange/black in 1984)
Number built: 1,108
Price: $6,995

XR-1000 (1983) AND XLX-61 (1983)

No matter the national economic conditions, or the shifting fortunes of the motorcycle market, there always remained in Milwaukee a core group of hot rodders. In this instance it was marketing director Clyde Fessler, racing manager Dick O'Brien and design chief Willie G. Davidson. The result was the XR-1000.

Harley-Davidson had lost sizeable chunks of several market segments to the Japanese motorcycle manufacturers. Giving up the street rod market was rather like adding salt to the wounds. The high-performance fans had lobbied Milwaukee for years to build a street version of the racing XR-750, but to no avail. The XLCR had been considered little more than a cosmetic gesture. Real horsepower was the demand, in traditional Sportster trim.

The factory did consider the possibilities, but the costs involved in outfitting the racer for the street were much higher than projected sales would warrant. So the focus shifted to the existing Sportster, since the new chassis could handle more power and most of the necessary components were in house. Since the Evolution engine project had top priority at the time, the XR-1000 had to be a back room project.

Dick O'Brien enlisted the aid of California

Right: Belt drive arrived just in time for the last of the Shovelhead dressers. Production ran half way through 1984, when the Evolution engine superseded the Shovel. Another collectible, shown here in vivid blue.

flowmeister Jerry Branch, who made sure the new alloy heads breathed properly. Since the heads were larger, the new cast iron cylinders had to be shortened a half-inch (12.7mm) to fit the engine into the Sportster frame. The motor was rated at 70 horsepower, ten more than the standard powerplant. The XR-1000 was quicker (sub-13 second quarter-mile) and faster (125mph, 201km/h) than the XLH, but was less than comfortable on the street. The potent engine made more mechanical clatter and stumbled at low speeds. And at nearly $7,000 the XR was much costlier than the crotch rockets from across the water.

Though no great success on the highway, the XR-1000 proved itself on the race track. O'Brien had the engine bolted into an old road-racing chassis, with competition suspension, brakes and full fairing, which was aptly dubbed "Lucifer's Hammer." Three-time national champ Jay Springsteen dusted the competition with it at

1983 FLH
Owner – Dennis Huggins
Lompoc, California

Right: The XR-1000 resulted from requests for a street version of the XR-750 racer. Thus the expression, "Be careful what you wish for, because you may get it."

1983 XR-1000
Owner – Oliver Shokouh
Harley-Davidson of Glendale
Glendale, California

1984 XR-1000
Owner – Duane Anderson
Arroyo Grande, California

Daytona. Later, under tuner Don Tilley and rider Gene Church, the machine went on to win three successive titles in the Battle of the Twins competition.

XLX-61

The XR-1000 did serve Milwaukee well as an image builder, and drew more than a few prospective customers into the showrooms. Usually, after the oohs and ahhs had subsided, the viewers looked at the price tag and bought an XLX-61.

By contrast, the baby brother from the bargain basement was an instant winner with the public. The XLX-61, with its traditional cubic-inch designation, was the Spartan warrior of the Sportster clan. And with a price below $4,000, it attracted attention.

The XLX recalled the "stripped stock" identification for early production bikes sold to amateur racers. The new Sportster was street-legal, of course, but for $3,995 it came with the bare minimum of accessories. Basic black was the standard color, with a solo seat, low handlebars and little chrome. No instrument panel, tachometer, centerstand or sissy bar. Just a bare-bones machine with a big engine, a tribute to the concept of the original XLCH.

Harley-Davidson had got a bit too tricky with the XR-1000, but the muscle-flexing exercise earned points with the high-performance crowd and created another instant collectible. The XLX, on the other hand, grabbed the attention of riders who had given up on Milwaukee for simple economic reasons. When the price came down, they took another look and became part of the evolutionary process.

Below: The XLX-61 was one of Milwaukee's most astute marketing maneuvers. The price of $3,995 put the Sportster within reach of more riders, and brought more customers into the showrooms. 1983 production: 4,892.

1983 XLX-61
Owner – Trev Deeley Museum
Vancouver, British Columbia

Above: The real venue for the XR-1000 was in Battle of the Twins roadracing. With 70 horsepower in street trim, the engine could be tuned for 95 on the track. As a road machine it was just too expensive and troublesome.

FLHX (1984), FXST (1984) AND FXEF (1984)

Evolution takes time. In the motorcycle business, money is also helpful. In the late 1960s, at the height of the motorcycle sales boom, Harley-Davidson had run out of time and money.

The Motor Company had survived Henry Ford, the Indian Motorcycle Company, the Great Depression, Hollywood and the Hell's Angels. But they were not prepared for Soichiro Honda. (Who knew?). American Machine and Foundry bought the time Milwaukee needed, and even helped finance the evolution. It took 15 years (a millisecond on the Darwinian scale), but by 1984 the newest member of the species *Milwokus motobikus* had evolved.

Even veteran insiders had given Harley-Davidson little chance of success. A dinosaur, they concluded, that had reached the end of its natural lifespan. AMF, an apparent expert in the "recreation" business, had bailed out. The Japanese, who could design, tool-up and build entirely new motorcycles in a period of 18 months, ruled the marketplace. Milwaukee was granted the proverbial snowball's chance in hell.

Then hell froze over.

To evolve is "to develop gradually by a process of growth and change." The Milwaukee process was nothing if not gradual. The company had, over the years, produced a few mechanical mutations that were rejected by the market organism. But given the span of time and weight of numbers – eight decades, millions of motor-

cycles – Harley had the one element essential for survival. Experience.

The brick walls on Juneau Avenue housed four generations of genetic information. Threatened with extinction, Harley-Davidson was forced to adapt or expire. Once the decision was made, the experience could be put to work. The result of that effort was called appropriately, the Evolution engine.

Experience, that great teacher, showed that the new Harley-Davidson had to have a V-twin engine. And that the motorcycle must look, sound and feel much the same as Milwaukee iron always had. And further, that it perform to contemporary standards in terms of comfort, safety, maintenance and reliability. And maintain its resale value.

The story of how Harley-Davidson accomplished this feat has been recounted elsewhere. This book is merely a hardware history, the existence of which testifies that the New Harley-Davidson Motor Company achieved enormous success. The engine was the single most important part of Milwaukee's salvation equation. So how'd they do it?

Gradually, of course. They crafted an alloy engine with iron cylinder liners, squish band combustion chambers, flat-top pistons, stronger rods, closer tolerances, better oiling, tighter joints, stronger valve train, smaller valves set at 58 degrees, and computerized ignition. The technical data is beyond the scope of this survey, but the result was a lighter, tighter, stronger, cooler, higher-power, longer-lasting and more fuel-efficient engine. The engineering was exhaustive, expensive and the testing was elaborate to the point of brutality. That done, the Evo team took two machines to Alabama's Talladega Speedway and ran them for four days straight at 85mph (137km/h). They didn't break.

The everlasting story has a new chapter:
Starship Milwaukee: The Next Generation.

1984 FXST

SPECIFICATIONS

ENGINE/DRIVETRAIN
Engine: OHV 45° V-twin
Displacement: 81.65ci (1338cc)
Bore & stroke: 3.5 x 4.25in (89 x 108mm)
Compression ratio: 8.5:1
Horsepower: 55
Carburetion: 38mm Keihin
Transmission: 4-speed
Primary drive: Duplex chain
Final drive: Chain
Brakes: F. Disc. R. Drum
Battery: 12-volt
Ignition: CDI

CHASSIS/SUSPENSION
Frame: Steel, double downtube
Suspension: F. Telescopic fork. R. Shocks
Wheelbase: 66.3in (168.4cm)
Weight: 628lb (285kg)
Fuel capacity: 5gal (18.9lit)
Oil capacity: 3.5qts (3.3lit)
Tires: F. 3.00 x 19in (7.62 x 48.26cm). R. 5.00 x 16in (12.7 x 40.64cm)
Top speed: 110mph (177km/h)
Colors: Vivid black with pinstripes; candy red with pinstripes
Number built: 5,413
Price: $7,999

Right: The transition from the Shovelhead to the Evolution engine began in 1984. One of the five models with the new Evo motor was the FXST Softail, featuring the look but not the ride of the old rigid chassis.

Above: The rigid looking frame section belies the shock absorbers cleverly hidden below the transmission.

Below: The Softail was traditional in more than just appearance: the engine may have been all new inside, but it was still mounted solidly to the frame and had a four-speed transmission. And a kickstarter.

1984 FLHX
Owner – Trev Deeley Museum
Vancouver, British Columbia

Above: The FLHX Electra Glide was built as a limited edition model for 1984. This marks the final chapter for the solid-mount four-speed Shovelhead. The production total was 1,258.

Left: The 1984 Fat Bob was the last Shovel in the Super Glide series. It was also the curtain call for chain drive.

1984 FXEF
Mathews Harley-Davidson
Fresno, California

1984 FXST Softail
Dudley Perkins Company
San Francisco, California

1985 FLHTC

SPECIFICATIONS
ENGINE/DRIVETRAIN
Engine: OHV 45° V-twin
Displacement: 81.65ci
(1338cc)
Bore & stroke: 3.5 x 4.25in
(89 x 108mm)
Compression ratio: 8.5:1
Horsepower: 55
Carburetion: 38mm Keihin
Transmission: 5-speed
Primary drive: Duplex chain
Final drive: Belt
Brakes: F. Dual discs. R. Disc
Battery: 12-volt
Ignition: CDI

CHASSIS/SUSPENSION
Frame: Steel, double downtube
Suspension: F. Telescopic fork.
R. Shocks
Wheelbase: 62.9in (159.8cm)
Weight: 760lb (345kg)
Fuel capacity: 5gal (18.9lit)
Oil capacity: 4qts (3.8lit)
Tires: F. 3.00 x 19in
(7.62 x 48.26cm).
R. 5.00 x 16in (12.7
x 40.64cm)
Top speed: 110mph
(177km/h)
Colors: Vivid black;
candy red; candy blue;
tan/cream; candy
burgundy/slate gray (all
with pinstripes); candy
burgundy/candy pearl
Number built: 3,409
Price: $9,199

FLHT (1985) AND FXST (1986)

When the Evo engine became the only big twin in 1985, design variations arrived to identify them by type and function. The FXRS Low Glide had the rubber-mount system, 5-speeds, belt drive and triple disc brakes. The Heritage Softail joined the FL series in 1986, expanding the retro-look of the 1950s and retaining the solid-mount chassis.

Testing its abilities (characteristic of newly evolved species), Harley-Davidson sought to learn how many levels of the custom/cruiser/touring/sport market were out there. Things had changed. The niche segments of the riding spectrum had been redefined by the motorcycle boomers of the 1960s and 1970s, so Milwaukee developed a new interest in demographics. The engineers and engine builders had done their jobs, now it was time for the boys in marketing.

Even though the Evolution engine received favorable coverage in the enthusiast press, the new models didn't claim overnight success. Not until 1988 did production approach the levels it had reached in the 1970s. Styling, market research and advertising employees took responsibilty for the next phase of the natural selection process.

1986 FXSTC
Owner – John Kingston
Atascadero, California

Left: Combined with the saddlebags, the top box provided plenty of cargo capacity for the touring rider.

Below: In its continuing effort to make large motorcycles more user-friendly, Milwaukee worked to lower the seat height. Balancing a heavy motorcycle on tiptoes does little to induce confidence in the rider.

Right: The FLHTC Electra Glide Classic heralded the advent of longer letter and name designations. It also marked a great step forward in touring comfort, roadworthy performance, engine reliability and reduced maintenance.

Left: The Softail was joined by a Custom model in 1986, featuring a disc rear wheel. Both models had the new five-speed transmission and belt drive.

Left: More riders were coming to appreciate the wind protection offered by a windshield.

Left: The bar-mounted fairing had changed little in 25 years, and remained more popular than the larger touring fairing.

Above: The V2 Evolution engine proved to be driving force in the revitalization of Harley-Davidson.

The FLHT Electra Glide Classic wore the traditional bar-mount fairing in 1985, and the styling was unchanged but for the old-time bar-and-shield tank emblem. An improved diaphragm clutch had been introduced the year before, designed for cooler running, less slippage and easier operation. With the 5-speed and belt drive, the big twins required less effort of the rider. The FLTC Tour Glide Classic with frame-mount fairing had gained popularity, the FXRS Low Glide replaced the Super Glide II and the Fat Bob made its final appearance.

The FXST Softail, introduced in 1984, had struck the right balance of contemporary engineering and nostalgic design. Between the FX and FL renditions, the Softail accounted for nearly 9,000 machines in 1986. The rear frame section, designed to emulate the old rigid or "hard tail" frames, hid the shock absorbers beneath the transmission. And the new Harely not only resembled the old in appearance, with the engine solidly connected to the frame it rode more like its ancestor. Of course the Evo didn't shake with nearly the vigor of a Knucklehead.

The FX softie was presented in a custom version for 1986 (FXSTC), distinguished by the solid disc rear wheel, sissy bar, black engine and old-timey lettering on the fuel tank. The Custom accounted for 3,782 motorcycles, compared to 2,402 for the standard Softail. In 1987 the Custom outsold the ST better than two to one.

The FL series lagged behind in the market crowded with touring bike choices. The Electra Glide Classic had jumped to 3,409 machines in 1985, but dropped to 1,879 the following year. For 1986, Harley-Davidson cross-bred the Softail chassis and the Electra Glide front end to create the FLST Heritage Softail. The 1950s styling included the two-tone paint of that era. A Special version included windshield, leather saddlebags, wire wheels and footboards.

Both the FX and FL Softails enjoyed early success and continued selling well in the 1990s. In 1987 The Harley-Davidson Motor Company was listed on the New York Stock Exchange. Milwaukee was over the hump, and celebration plans were made for the company's 85th anniversary party in 1988.

1985 FLHTC
Bartels' Harley-Davidson
Marina Del Rey, California

FLST (1986) AND XLH-1100 (1987)

The Electra Glide had added considerable bulk over the years, and the FX Softails had subtracted a few pounds in the cruiser category. Which meant there was room in between for an updated version of the Hydra-Glide. Enter the FLST Heritage Softail.

With the Evolution engine solidly in place (not rubber-mounted as it was in the FX series), the Heritage Softail mixed Milwaukee tradition with contemporary technology and design. The rigid-look rear frame section complements the Hydra-Glide front end, with its deeply skirted fender, large headlight and sergeant-stripe cowling. The deeply stepped saddle reflects more modern tastes, and puts the seat height at only 26.5 inches (67.3cm).

1986 FLST

SPECIFICATIONS
ENGINE/DRIVETRAIN
Engine: OHV 45° V-twin
Displacement: 81.65ci (1338cc)
Bore & stroke: 3.5 x 4.25in (89 x 108mm)
Compression ratio: 8.5:1
Horsepower: 55
Carburetion: 38mm Keihin
Transmission: 5-speed
Primary drive: Duplex chain
Final drive: Belt
Brakes: F. & R. Disc
Battery: 12-volt
Ignition: CDI

CHASSIS/SUSPENSION
Frame: Steel, double downtube
Suspension: F. Telescopic fork. R. Shocks
Wheelbase: 62.5in (158.75cm)
Weight: 650lb (295kg)
Fuel capacity: 5gal (18.9lit)
Oil capacity: 3qts (2.84lit)
Tires: MT-90S-16
Top speed: 112mph (180km/h)
Colors: Signal red/creme; bronze/creme
Number built: 2,510
Price: $9,099

1987 XLH-1100

SPECIFICATIONS
ENGINE/DRIVETRAIN
Engine: OHV 45° V-twin
Displacement: 67.2ci (1100cc)
Bore & stroke: 3.35 x 3.81in (85 x 97mm)
Compression ratio: 8.5:1
Horsepower: 63
Carburetion: Keihin
Transmission: 4-speed
Primary drive: Chain
Final drive: Chain
Brakes: F. & R. Disc
Battery: 12-volt
Ignition: CDI

CHASSIS/SUSPENSION
Frame: Steel, double downtube
Suspension: F. Telescopic fork. R. Dual shocks
Wheelbase: 60in (152.4cm)
Weight: 492lb (223kg)
Fuel capacity: 2.25gal (8.52lit)
Oil capacity: 3.5qts (3.3lit)
Tires: F. MJ90-19. R. MT90-16
Top speed: 112mph (180km/h)
Colors: Black and orange (Anniversary); vivid black; candy brandywine; candy bronze; metallic blue and silver; brandywine/crimson
Number built: 4,618
Price: $5,199

Right: With the success of the FX-series Softails, the next logical step applied the same technology to the FL.

1987 XLH-1100
Dudley Perkins Company
San Francisco, California

Left: Of the 4,618 XLH-1100 Sportsters built for 1987, 600 were specials celebrating the model's 30th anniversary. The model featured orange and black paint and a black and chrome engine.

Above: Like the FXST, the Heritage Softail hid its shock absorbers out of sight below the transmission. Brakes were single disc at each end.

Below: The Heritage handlebar had plenty of pullback to put controls within easy reach of the rider, who was positioned relatively far aft on the machine.

The seat put the rider farther aft than the FXR perch, so the handlebar was pulled back for comfort. The riding position was designed to accommodate the traditional footboards, locating the feet between the standard touring posture and the recliner mode of highway pegs.

Although it shared many components with the FXR Low Rider, the Heritage Softail was a quite different machine. With some two inches (5cm) less wheelbase, 16-inch (40.64cm) front wheel, more trail, reduced ground clearance and 50-pound (22.7kg) weight surplus, the FLST was hardly a nimble sport bike. The

Heritage Softail was designed for stately motoring, which was reflected by the 1950s styling.

In the FLST Milwaukee had brought forth a modern classic, a retro-look with clean, uncluttered lines and modern, low-mainte-nance engine and running gear. Naturally it was followed a year later by the Heritage Softail Classic, with paint schemes from the past, rocket-fin mufflers, studded seats and saddlebags.

The Sportster was awarded an Evolution engine in 1986. The 883cc version was soon joined by an 1100 with larger valves and 63 horsepower, a ten-horse jump. The Sporties got new clutches and trannies, and a slightly revised frame.

In 1987 the XLH-883, including the lowered Hugger model, represented the bulk of Sportster production with 9,356 machines. The 1100 accounted for 4,618 bikes, 600 of which were the Anniversary edition shown here. The special celebrated the Sportster's 30th birthday with a black and chrome engine, orange and black paint and commemorative graphics.

The Hugger, so named for its abbreviated seat height, was aimed at women riders and males in the inseam-disadvantaged category. Short guys. By shortening the fork tubes two inches (5cm), revising the shock absorber angle and offering a softer seat, the seat height came down to 26.75in (68cm). That was 1.75in (4.4cm) lower than the standard Sportster, and allowed more folks to plant their feet securely when stopped. A deluxe version of the 883 was also offered, with dual seat and wire wheels.

Harley-Davidson made another decisive marketing move in 1987. Buyers of the XLH-883 were guaranteed an exchange value of $3,995 if they traded within two years for an FL or FX model. Milwaukee was determined to post a clear demonstration of their own confidence in the new machines. People noticed.

Below: The architecture of the large headlight and squared aluminium fork cover replicated the front end of the Hydra-Glide from 1949. The three ribs are 1955-style.

Below: The bespoke wheels, hub cap and 1950s-style fender mark the nostalgia for an earlier era, when "life was simpler."

1986 FLST
Owner – Harley-Davidson Motor Co.
Milwaukee, Wisconsin
© Harley-Davidson Archive photo

1988 FXRS

SPECIFICATIONS
ENGINE/DRIVETRAIN
Engine: OHV 45° V-twin
Displacement: 81.65ci
(1338cc)
Bore & stroke: 3.5 x 4.25in
(89 x 108mm)
Compression ratio: 8.5:1
Horsepower: 55
Carburetion: 38mm Keihin
Transmission: 5-speed
Primary drive: Duplex chain
Final drive: Belt
Brakes: F. Dual discs. R. Disc
Battery: 12-volt
Ignition: CDI

CHASSIS/SUSPENSION
Frame: Steel, double downtube
Suspension: F. Telescopic fork.
R. Shocks
Wheelbase: 63.1in (160.3cm)
Weight: 580lb (263kg)
Fuel capacity: 4.5gal (17lit)
Oil capacity: 3qts (2.8lit)
Tires: F. MT90-19. R. MT90-16
Top speed: 110mph (177km/h)
Colors: Vivid black; candy
brandywine; bright candy plum;
candy brandywine/candy
crimson; bright cobalt/candy
blue/silver; champagne gold/black
(Anniversary)
Number built: 2,637 (Sport:
818; Anniversary Edition: 519)
Price: $9,245

FXRS (1988), XLH 1200(1988) AND XLH 883 (1989)

With the Evolution (Darwinhead?) engine powering the entire Harley-Davidson lineup, attention in Milwaukee turned to variations on the theme. A frenzy of new names and letters arrived to identify the assortment of Super Glide/Low Rider derivations that multiplied each year.

With the addition of hybrids like the FXSTC (Softail Custom) and FLSTC (Heritage Softail Classic), the model chart grew increasingly complex. There was the standard FXR Super Glide, FXRS Low Rider, FXRS-SP Low Rider Sport, FXLR Low Rider Custom and FXRT Sport Glide. Then the FXRS Convertible, followed by the FXDB Dyna Glide Sturgis. One had to pay attention.

In 1985 the FXRS had returned with the longer suspension and dual-disc front brakes it had worn three years earlier. Now it was enhanced with the Evo engine and belt drive. The new version was slightly lighter despite the larger 4.5-gallon (17lit) fuel tank, and was rated at 55 horsepower. The price was $8,149.

By 1988 the Low Rider's popularity had been eclipsed by the Softail models, but performance-minded riders preferred the FXRS for its rubber-mount engine and sporting road manners. And they had the choice of more traditional styling in the standard model, which put the instruments on a tank panel rather than the handlebar. The Low Rider had a single disc brake on the front wheel and came standard with forward-mounted highway pegs. The turn signals were now attached to the mirror mounts rather than the handlebar. Fork tube diameter increased from 1.38in to 1.54in (3.5 to 3.9cm).

The Sport Edition still wore its instruments on the handlebar and the gas cap in the center of the tank. The sporty version featured a new version of the air-assisted fork first seen in 1983 on the Sport Glide. Using the handlebar as an air resevoir, the system incorporated an anti-dive feature to reduce nosedive under braking. Air volume was adjusted using a Schrader valve at the left end of the handlebar.

Dual disc front brakes were standard on the Sport Edition, which had 1.4in (3.56cm) more wheelbase than the standard model. Steering geometry was different as well, the sport fork set at 31 degrees rather than 29, and the handlebar was lower and flatter. Despite its handling advantages, the Sport Edition enjoyed far less popularity than the Super Glide and Low Rider versions. Only 818 of the sporties were made in 1988.

XLH 1200

The Sportster climbed another rung on the muscle ladder in 1988 with the introduction of a 1200cc model. The 1100 cylinder bore was taken out to 3.50 inches (89mm), which combined with new combustion chambers, smaller valves and a 40mm carburetor produced 12 percent more power.

Naturally the 1200 was quicker and faster than its predecessor. The ratios between the first three gears had been tightened up the year before, which helped with acceleration. The new carburetor also featured an enrichening circuit that allowed smoother running in city riding and improved throttle response. The Sportsters also got the larger fork tubes awarded to the FX series, and for the first time came fitted with two rear view mirrors.

For 1989 the Sportster roster remained at four models: the XLH 883 with solo seat and speedo only, with the price up to $3,999; the similarly equipped Hugger with buckhorn bars; the 883 Deluxe with wire wheels, dual seat and passenger pegs, and the 1200 with Deluxe accoutrements and more ponies. All models featured a new kickstand that was farther aft and an easier reach.

Right: In 1988 the FXRS was awarded a traditonal fat bob fuel tank, but it still retained the dual disc brakes on the front wheel. This machine has an accessory exhaust system, shorter shock absorbers and spoked rather than cast wheels.

Below: The standard FXR was now labeled the Super Glide, the FXRS the Low Rider and the FXRS-SP was the Low Rider Sport Edition, with longer travel suspension. The FXR was produced as one of four special anniversary editions in 1988, commemorating the 85th anniversary of Harley-Davidson. Only 519 of the specials were built.

Below: The 1200cc Sportster produced a good measure more of both torque and horsepower over the 1100. The '88 Sporties also got the 39mm fork tubes.

1988 XLH 1200
Bartels' Harley-Davidson
Marina Del Rey, California

Below: The Evolution Sportster was offered in multiple configurations, with cast or spoked wheels, solo or dual seat, and 883 or 1200cc engine.

1989 XLH 883
Harley-Davidson of Atascadero
Atascadero, California

1988 FXRS
Dudley Perkins Company
San Francisco, California

1988 FXSTS

SPECIFICATIONS
ENGINE/DRIVETRAIN
Engine: OHV 45° V-twin
Displacement: 81.65ci
(1338cc)
Bore & stroke: 3.5 x 4.25in
(89 x 108mm)
Compression ratio: 8.5:1
Horsepower: 55
Carburetion: 38mm Keihin
Transmission: 5-speed
Primary drive: Duplex chain
Final drive: Belt
Brakes: F. and R. Disc
Battery: 12-volt
Ignition: CDI

CHASSIS/SUSPENSION
Frame: Steel, double downtube
Suspension: F. Springer fork.
R. Shocks
Wheelbase: 64.5in (163.8cm)
Weight: 635lb (288kg)
Fuel capacity: 6.4gal (24.2lit)
Oil capacity: 3qts (2.8lit)
Tires: F MT90-21. R. MH90-16
Top speed: 114mph (183km/h)
Colors: Black with red pinstripes
Number built: 1,356
Price: $10,279

Right: The FXSTS Softail
Springer first appeared in
1988. In blending vintage
styling with contemporary
engineering and materials,
Milwaukee created yet
another popular piece of
functional nostalgia.

FXSTS (1988) AND FLHTC (1989)

Harley-Davidson took nostalgia another step into the past with the Softail Springer in 1988. Having made the rear suspension look just like the no-suspension frames of earlier years, Milwaukee decided to retro-style the front end as well. So the fork appeared to be right out of the 1940s, with the leading link/spring assembly characteristic of the Knucklehead era.

But while the look was 1948, the performance proved to be surprisingly contemporary. Harley engineers worked diligently to give the Springer fork modern manners on the road. And while they couldn't provide the same travel or damping provided by a telescopic fork, the result was a decent compromise between comfort and style.

With the help of computers, Teflon bearings and extensive testing, Milwaukee created a modern version of a design first used nearly 60 years earlier. Critics of retro-style motorcycles were skeptical, but most were forced to admit that the new/old fork worked better than expected. Braking performance was acceptable, limited by the narrow front tire, not by the fork's design.

Below: The Springer successfully combined styling cues from the 1940s to the 1970s, adding '90s reliability.

Above: Like its FX brethren, the Springer runs the 80in (1340cc) Evolution engine with belt drive and hidden rear shocks. A triangular swing arm provides 3.4 inches (8.6cm) of rear wheel travel.

Once again Milwaukee tested the market with caution, building a total of 1,356 Springers for 1988. The release was timed to coincide with Harley-Davidson's 85th anniversary celebration, and the FXSTS featured commemorative graphics on the tank and front fender. The styling was an immediate hit, and Milwaukee was encouraged to crank up the production line for 1989. Which they did, fashioning 5,387 Springers for the next season.

Harley-Davidson was obviously on a retrospective roll, creating one piece of motorized memorabilia after another. The Springer didn't overtake the cruiser champion, the Softail Custom, but the numbers were close and the balance sheets properly weighted. The only recurring complaint from the field concerned the front fender; its height above the tire reminded people of a dirt bike. So the mounting brackets were changed and the gap closed.

1989 FLHTC
Harley-Davidson of Atascadero
Atascadero, California

1988 FXSTS
Owner – Harley-Davidson Motor Co.
Milwaukee, Wisconsin
© Harley-Davidson Archive photo

Above: The Classic Electra Glide was number five in Milwaukee production for 1989, with 3,969 built. The FL touring models all got self-canceling turn signals, a stronger alternator and a redesigned fuel tank. The Ultra models were fitted with cruise control.

Left: The 21-inch (53.3cm) wheel enhances the long and lean look. The front fender was later lowered in response to customer demand.

The first Softail was an immediate hit with the craftsfolk in the customizing realm. The uncluttered back end provided a clean backdrop for stylish seat and fender formulations, and put more of the rear wheel on display. The low seating position offered by the frame was perfectly suited to the easy-chair riding position favored by most of the cruiser crowd, and no cutting or welding was required.

Grafting on the Springer front end added another dimension to the Softail's multi-faceted personality. In addition to giving it some of the Knucklehead panache of the 1940s, the configuration offered yet another direction for custom treatments. The Knuckle had attracted many fans in the modified motorcycle trend that grew up following World War II, and the later generation was attracted to the Softail Springer for the same reasons. The straight line from rear axle to steering head provided an open framework for the engine and drivetrain; and the traditional leading link fork and exposed springs put the suspension's working hardware in plain view. And it worked pretty well.

SPRING BACK TO THE FUTURE

The spring fork worked much newer than it looked. The design, though a couple of generations old, had been good in the first place. And with the advantages of computer-aided engineering and better materials, this incarnation was superior on the road.

Although the Springer carried a 20 percent disadvantage in terms of wheel travel compared to the telescopic fork, it offered a more rigid attachment between the frame and axle. And despite its added weight penalty, the girder-and-yoke assembly didn't suffer the stiction problems of hydraulic tubes. Plus, the 21-inch (53.3cm) front wheel traversed potholes with less drama than the smaller hoops.

Pivoting-link forks, with the axle either ahead or behind the pivot, were used on the earliest motorcycles. The Harley system hinged the suspension arm at the rigid fork, with the axle in front and the sprung yoke fitted at the fulcrum. Spring action is damped by a small hydraulic shock, and the wheel is braced by four fork legs rather than the telescopic's two.

The new fork had to meet higher performance standards than the old lower-case springer, including more than double the wheel travel. This dictated the need for strong bushings and close tolerances at the pivot points. Harley engineers solved the problem with adjustable Teflon bushings that proved efficient and durable. Then they cleverly incorporated a compact disc brake carrier above the axle. A dandy piece of work, all told.

1990 FLTC

SPECIFICATIONS
ENGINE/DRIVETRAIN
Engine: OHV 45° V-twin
Displacement: 81.65ci
(1338cc)
Bore & stroke: 3.5 x 4.25in
(89 x 108mm)
Compression ratio: 8.5:1
Horsepower: 55
Carburetion: 38mm Keihin
Transmission: 5-speed
Primary drive: Duplex chain
Final drive: Belt
Brakes: F. Dual discs. R. Disc
Battery: 12-volt
Ignition: CDI

CHASSIS/SUSPENSION
Frame: Steel, double downtube
Suspension: F. Telescopic fork.
R. Dual shocks
Wheelbase: 63.1in (160.3cm)
Weight: 780lb (354kg)
Fuel capacity: 5gal (18.9lit)
Oil capacity: 3qts (2.8lit)
Tires: F. MT90-19. R. MT90-16
Top speed: 110mph (177km/h)
Colors: Vivid black; dark hi-fi
blue; candy hi-fi blue; dark
ruby/candy ruby
Number built: 3,082
Price: $13,695

Above: The cockpit of the
Tour Glide Ultra Classic was
loaded with amenities. With
built-in citizen's band radio,
intercom system, 80-watt
stereo and cruise control, the
FLTC was the flagship of
long-distance tourers.

Right: Large travel trunk and
saddlebags carry enough gear
for two people on the road
for extended periods. Triple
disc brakes ensure that heavy
loads can be slowed down in
a reasonable distance.

FLTC ULTRA (1990) AND XLH (1992)

Following the design and development efforts devoted to the FX series, Harley-Davidson refocused attention on the Electra Glide. The FLHS Sport model was produced in limited numbers for 1987 and 1988, but didn't light large fires of enthusiasm with the sport-touring crowd. The FL Softail was far more popular.

For 1989 Milwaukee introduced the Tour Glide and Electra Glide Ultra Classics, the Ultra indicating full-dress and then some. The Tour Glide featured the frame-mount fairing and the Electra Glide retained the bar-mount fairing. Both models got cruise control, 80-watt four-speaker stereo system with tuning controls for the passenger, CB radio/voice-activated intercom and fairing lowers.

The Ultras were distinguished by silver and black paint schemes, circular graphics on the tank and Ultra Classic nameplates on the front fender and saddlebags. All the touring models got new fuel tank designs, high-output alternator and self-canceling turn signals.

The luxury touring market, much like its automobile counterpart, had been steadily redefined by the Japanese manufacturers. Electra Glide sales were back on the rise and Milwaukee wanted to see that direction maintained. The popularity of long-distance touring, in considerable style and comfort, was showing signs of strength once again. Customer's requirements had expanded in hand with the manufacturers' abilities to produce deluxe machines. Amenities that Harley-Davidson had previously consigned to the aftermarket suppliers were now expected as original equipment.

And passengers were now getting more attention than ever before. (If the saddlepal is unhappy, the rider is soon informed). More creature comforts were being built into the pillion perch every year. Seat shapes and heights, backrests, armrests, footboards and grab rails all were reexamined and redesigned. Touring, after all, is largely a family activity.

Below: Both rider and passenger were
awarded comfortable seats. The rider's
backrest is removable.

1992 XLH
Owner – Val Bassetti
Bradley, California

The Electra Glide family came in for incremental revisions and improvements in 1990. The clutch was beefed, or maybe in this case porked, up and the cruise control was awarded some fine adjustment. The Electra Glide, with its traditional bar-mounted fairing and small windscreen, had continued outselling the Tour Glide better than five to one. But in 1991, partly owing to Milwaukee's demonstration ride program at major rallies, the Tour Glide and its frame-mounted fairing picked up the pace.

For riders unaccustomed to full fairings (a sizeable segment of Harley enthusiasts), the first experience with one is awkward. The bar-mount fairing sits much closer to the rider, and blocks little of the view immediately ahead. The larger unit at first seems an unwieldy overhang and an obstruction during low speed maneuvers. But out on the open road it affords much better wind protection, quieter ride and helps reduce fatigue on long hauls. And once accustomed to the fairing, most riders don't notice its presence.

Of course other riders don't mind life in the wind, and need only the minimal amount of protection from the elements. Which is why Harley-Davidson continues to offer touring machines in the minimal, medium and full-toot configuration.

In 1992 the FL models had the oil filter relocated to the front of the engine for improved access. New materials in the disc rotor and brake pads enhanced feel at the brake lever, and the saddlebags got better gaskets to keep the contents dry.

Above: This Sportster has been modified with a number of custom touches to suit the owner's style: a larger tank, studded seat, aftermarket exhaust system and fancy laced wheels give the Sporty a whole new look.

1990 FLTC Ultra Classic
Owner – Howard Mahler
Studio City, California

Above: The Tour Glide looked little changed in ten years, but the Evolution engine and upscale creature comforts made quite a difference

1990 FLSTF

SPECIFICATIONS
ENGINE/DRIVETRAIN
Engine: OHV 45° V-twin
Displacement: 81.65ci (1338cc)
Bore & stroke: 3.5 x 4.25in (89 x 108mm)
Compression ratio: 8.5:1
Horsepower: 55
Carburetion: 38mm Keihin
Transmission: 5-speed
Primary drive: Duplex chain
Final drive: Belt
Brakes: F. and R. Disc
Battery: 12-volt
Ignition: CDI

CHASSIS/SUSPENSION
Frame: Steel, double downtube
Suspension: F. Telescopic fork. R. Shocks
Wheelbase: 62.5in (158.7cm)
Weight: 665lb (302kg)
Fuel capacity: 4.7gal (17.8lit)
Oil capacity: 3qts (2.8lit)
Tires: F. and R. MT90-16
Top speed: 114mph (183km/h)
Color: Metallic silver
Number built: 4,440
Price: $10,995

FLSTF (1990) AND BUELL RR1200 (1990)

The evolutionary retro-revolution produced a chubby new member of the species in 1990, the Fat Boy. Genetically engineered with components from the Softail Custom and Heritage Softail Classic, the portly FLSTF was an instant crowd pleaser.

The Fat Boy took the Softail series into still another quasi-historical realm, the Flash Gordon era of science fiction space travel in the late 1940s. The silver custom dresser personified the ideal craft for solo interplanetary travel, or a funky little shuttle for delivering recruits to outposts on frontiers of the galaxy, or, in real life, to the diner across town.

Harley-Davidson had invented fantasy bikes from the factory, but the Fat Boy was still something of a first. The Super Glide, Low Rider, Fat Bob and Springer were all contemporary takes on historical or existing themes that were established, motorcycles modified to achieve a look. Derivative, in other words. The genius of the Fat Boy was not only that the look came before the machine, but that it emerged from a retouched Heritage Softail. New and old were combined not to replicate a motorcycle, but to create something new.

The Fat Boy was Milwaukee's first novelty bike, but it didn't fit the category of cautionary market experimentation. Harley-Davidson built 4,440 examples in the first year of production, not numbers associated with testing the waters. The Softail had already proven itself for four years running, so only the industrial-cosmic styling qualified as a risk factor.

Of course had it failed, the bike could readily be retrofitted with Heritage Softail components and probably not oversupply the market. But the production numbers indicate otherwise; that someone knew the brash Fat Boy would succeed on its own. That someone would be Willie G. Davidson, who designed this one for himself.

BUELL RR1200

This is a Harley from an entirely different hogpen. Actually only the engine is from Harley-Davidson; the rest originated in the imagination of ex-Milwaukee engineer Erik Buell. The handcrafted motorcycles are built in Mukwonago, Wisconsin.

Buell, a former roadracer, had been part of the design team on the FXR rubber-mount chassis. He had left Milwaukee in 1985 to build racing machines, one of which became a Sportster-engine Battle of the Twins bike, appropriately called the RR-1000 Battle Twin. With the advent of the Evolution engine, the Buell in turn evolved as the RR-1200 in 1988, followed by the RS model with less bodywork.

Below: The seat features an insert of pigskin, with a touch of leather lace on the side and the gas tank strap.

Right: Willie and the Fat Boy. For 1990 Willie G. composed a "two-wheeled testament to American industrial art." And just to demonstrate that the craft of mechanical design is not devoid of humor, he called it the Fat Boy.

Above: Echoes of the Vincent Black Prince are evident in Erik Buell's Harley-powered RR 1200. Later models lost most of the bodywork.

1990 Buell RR 1200
Owner – Mike Lady
Arroyo Grande, California

The Buell chassis is a birdcage frame of chrome-moly tubing, from which the Sportster engine is hung by a four-point mounting system. The mounts employ rubber dampers and Heim-joint rods to absorb the V-twin's vibrations. A Marzocchi fork suspends the front end and a Works Performance shock absorber, mounted below the engine, dampens the rear wheel. The exhaust pipe is also routed beneath the powerplant.

Most of the hardware is handmade for the sport bike, including the Buell-designed four-piston front brakes. The wheel rims were furnished by Performance Machine, with spoke design and hubs by Erik Buell. The price of the RR1200 was $13,695. Harley-Davidson later purchased part interest in Buell's company, effectively making it Milwaukee's sport bike division.

Below: Disc wheels and flared fenders recall the techno-deco futurism of the 1950s.

1990 FLSTF
Bartels' Harley-Davidson
Marina Del Rey, California

FXDB STURGIS (1991) AND FXDB DYNA DAYTONA (1992)

1992 FXDB DYNA DAYTONA

SPECIFICATIONS
ENGINE/DRIVETRAIN
Engine: OHV 45° V-twin
Displacement: 81.65ci (1338cc)
Bore & stroke: 3.5 x 4.25in (89 x 108mm)
Compression ratio: 8.5:1
Horsepower: 72 @ 4,000rpm
Carburetion: 40mm Keihin
Transmission: 5-speed
Primary drive: Duplex chain
Final drive: Belt
Brakes: F. Dual discs. R. Disc
Battery: 12-volt
Ignition: CDI

CHASSIS/SUSPENSION
Frame: Steel, double downtube
Suspension: F. Telescopic fork. R. Shocks
Wheelbase: 65.5in (166.4cm)
Weight: 630lb (286kg)
Fuel capacity: 4.9gal (18.5lit)
Oil capacity: 3qts (2.8lit)
Tires: F. 100/90-19. R. 130/90-16
Top speed: 103mph (166km/h)
Color: Gold pearlglo/indigo blue metallic
Number built: 1,700
Price: $12,120

Following the whimsical styling of the Fat Boy, what might be the next costume drama in the Willie G. bag of tricks? And what could the next name be – Chub Hog? Glide Rider? Super Low Glider? None of that, thank you, and in fact the bike was a revival of the Sturgis. Would the G-man repeat himself?

Yes and no. The Sturgis styling had been enormously popular ten years earlier, and now Milwaukee had the technology to present it in new and improved form. Thus the Dyna Glide chassis, the result of computer-aided design work. The square-section frame backbone runs from the steering head to the swingarm pivot, and the engine-mount system uses two rather than four rubber mounts. All major frame junctions are forged rather than stamped, and the oil tank has been relocated below the transmission.

As a third-generation Low Rider, this version of the Sturgis was another limited edition model, built only a single year with a production run of 1,546. The reborn Sturgis served as a handsome platform to introduce the Dyna Glide chassis, and to satisfy the many requests to offer the model once again. The belt drive system had been simplified and improved since its inception, and now included an improved drive sprocket retainer that had better retention.

The new Sturgis resembled the original in most respects, but numerous differences appeared in the details. The Dyna version got only one disc brake in the front, and both the new seat and handlebar were higher than the old. Both machines weighed in at 610 pounds (277kg), but the new model has nearly an inch (2.5cm) more wheelbase. Of course the new one was smoother, more comfortable and ran longer between tune-ups. And cost more. (1981: $5,687 – 1991: $11,520).

DAYTONA

The next model to carry the Dyna Glide chassis was still another limited edition, named the Daytona in honor of the 50th anniversary in 1991 of the Daytona 200. Released in 1992, the Daytona shared its running gear with the Sturgis but carried dual disc brakes in front.

The Daytona was heralded as the first Harley-Davidson to feature a true pearl paint. The two-tone scheme was gold pearl-glo with indigo blue metallic. The cast wheels and rear drive pulley were painted a complementary gold, and the tank featured a special 50th anniversary graphic. An inscription on the air cleaner cover also noted the exclusivity.

The electrical components hid in a chrome-capped boxed under the seat's left side, where the oil tank formerly fit. The battery, also encased in chrome, sat in its original position on the right. The Daytona received Milwaukee's new self-canceling turn signals and a horn loud enough to wake up car drivers. The

Below: The Sturgis seat put the rider 29 inches (74cm) from the road. The price of the ticket was $11,520.

Right: The Sturgis returned for an encore in 1991, this time with an entirely new chassis and the Evolution engine. The FXDB Dyna Glide Sturgis was the first Harley constructed using computer-aided design.

1991 FXDB Sturgis
Bartels' Harley-Davidson
Marina Del Rey, California

exhaust crossover pipe was nicely hidden away below the transmission. Other modifications included continuous venting for the fuel tanks to ensure constant fuel supply to the 40mm carburetor, which was recalibrated to make starting easier in cold weather.

The next version of the Dyna Glide would be designated the FXDC Custom. This model shared all the components of the Daytona, but was painted metallic silver and black, with a silver powder-coated frame. The Custom's engine was left unpainted. For 1993 the Dynas evolved as the FXDL Low Rider and FXDWG Wide Glide.

1992 FXDB Daytona
Owner – Trev Deeley Museum
Vancouver, British Columbia

Below: The 32-degree fork rake was standard cruiser profile. The Sturgis wore only one front disc brake as original equipment; a second disc greatly improved braking.

Above: The Dyna Daytona was a limited edition commemorating 50 years of motorcycle festivities at Daytona Beach, Florida. Production was confined to 1,700 copies.

Below: Dual front disc brakes were standard on the Daytona. The two-tone color scheme featured Harley's first "true pearl paint." The engine was finished in black and chrome.

Above: The Dyna Glide chassis situated the engine farther forward in the frame and tilted it 4 degrees aft. The oil tank fit beneath the transmission.

FXDWG (1993), FXRS (1991) AND FXSTS (1992)

1993 FXDWG

SPECIFICATIONS
ENGINE/DRIVETRAIN
Engine: OHV 45° V-twin
Displacement: 81.65ci
(1338cc)
Bore & stroke: 3.5 x 4.25in
(89 x 108mm)
Compression ratio: 8.5:1
Horsepower: 72 @ 4,000rpm
Carburetion: 38mm Keihin
Transmission: 5-speed
Primary drive: Duplex chain
Final drive: Belt
Brakes: F. Dual discs. R. Disc
Battery: 12-volt
Ignition: CDI

CHASSIS/SUSPENSION
Frame: Steel, double downtube
Suspension: F. Telescopic fork.
R. Shocks
Wheelbase: 66.1in (167.9cm)
Weight: 615lb (279kg)
Fuel capacity: 5.2gal (19.7lit)
Oil capacity: 3qts (2.8lit)
Tires: F. MH90-21.
R. 130/90-16
Top speed: 110mph (177km/h)
Colors: Vivid black; victory
red/sun-glo; aqua sun-glo/silver
Number built: 5,602 (including
1,993 Anniversary)
Price: $12,550

Above: Harley-Davidson marked its 90th birthday with a major celebration in Milwaukee. Limited edition anniversary models were customized with special silver/charcoal paint, serialized nameplates and cloisonné tank emblems.

Right: Just as the Sturgis was reborn in updated form, the Wide Glide also returned with the Dyna chassis and Evolution engine. The fat bob format was apparent in the wide fuel tank (fat) and trimmed (bobbed) rear fender.

With the arrival of 1993 it was obviously time to celebrate Harley-Davidson's 90th anniversary in the motorcycle business. A large party was planned for Milwaukee, with group rides arriving from across the continent, parades, motorycle races, rock 'n roll shows and assorted revelries. And six Anniversary Edition motorcycles.

Foremost among the commemorative models was the FXWDG Dyna Wide Glide. With its 32-degree fork rake, 21-inch (53.3cm) front wheel and officially trademarked Ape Hanger handlebars, it was fat bob fashion revisited. Once again Milwaukee had blurred the distinction between civilian and factory choppers. For more conservative cruisers, Harley-Davidson offered the FXDL Dyna Low Rider.

The Wide Glide represented a salute to the chopper revival of two decades prior, the kicked-out, laid-back Easy Rider posture of bike and rider. The minimalist's recliner for the open road, headed for adventure feet first. Maybe not the most comfortable posture for long hours in the saddle, but just right for cruising the back roads or boulevards. New motor mounts and support plates brought reduced vibration.

The bobtail rear fender housed a tucked in tail light ("Frenched" was the 1950s term). The slim front fender sat in the 8-inch (20.3cm) gap between the fork tubes, accounting for the Glide's wideness. From the custom "pillow-soft" seat to the forward-mounted shifter and brake levers was a long span for the short of leg.

The Anniversary Editions were all fitted with serialized nameplates, "jeweled" cloisonné fuel tank emblems

and two-tone silver/charcoal satin-brite paint schemes. The FXDWG special was limited to production of 1,993 machines.

FXRS

With the addition of the Convertible in 1989, the Super Glide/Low Rider family had grown to six models. The Low Rider remained the most popular member of the family, followed by the Custom and Super Glide. The Sport model, with its longer suspension travel, ran a distant third, but the Convertible was matching numbers with the standard FXR.

The Convertible was simply a Sport model with adjustable/detachable windshield and quick-release saddlebags. The dual-function option would later be used in similar fashion for the FLHR Road King. The Convertible was Milwaukee's rendition of a sport-touring machine, which was easily rigged to suit (or disrobe) for either end of the functional scale. A motorcycle with fewer long-haul comforts than the Electra Glide, and more capacity and amenities than the Sportster.

The motorcycle press held general consensus that the FXR Sport was the best handling and most versatile of all the big Harleys. Though a broad accord among the H-D faithful held that the motorcycle press was comprised largely of wheelie-mad dilberts, street-racing rabble and draft dodgers.

The Springer was not elected to carry anniversary edition status in 1993. But it did receive, in response to continued urging, a front fender that more closely conformed with the tire. The new fender attached via chromed dog-bone links to the sprung yoke, so the fender moved with the wheel. A new more tapered headlamp was added to complement the Springer's suspension hardware.

1993 FXDWG
Los Angeles Harley-Davidson
South Gate, California

Below: The latest Wide Glide was *déjà vu* all over again, with a 21-inch (53.3cm) wheel bolted to a kicked-out fork topped by ape hanger handlebars. The social stigma of earlier apes having passed to history, the high-rise tillers became Ape Hangers®, a Milwaukee trademark.

Below: The FXRS Low Rider had established itself as the most popular model on the Super Glide roster. After 15 years, and numerous upgrades, still king of the cruisers.

1991 FXRS
Harley-Davidson of Sacramento
Sacramento, California

1992 FXSTS
Dudley Perkins Company
San Franscisco, California

Left: The Softail Springer looks even more traditional with the studded seat and saddlebags.

Above: Forward-mount foot controls allow the laid-back riding position essential to easy chair cruising.

1993 FLHTC ULTRA CLASSIC

SPECIFICATIONS
ENGINE/DRIVETRAIN
Engine: OHV 45° V-twin
Displacement: 81.65ci
(1338cc)
Bore & stroke: 3.5 x 4.25in
(89 x 108mm)
Compression ratio: 8.5:1
Horsepower: 72 @ 4,000rpm
Carburetion: 38mm Keihin
Transmission: 5-speed
Primary drive: Duplex chain
Final drive: Belt
Brakes: F. Dual discs. R. Disc
Battery: 12-volt
Ignition: CDI

CHASSIS/SUSPENSION
Frame: Steel, double downtube
Suspension: F. Telescopic fork.
R. Shocks
Wheelbase: 62.9in (159.9cm)
Weight: 774lb (351kg)
Fuel capacity: 5gal (18.9lit)
Oil capacity: 4qts (3.8lit)
Tires: F. and R. MT90-16
Top speed: 110mph (177km/h)
Colors: Vivid black; victory red
sun-glo; two-tone aqua sun-
glo/silver; two-tone victory red
sun-glo/silver (option: 90th
anniversary livery)
Number built: 3,702
Price: $15,349

Above: The Electra Glide's jumbo travel trunk is hinged on the left, opening sideways. The luggage carrier was optional. Flexible antennas for radio and CB radio attach at the trunk's corners. The saddlebags gained 15 percent more capacity for 1993.

Right: With the battery relocated under the seat, it no longer intruded on space in the right saddlebag. New lockable latches operate with the same key used for the ignition and fork lock.

FLHTC (1993), FLSTC (1994) AND FLHTC(1994)

Another of the six 90th Anniversary limited editions was the FLHTC Electra Glide Ultra Classic, of which 1,340 were made. A new automotive-style cruise control, with a tap-feature for raising and lowering speeds was introduced, and a new American-made CB radio was installed. The silver/gray/black paint, cloisonné tank emblems and serialized nameplate put the Anniversary model price at $16,099.

All the touring machines had the new oil pan below the engine, which afforded better oil cooling and a lower center of gravity. Maintenance was also simplified, and the oil was checked with a dipstick. The battery, formerly housed in the saddlebag, had a new position below the seat. The tourers also got the ergonomically contoured (dog-leg) brake and clutch levers, for easier reach and better feel.

The saddlebag lids, now permanently attached, received new hinges and a nylon tether. The guard rails surrounding the bags were redesigned for both strength and appearance. The new latch mechanism was fashioned for both secure sealing and ease of operation.

The Ultras (Electra and Tour Glide) shared with the rest of the FL series an air-suspension system at both front and rear. Air pressure settings at both ends could be balanced to accommodate varying loads and road conditons.

FLSTC

The Heritage Softail Nostalgia was first shown to the public during Bike Week in Daytona Beach. It was quickly dubbed the Cow Glide for its natural cowhide inserts on the seat and saddlebags. The bovine motif was complemented by wide Dunlop whitewall tires on wire wheels and a black and white paint scheme.

The Nostalgia was the only non-Anniversary model to wear the chrome and fired-enamel cloisonné tank emblems. The FLSTN shared the Fat Boy's "shotgun" dual exhausts. Also a limited edition, the production line rolled out 2,200 Nostalgias.

The Softails shared many of the engineering improvements to the controls and drivelines of the other models. The Heritage Softail Classic retained the vintage character of the 1950s with two-tone paint and studded seat and saddlebags. The Classic managed to look a bit like every big twin built since 1949, and what looked good then would look good again.

The Heritage Softail lacked the touring refinements of the Electra Glide Ultra Classic, but it was lighter by 55 pounds (25kg),

Below: The rider's backrest is detachable. The passenger seat is comfortably outfitted with armrests, stereo speakers and separate radio controls.

1994 FLHTC
Dudley Perkins Company
San Francisco, California

1993 FLSTN "Cow Glide"
© Harley-Davidson photo

Below: The Heritage Softail Classic echoes an earlier era, with its fishtail mufflers, spoked wheels and studded seat and saddlebags. Full windshield, passing lamps and floorboards complete the historical portrait.

1994 FLSTC
Bartels' Harley-Davidson
Marina Del Rey, California

Above: The Electra Glide Classic shares most components with the Ultra Classic except the CB radio and cruise control.
The Classic is likewise some 25 pounds (11kg) lighter and several dollars less expensive.

Below: Instruments and radio are shielded from the elements by the fairing. Sound system controls are fitted to the handlebar.

a tad faster and didn't cost as much. And it was easier to handle around town. The stylish half-dresser marked its eighth year of production, and remained popular for several fundamental reasons. Between touring luxury and sport-touring compromise stretches the broad landscape of all-purpose big bikes.

The 4.2-gallon (15.9lit) fuel tank is sufficient for all-around travel, the seat is less than 28 inches (71cm) off the pavement and the motor feels good. The massive V-twin does not float in the middle of the chassis, but is bolted directly to the frame. For many more than a few Harley enthusiasts, feeling the motor is a large portion of the appeal. The Heritage Softail delivered a balanced package of past and present, and put more than several Shovelheads in the classified columns.

The Classic arrived fitted with high-rise handlebars that sweep back to the rider and a king-size Lexan windshield. The Hydra-Glide fork cover and leather saddlebags are directly from the 1950s, and the fishtail mufflers date back farther. The Classic was offered in black, red, blue, or two-tone victory red sun-glo, aqua sun-glo/silver, wineberry sun-glo or black/scarlet red.

Left: The air suspension system allows air pressure settings to be altered to suit loads and road conditions.

1993 FLHTC Ultra
Bartels' Harley-Davidson
Marina Del Rey, California

1994 VR 1000

SPECIFICATIONS
ENGINE/DRIVETRAIN
Engine: DOHC 60° V-twin
Displacement: 61ci (1000cc)
Bore & stroke: 3.86 x 2.6in (98 x 66mm)
Compression ratio: 11.6:1
Horsepower: 135 @ 10,000rpm
Fuel injection: Weber EFI
Transmission: 5-speed
Clutch: Multi-disc, dry
Primary drive: Gear
Final drive: Chain
Brakes: F. Dual discs. R. Disc
Ignition: Electronic

CHASSIS/SUSPENSION
Frame: Aluminum 2-spar perimeter
Suspension: F. Inverted fork. R. Single shock
Wheelbase: 55.5in (141cm)
Weight: 390lb (176.9kg)
Fuel capacity: 4.5gal (17lit)
Oil capacity: 3qts (2.84lit)
Tires: F. Dunlop 120/70ZR17. R. 150/70ZR17
Top speed: 170mph (274km/h)
Color: Orange/black
Number built: 50
Price: $49,490

Above: View from the VR 1000 cockpit shows the centered analog tachometer. The LED panel below the tach displays speed, mileage, oil pressure, engine temperature and battery condition.

Right: The street-legal version of the Superbike racer includes a few concessions to civility. A single muffler replaces the racer's duals, and lights, turn signals, mirrors and horn are fitted.

VR 1000 (1994) AND 883 RACERS (1996)

The 1994 VR 1000 was the first pure racing motorcycle Harley-Davidson ever built. Every other Harley racer, from 1915 through 1993, had been a modified production machine. The VR was purpose-built from the ground up.

Milwaukee has never been comfortable with the concept of pure-bred competition machines. Eighty years earlier the founders had been dragged mumbling into the racing game, convinced of its necessity only after Indian had captivated the sporting enthusiasts of the 1910s and 1920s. But once installed in the Milwaukee hierarchy, the racing department proved itself a continuing resource of team spirit and public good will. People rode their motorcycles to the races, and supported their favorite riders and manufacturers.

Harley-Davidson had maintained its support of dirt tack, the traditional American fairgrounds racing, and built a few XR 1000 production-based roadracers. But nothing on Milwaukee's menu

1996 883 Twin Sport
Bartels' Harley-Davidson
Marina Del Rey, California

1996 883 Dirt Track
Bartels' Harley-Davidson
Marina Del Rey, California

Above: The 883 Twin Sports roadracing class features lightly modified Sportsters in close competition. Footpegs are raised and moved aft, shift lever reversed and unnecessary hardware removed.

Left: The 883 Dirt Track series runs in conjunction with the AMA Grand National Championship races. These are also moderately modified Sportsters set up for the demands of half-mile and mile dirt ovals.

Above: The VR 1000 engine is a dual overhead cam, liquid-cooled, 60-degree V-twin with four valves per cylinder. Initial horsepower rating was 135 at 10,000 rpm.

suited the demands of Superbike racing in the 1990s. At the upper outposts of "street bike" competition, the track-wise roadsters weigh 375 pounds (170kg) and produce 150 horsepower. Handling and braking factors are tuned to millisecond response margins. All of which is enormously expensive to achieve.

With some money in the bank, Harley decided to build its second eight-valve racer, with an American engine, chassis and brakes. Engineer Steve Scheibe headed the team, and called in experienced help from NASCAR and Indy Car racing. The project took five years and produced a double-overhead-cam, 60-degree V-twin, with 4-valve heads, Weber-USA electronic fuel injection and liquid cooling. Power went by gear to a multi-disc dry clutch and through a 5-speed transmission.

The first bikes used a Penske inverted fork and Wilwood six-piston brake calipers. The road model carries an Ohlins fork with titanium-coated stanchions. The body work is constructed of carbon fiber, and the factory listed the dry weight at 390lb (176.9kg). The production schedule was set for 50 copies of the VR 1000, the price of each listed at $49,490.

The VR first appeared on the racetrack for the Daytona Superbike race in 1994. There were few illusions about the early chances, and teething problems were anticipated, but the motor-cycle handled remarkably well. Top speed was not at the level of frontrunners, though rider Miguel Duhamel turned in good results on some of the tighter circuits. Results for the 1995 season were disappointing, and rider Doug Chandler had difficulty coming to terms with the machine. National dirt track champion Chris Carr was also on the team and showed a quick learning curve.

Rumors circulated during the off-season that management disputes in Milwaukee cast doubts on the future of the VR 1000. The factions split as they had a half-century before; the economic rationale perceives big-league factory racing as large expense versus small return. The sporting enthusiast segment says racing pays huge dividends in public relations, and puts the company logo on television. And wins hearts and minds.

Harley-Davidson continued the support of two Sportster-based production racing divisions; Twin Sports Roadracing and 883 Dirt Track. These all-Harley contests serve racers as a semi-pro league, attract the faithful to the race tracks, and offer more tangible coporate benefits than Superbike racing. Without a street-legal counterpart to the VR 1000, where's the profit?

The Superbike project was still operational for the 1996 season. No expensively talented racer/development rider had been hired to bring the bike up to speed, but Chris Carr did manage a tenth place at Daytona. New cylinder heads upped horsepower as the '96 season began, which suggests more investment from either Milwaukee or outside sponsors, or both. Time and money will tell. Keep the faith.

Below: Even though the Superbike racer is outfitted for civilian use, the riding position necessarily enforces the racer's crouch. Road riders would likely opt for higher handlebars, or limit the distances of their rides.

Left: Most of the bodywork is constructed of light, and expensive, carbon fiber. The frame design came from Oregon mountain-bike builder Mike Etough.

1994 VR 1000
Petersen Automotive Museum
Los Angeles, California

Left: Huge rotors and six-piston Wilwood brake calipers help slow the VR 1000 down from upwards of 170mph (275km/h). With authority.

Above: The front fork is built by suspension specialist Ohlins. Stanchions are coated with titanium. Wheel travel is 4.7 inches (11.94cm).

1995 FLHR

SPECIFICATIONS
ENGINE/DRIVETRAIN
Engine: OHV 45° V-twin
Displacement: 80ci (1340cc)
Bore & stroke: 3.5 x 4.25in
(89 x 108mm)
Compression ratio: 8.5:1
Torque: 77lb-ft @ 4,000rpm
Carburetion: 40mm Keihin
Transmission: 5-speed
Primary drive: Duplex chain
Final drive: Belt
Brakes: F. Dual disc. R. Disc
Battery: 12-volt
Ignition: Electronic

CHASSIS/SUSPENSION
Frame: Steel, double downtube
Suspension: F. Air-adjustable
fork. R. Dual air-adjustable shocks
Wheelbase: 62.9in (159.8cm)
Weight: 719lb (326kg)
Fuel capacity: 5gal (18.9lit)
Oil capacity: 4qts (3.8lit)
Tires: F. and R. MT90B-16
Top speed: 112mph (180km/h)
Colors: Vivid black; two-tone
aqua pearl/silver; two-tone vivid
black/silver; two-tone burgundy
pearl/silver
Number built: 7,910
Price: $13,475

The F series has gone through more permutations over the years than any other Harley-Davidson. The Kings of the Road are in continuous process, with subtle changes in accessory groups, paint schemes and comfort amenities. The '95 FLHR Road King boasts what Milwaukee calls "the ultimate in traditional styling."

The FLHR replaced the Electra Glide Sport in 1994. The new 5-gallon (18.9lit) tank had an electronic speedometer and digital odometer mounted at the top. The passenger seat detached easily, for kingly solo rides. Also detachable were the saddle bags and new Lexan windshield, easily turning the highway monarch into a boulevard emperor.

The Road King also received the appointments of its subordinates in the big twin royal family. The new wiring harness featured waterproof connectors, the accessory plug activated with an illuminated switch, and the petcock was vacuum-operated. Also in common with its big brethren was a taller overall gear ratio.

To trace its royal lineage more specifically, the Road King is descended from the Electra Glide Sport, for ten years the econo-tourer in the FL roster. At 692lb (314kg) dry, it was also the lightweight among the heavyweights, and the Road King, despite the higher luxury quotient, weighs in at exactly the same. Better doesn't necessarily have to mean bigger.

The Road King has an air-adjustable front fork and stout 11.5in (29.2cm) brake discs at the bottom of each leg. But despite the modern techno-trickery, with those wide whitewalls, from a distance you'd swear it was an Electra Glide from the 1960s. It just works a whole lot better.

Given the longevity of the Electra Glide Sport, the Road King is likely to have a similar lifeline. The convenience factor of a motor-cycle that can be quickly switched from cruising to touring mode has broad appeal. For 1996 the FLHR came available with the fuel-injection system first offered on the '95 Ultra Classic Electra Glide. ESPFI (electronic sequential port fuel injection) was also fitted to the Classic and Ultra Classic Glides for 1996.

FXDL

The Dyna Low Rider continued its role as the standard cruiser of the FX series. The machine appealed to both the creative customizers and the cruising comfort segments of a broad market. The easier riders now accounted for 35 percent of the street-legal motorcycles sold nationwide. And Harley-Davidson, which had effectively re-engineered the cruiser division, held the lion's share of the category.

The imports were coming closer in terms of style, and even a greater portion of the substance than they had previously managed. But, whether imitation is the highest form of either praise or incompetence, the derivatives lacked that intangible element of the Harley identity. "Things Are Different on a Harley" asserted the ad slogan. And the price for those differences was about 30 percent more than the competition charged.

The Dyna Low Rider received an electronic speedometer in 1995, and seat height was down a half-inch to 26.5 inches (67.3cm). The 32-degree front fork maintained the long and low look, and the dual disc front brakes help decelerate the Dyna's 615-pound (279kg) mass. The FXDL was priced at $12,475 for solid colors, with a $75 premium for metallic paint and another $150 for the choice of two-tone victory red/sun-glo or aqua pearl/silver.

Below: The saddlebags are closely integrated with the machine. A common key fits the bags, fork lock and ignition.

Below: A quick-detach passenger pillion attaches to the fender behind the solo saddle. The stud pattern carries back to the passenger perch.

Right: The FLHR Road King combined contemporary engineering with the stately styling of the 1965 Electra Glide. Period touches include the traditional windshield, whitewall tires and deeply skirted fenders.

1995 FLHR
Owner – Mike Lady
Arroyo Grande, California

Right: The look established by the Low Rider in 1977 had not gone out of style with the passage of two decades. Handling and reliability improved.

Below: The FXDL Dyna Low Rider carried the cruiser tradition to lower heights by bringing the seat even closer to the road.

1995 FXDL
Los Angeles Harley-Davidson
South Gate, California

Below: Dual disc brakes remained standard on the Low Rider. Cast wheels were fitted as standard equipment, spoked rims optional.

Left: The Road King's windshield detaches easily for low-speed cruising around town.

Left: The S2 adapts to sport-touring mode with the addition of saddlebags. The factory version, S2T, comes with fairing lowers, higher handlebars and lower footpegs.

Above: The Buell S2 Thunderbolt features unique Uniplanar rubber-mount engine system, underslung shock absorber and muffler.

1995 Buell S2
Owner – Ray Earls
Foster City, California

Above: The 1340cc Evolution V-twin is common to the entire FL and FX series. For 1996 the Road King received the optional fuel injection system.

Buell S2 Thunderbolt

In 1993 Harley-Davidson became almost-half owner of the Buell Motorcycle Company. Milwaukee, in a refreshing bit of candor, admitted its specialized factory sport bikes had achieved little success. Better to assist someone well-suited to the design, chassis and assembly requirements of those machines, with Harley-Davidson acting only as the engine supplier.

The timing was right. Buell was under-capitalized, Harley needed a sport bike and an investment opportunity. In 1994 the Thunderbolt was the first product of the new partnership between Milwaukee and Mukwonago. The chassis' wheelbase and steering geometry were unchanged, but the new design left more of both the engine and frame visible. The riding position became something of a compromise between the racer's crouch and the cruiser's slouch.

The Thunderbolt bristles with tasty techno-pieces, from the frame and engine mounts, huge disc brake with 6-piston caliper, inverted fork, to the subverted shock absorber and carbon-fiber air cleaner cover. The oversize muffler permits some tweaking of the 1200 Sportster's performance profile, and the horsepower rating bumps up to 76 at 5,200 rpm, with exactly matching figures for torque. The curb weight is 481 pounds (218kg). The production schedule was set for 300 Thunderbolts in its debut year.

In 1996 the S2T was introduced with color coordinated saddlebags and fairing lowers, with touring handlebars and footpegs. Another example of Harley-Davidson's support showed in the prices; the S2 listed for $11,995 and the touring model for $12,795, well in line with the competition.

FXDS (1996), FLSTN(1996) AND FXSTC (1996)

The FXRS Convertible Low Rider had proven more popular than its stablemate the Sport Edition. With the switch to the Dyna Glide chassis, the Sport was deleted in favor of the FXDS Convertible. The motorcycles had been too similar to warrant separate models, and without its windscreen and saddlebags the Convertible was a Sport.

The Dyna transition did effect some modifications to the sport-touring member of the Milwaukee roster. The steering head angle diminished from 31 to 28 degrees, and wheelbase shrank about an inch to 63.9 inches (162cm), giving the newer generation quicker handling in the tighter turns. And the Dyna had a quarter-inch (0.63cm) more ground clearance. But the FXDS also managed to gain 35 pounds (15.9kg) in the process.

The obvious appeal of the Dyna Glide Convertible, just as its predecessor, was the quick-change capability. The windshield and saddlebags detach readily in a few minutes, swapping the Convertible's character from tourer to boulevardier in short order. Most commuters and weekend recreation riders tend to leave the windshield in place, since it offers a significant reduction in wind buffeting. The leather-topped saddlebags feature a nylon liner and hard plastic frame to retain their shape.

With the Low Rider Sport gone, the series dropped to four models. The FXD Dyna Super Glide shared the Convertible's steering geometry, but had slightly less wheelbase, only one front disc brake and an engine in milder tune. The Dyna Wide Glide and Low Rider retained the 32-degree fork and longer wheelbase.

1996 FXDS

SPECIFICATIONS
ENGINE/DRIVETRAIN
Engine: OHV 45° V-twin
Displacement: 81.65ci (1338cc)
Bore & stroke: 3.5 x 4.25in (89 x 108mm)
Compression ratio: 8.5:1
Horsepower: 72 @ 4,000rpm
Carburetion: 38mm Keihin
Transmission: 5-speed
Primary drive: Duplex chain
Final drive: Belt
Brakes: F. Dual discs. R. Disc
Battery: 12-volt
Ignition: CDI

CHASSIS/SUSPENSION
Frame: Steel, double downtube
Suspension: F. Telescopic fork. R. Shocks
Wheelbase: 63.9in (162.3cm)
Weight: 638lb (289kg)
Fuel capacity: 4.9gal (18.5lit)
Oil capacity: 3qts (2.8lit)
Tires: F. 100/90-19. R. 130/90HB-16
Top speed: 112mph (180km/h)
Colors: Vivid black; patriot red pearl; states blue pearl; violet pearl; two-tone victory sun-glo/platinum; two-tone violet/red pearl; two-tone platinum silver/black
Number built: n/a
Price: $13,330

Right: The FXSTC Softail Custom runs a disc rear wheel, kicked-out 34-degree fork and deeply stepped seat. The bobtail fender, buckhorn handlebar on risers and 21-inch (53.3cm) front wheel are straight from chopper central.

1996 FXSTC
Bartels' Harley-Davidson
Marina Del Rey, California

Right: The FXDS CONV Dyna Convertible takes longer to say than to switch the bike from touring to sport mode. Both the saddlebags and windshield feature quick-release hardware for instant personality changes.

Above: The Dyna Convertible's staggered shorty dual exhausts are connected by a tube hidden below the transmission.

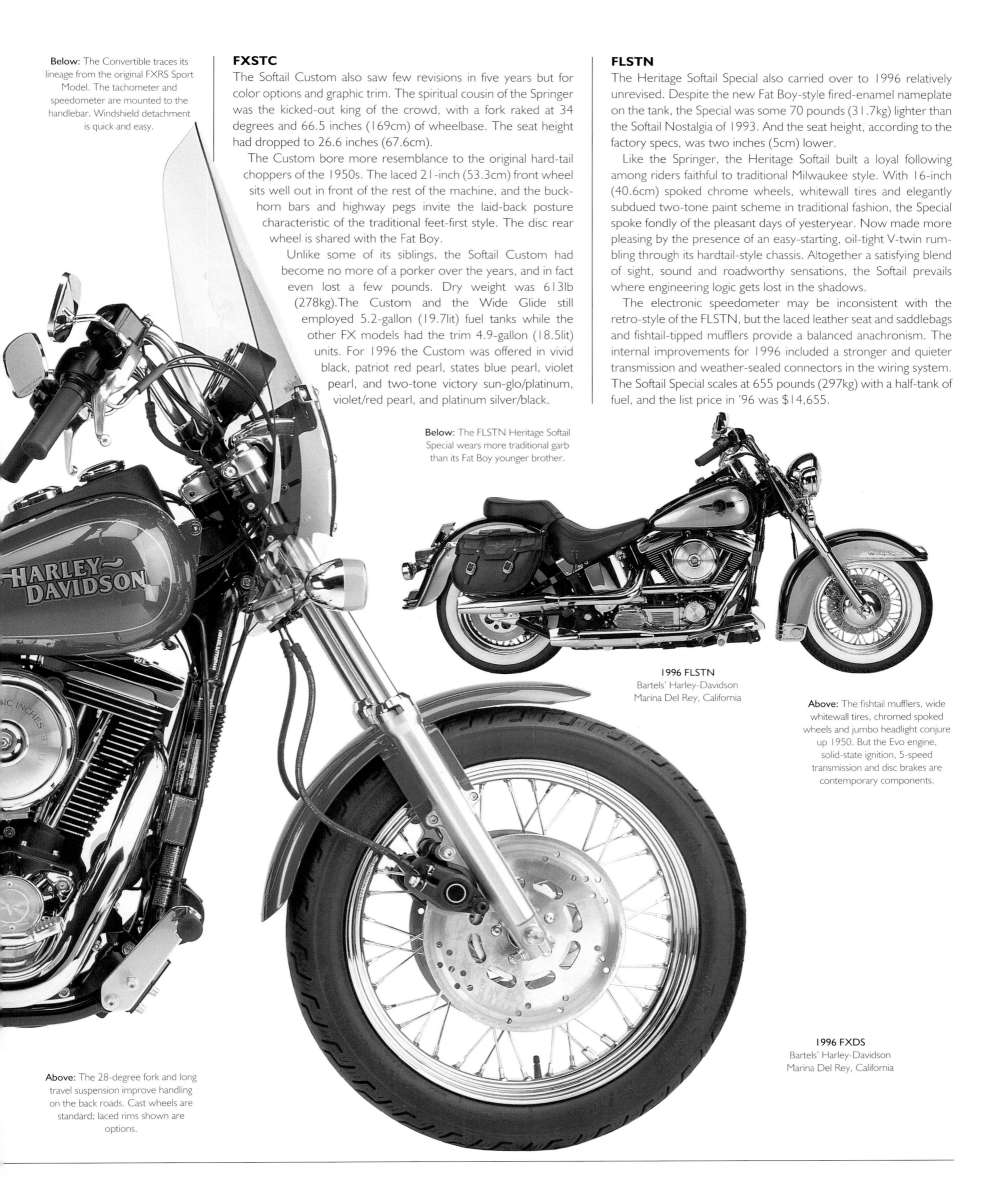

Below: The Convertible traces its lineage from the original FXRS Sport Model. The tachometer and speedometer are mounted to the handlebar. Windshield detachment is quick and easy.

FXSTC

The Softail Custom also saw few revisions in five years but for color options and graphic trim. The spiritual cousin of the Springer was the kicked-out king of the crowd, with a fork raked at 34 degrees and 66.5 inches (169cm) of wheelbase. The seat height had dropped to 26.6 inches (67.6cm).

The Custom bore more resemblance to the original hard-tail choppers of the 1950s. The laced 21-inch (53.3cm) front wheel sits well out in front of the rest of the machine, and the buck-horn bars and highway pegs invite the laid-back posture characteristic of the traditional feet-first style. The disc rear wheel is shared with the Fat Boy.

Unlike some of its siblings, the Softail Custom had become no more of a porker over the years, and in fact even lost a few pounds. Dry weight was 613lb (278kg).The Custom and the Wide Glide still employed 5.2-gallon (19.7lit) fuel tanks while the other FX models had the trim 4.9-gallon (18.5lit) units. For 1996 the Custom was offered in vivid black, patriot red pearl, states blue pearl, violet pearl, and two-tone victory sun-glo/platinum, violet/red pearl, and platinum silver/black.

Below: The FLSTN Heritage Softail Special wears more traditional garb than its Fat Boy younger brother.

FLSTN

The Heritage Softail Special also carried over to 1996 relatively unrevised. Despite the new Fat Boy-style fired-enamel nameplate on the tank, the Special was some 70 pounds (31.7kg) lighter than the Softail Nostalgia of 1993. And the seat height, according to the factory specs, was two inches (5cm) lower.

Like the Springer, the Heritage Softail built a loyal following among riders faithful to traditional Milwaukee style. With 16-inch (40.6cm) spoked chrome wheels, whitewall tires and elegantly subdued two-tone paint scheme in traditional fashion, the Special spoke fondly of the pleasant days of yesteryear. Now made more pleasing by the presence of an easy-starting, oil-tight V-twin rumbling through its hardtail-style chassis. Altogether a satisfying blend of sight, sound and roadworthy sensations, the Softail prevails where engineering logic gets lost in the shadows.

The electronic speedometer may be inconsistent with the retro-style of the FLSTN, but the laced leather seat and saddlebags and fishtail-tipped mufflers provide a balanced anachronism. The internal improvements for 1996 included a stronger and quieter transmission and weather-sealed connectors in the wiring system. The Softail Special scales at 655 pounds (297kg) with a half-tank of fuel, and the list price in '96 was $14,655.

1996 FLSTN
Bartels' Harley-Davidson
Marina Del Rey, California

Above: The fishtail mufflers, wide whitewall tires, chromed spoked wheels and jumbo headlight conjure up 1950. But the Evo engine, solid-state ignition, 5-speed transmission and disc brakes are contemporary components.

1996 FXDS
Bartels' Harley-Davidson
Marina Del Rey, California

Above: The 28-degree fork and long travel suspension improve handling on the back roads. Cast wheels are standard; laced rims shown are options.

XL 1200S (1996), FLHTC UI (1996) AND XL 1200C (1996)

1996 FLHTC UI

SPECIFICATIONS
ENGINE/DRIVETRAIN
Engine: OHV 45° V-twin
Displacement: 81.65ci
(1338cc)
Bore & stroke: 3.5 x 4.25in
(89 x 108mm)
Compression ratio: 8.5:1
Torque: 77lb-ft @ 4,000rpm
Carburetion: Electronic fuel
injection
Transmission: 5-speed
Primary drive: Duplex chain
Final drive: Belt
Brakes: F. Dual discs. R. Disc
Battery: 12-volt
Ignition: CDI

CHASSIS/SUSPENSION
Frame: Steel, double downtube
Suspension: F. Telescopic fork.
R. Shocks
Wheelbase: 62.7in (159.3cm)
Weight: 781lb (354kg)
Fuel capacity: 5gal (18.9lit)
Oil capacity: 4qts (3.8lit)
Tires: F. and R. MT90B-16
Top speed: 110mph (177km/h)
Colors: Vivid black; states blue
pearl; platinum victory sun-glo;
two-tone victory sun-
glo/platinum; two-tone blue
pearl/platinum silver; two-tone
mystique green/black
Number built: n/a
Price: $17,500

1996 XL 1200S

SPECIFICATIONS
ENGINE/DRIVETRAIN
Engine: OHV 45° V-twin
Displacement: 73.2ci (1200cc)
Bore & stroke: 3.5 x 3.81in
(89 x 97mm)
Compression ratio: 9:1
Horsepower: 63
Carburetion: 40mm Keihin CV
Transmission: 5-speed
Primary drive: Triple-row
chain
Final drive: Chain
Brakes: F. Dual disc. R. Disc
Battery: 12-volt
Ignition: CDI

CHASSIS/SUSPENSION
Frame: Steel, double downtube
Suspension: F. 1.53in (3.9cm)
cartridge fork. R. Dual gas-
reservoir shocks
Wheelbase: 60.2in (152.9cm)
Weight: 512lb (232kg)
Fuel capacity: 3.3gal (12.5lit)
Oil capacity: 3qts (2.8lit)
Tires: F. 100/90-19.
R. 130/90-16
Top speed: 120mph (193km/h)
Colors: Vivid black; patriot red
pearl; states blue pearl; violet
pearl; two-tone victory sun-
glo/platinum; two-tone violet/red
pearl; two-tone platinum
silver/black
Number built: n/a
Price: $7,910

Since joining the Evolutionary family in 1986, the Sportster had been awarded doses of the technology advanced by the heavyweights. Belt drives and 5-speed transmission were standard on both the 883 and 1200cc models, and in 1996 the Sporties had five models in the lineup.

The standard XLH 883 with solo seat, laced wheels and low handlebar was the price leader at $5,095, and the buckhorn-barred Hugger followed in line at $5,760. The two new members of the group were the 1200cc Sport and Custom. The latter featured a 21-inch (53.3cm) wire wheel in front, 16-inch (40.6cm) slotted disc wheel at the rear and an embroidered dual seat. The Custom got handlebar risers, chromed highlights and a fired-enamel tank emblem. This top shelf Sportster listed for $8,360.

The XL1200S offered to put more of the sport back in Sportster, thus its full moniker, XL 1200S Sportster 1200 Sport. All the 1200s shared common upgrades for '96; the more efficient high-contact transmission gears, better switchgear and 13-spoke cast wheels. Laced wheels became an option. The S model added several bonuses for the corner-strafers on the back country roads. Adjustable suspension made its Sportster debut, with gas reservoir shocks and cartridge-type front fork from Showa. Both were adjustable for spring pre-load and compression and rebound damping.

To complement the newly compliant suspension,

Milwaukee fitted the Sportster front wheel with two 11.5-inch (29.2cm) floating discs and a redesigned master cylinder. The new braking system, in concert with Dunlop Sport Elite tires, gives new zeal and energy to the deceleration process. The slowing distance is compressed by better equipment and the feedback it offers the rider through the chassis. The suspension, brakes and tires render the sporting Sportster a more stable and comfortable platform at brisk rates on the twisty roads.

FLHTC UI

Milwaukee unveiled its first fuel-injected tourer with the 30th Anniversary Ultra Classic Electra Glide in 1995. The next year the Weber Marelli spritzer system was standard on the Ultra Classic Tour Glide and optional for the Classic and Ultra Classic Electras.

In addition to performance gains at all speeds, the injecta-Glides ran clean enough to meet the California emission standards without a catalytic converter. And fuel mileage went up by two miles per gallon (0.85km/lit) in city and country riding. The two-tone Tour Glide commanded a price of $18,160. With the optional injection, the Electra Ultra was priced the same, while the Classic Glide was tagged at $15,210 injected and $14,410 carbureted.

The Ultra Classic Electra Glide naturally boasts features and amenities not found on the smaller, less expensive machines. Twin spotlights operate with the headlight's low beam, and running lights adorn the front fender and rear luggage. The AM/FM/cassette stereo has four speakers, a weather band and separate controls for the passenger. The built-in citizen's band radio

Below: The FLHTC UI Ultra Classic Electra Glide is long on syllables and touring refinements. Including cruise control, 80-watt stereo with weather band, CB radio and standard helmet-mount headset. Plush.

features a voice-activated intercom with helmet-mounted headsets. Electronic cruise control is also standard equipment.

The Electra Glide has shown a steady curve of refinement during its 31 years in service. The successful adoption of fuel injection heralds an even longer life for the venerable air-cooled V-twin. And given the Harley history of technological cross-pollination within the extended family of twins, fuel injection will likely appear on other models in the near future.

Below: The bar-mounted fairing has been a favorite of Harley touring riders since 1969. Styling of the fairing and luggage has changed only slightly in the past 27 years.

Below: The XL 1200S Sportster 1200 Sport raised eyebrows and expectations with its adjustable suspension at both ends, twin floating discs and Dunlop Sport Elite tires. The Sportster became considerably sportier.

Left: For fans of more saddle-time, the '96 Sportster made another wish come true with a 3.3-gallon (12.5lit) fuel tank. The instrumentation features an electronic tach and speedometer with odometer and resettable trip meter.

1996 XL 1200S
Los Angeles Harley-Davidson
South Gate, California

Below: Another new addition to the Sportster roster for 1996 was the XL 1200C Sportster 1200 Custom. The cruiser motif included a chrome and black engine treatment, chrome teardrop headlamp and disc rear wheel.

1996 XL 1200C
Bartels' Harley-Davidson
Marina Del Rey, California

Above: The Sporty Custom has a spoked 21-inch (53.3cm) front wheel and shorter suspension at both ends, so seat height is nearly two inches less than the Sport. The three-dimensional cloisonné tank emblem is unique to the Custom.

1996 FLHTC UI
Los Angeles Harley-Davidson
South Gate, California

Left: The Ultra Classic is designed to accommodate varying loads on the open road. Front and rear suspension are air adjustable, with an anti-dive system at the front. Rider and passenger footboards are also adjustable.

FXSTSB (1996), BUELL S1 (1996) AND FLSTF (1996)

1996 FXSTSB

SPECIFICATIONS
ENGINE/DRIVETRAIN
Engine: OHV 45° V-twin
Displacement: 81.65ci
(1338cc)
Bore & stroke: 3.5 x 4.25in
(89 x 108mm)
Compression ratio: 8.5:1
Torque: 76lb-ft @ 3,500
Carburetion: 38mm Keihin
Transmission: 5-speed
Primary drive: Duplex chain
Final drive: Belt
Brakes: F. and R. Disc
Battery: 12-volt
Ignition: CDI

CHASSIS/SUSPENSION
Frame: Steel, double downtube
Suspension: F. Telescopic fork.
R. Shocks
Wheelbase: 64.4in (163.6cm)
Weight: 635lb (288kg)
Fuel capacity: 4.2gal (15.9lit)
Oil capacity: 3qts (2.8lit)
Tires: F. MH90-21
R. MT90B-16
Top speed: 110mph (177km/h)
Colors: Vivid black with yellow,
purple or turquoise graphics
Number built: n/a
Price: $14,425

1996 BUELL S1

SPECIFICATIONS
ENGINE/DRIVETRAIN
Engine: OHV 45° V-twin
Displacement: 73.4ci (1203cc)
Bore & stroke: 3.9 x 3.81in
(99 x 97mm)
Compression ratio: 10:1
Horsepower: 91 @ 6,000rpm
Carburetion: 40mm Keihin CV
Transmission: 5-speed
Primary drive: Triplex chain
Final drive: Belt
Battery: 12-volt
Ignition: CDI

CHASSIS/SUSPENSION
Frame: Chrome-moly
perimeter
Suspension: F. WP inverted
fork, adjustable. R. WP extension
shock, adjustable
Wheelbase: 55in (140cm)
Weight: 440lb (200kg)
Fuel capacity: 4.0gal (15.1lit)
Oil capacity: 2.6qts (2.5lit)
Tires: F. 120/70-17.
R. 170/60-17
Top speed: 130mph (209km/h)
Colors: Red snap; carbon black;
high voltage yellow
Number built: 1,407
Price: $9,995

Right: The Buell S1 Lightning
is strong evidence that Erik
Buell's heart remains on Racer
Road. Swingarm, sub-fender
and seat/tail section are new.
The S1 is fitted with 17-inch
(43.2cm) Dunlop Sportmax II
tires front and rear.

If the name Softail Bad Boy seems a contradiction in terms, just call it the FXSTSB for short. Whatever the designation, the latest Springer is a stylistic nod to the Knucklehead and the black-and-white movies of the 1940s. Jimmy Cagney would have ridden a Bad Boy.

Introduced in 1995, the Softail Springer with-an-attitude traded chrome for the black outfit of the boulevard bandito. The Bad Boy wore the slotted disc rear wheel of the Custom and the smaller 4.2-gallon (15.9lit) fuel tank of the Springer. The studded, deeply-stepped saddle and forward-mount foot controls put the rider in the classic sit-up-and-beg posture. With seat height an inch (2.54cm) less than the Sportster Hugger, the rider sits more in than on the bike. The price was $13,850, available in any color so long as it was black.

The Bad Boy carried over to 1996 with only moderate revisions. More chrome had turned black, seat height dropped still lower to 25.75 inches (65.4cm) and the machine lost five pounds (2.27kg). The electronic speedometer arrived and the price went up by $575. The Black Bart color scheme remained the only option, but the tank and fender graphics were offered in choices of either yellow, purple or turquoise.

Designer Willie G. Davidson has shown an affinity for black motorcycles, as evidenced by the XLCR Cafe Racer and the Sturgis. The classic British machines such as the Brough Superior and Vincent Black Shadow were ebony-coated constructs with chrome and polished

Right: The Lightning is obviously designed for solo sailing on twisting roads. Passengers need not apply.

1996 FLSTF
Owner – Dave Ybarra
San Gabriel, California

Above: The FLSTF Fat Boy underwent few changes since its inception in 1990. The traditional horseshoe oil tank and big chrome headlamp evoke memories of yesteryear. The color chart grew to include states blue pearl.

Left: Disc wheels and a Hydra-Glide fork distinguish the Fat Boy from garden variety nostalgia bikes. The enlarged tank emblem was new for '96.

1996 Buell S1 Lightning
Buell Motor Company photo

Right: The FXSTSB Bad Boy is the leaner, and marginally meaner, cousin to the Fat Boy. Their vital specs are nearly identical, including the lowest seat of all the Harleys.

1996 FXSTSB
© Harley-Davidson photo

Below: The bullet headlight, black Springer front end and laced 21-inch (53.3cm) front wheel set the Bad Boy apart from the crowd. A polished cloisonné tank badge gleams in midnight neon lights.

Right: The Bad Boy owes a measure of its machismo to the massive slotted disc rear wheel.

Left: The Lightning's minimalist fairing barely covers the tach and speedometer. The 4-gallon (15.1lit) fuel tank is three inches (7.62cm) shorter than the Thunderbolt tank, putting the rider closer to the handlebars for improved handling.

Left: The cast Marchesini wheels have a titanium finish. The 340mm floating rotor is cast iron; the six-piston caliper is built for Buell by Performance Machine.

aluminum highlights. Something about big motorcycles and lustrous black finish complements both the mechanical bits and the shapes and lines of the overall design, without colors competing for attention.

The Bad Boy rekindles the imagery of the past framed in the hardware of the present. The Softail chassis geometry was revised for slightly more rear wheel travel, and the new quieter, smoother-shifting gearbox and slotted floating disc brakes bring standards of contemporary performance. But the Bad Boy sells on its bold profile and patent leather sheen; Milwaukee's version of the Batmobile.

Buell S1 Lightning

When Harley-Davidson acquired 49 percent interest in the Buell Motorcycle Company, the prospects for a genuine made-in-America sport bike dimmed somewhat. And the subsequent shift to the sport-touring configuration of the Thunderbolt underscored the concern. Would Harley-Davidson dictate the style and function of Buell motorcycles? Would the independent skunk works spirit fade with the pressure of Big Money from Milwaukee?

Naah. If anyone thought that Buell had gone soft, the S1 Lightning answered their concerns. The sportier, and $2,000 less expensive, model got 10:1 compression, 91 horsepower at 5,800 rpm and a curb weight of 440 pounds (200kg). That the Thunderbolt is designated S2 and the Lightning S1 indicates that sport performance had not been demoted as a priority.

Though the chassis are the same, the Lightning differs from the Thunderbolt in most other respects. The small windscreen, 4-gallon (15.1lit) tank, seat/tail section and rear fender are unique to the Lightning, which is 25 pounds (11.3kg) lighter than the Thunderbolt. Add the 15-horsepower increase and the S1 takes a large stride in acceleration and speed. With the footpegs two inches (5cm) farther aft, the Thunderbolt rider adopts a posture closer to the racing crouch.

Another obvious distinction is the Thunderbolt airbox, designed to flow more air to the high-performance engine and simultaneously subdue intake noise. The curiously low-tech muffler was also enlarged to exhaust spent gases quickly and quietly. The S1 turns in quarter-mile times under 12 seconds at 114 mph (183km/h), with a top speed of 130 (209km/h).

With Harley-Davidson as partner, engine supplier and distribution network, the future of Buell's American sport bike looks uncommonly bright.

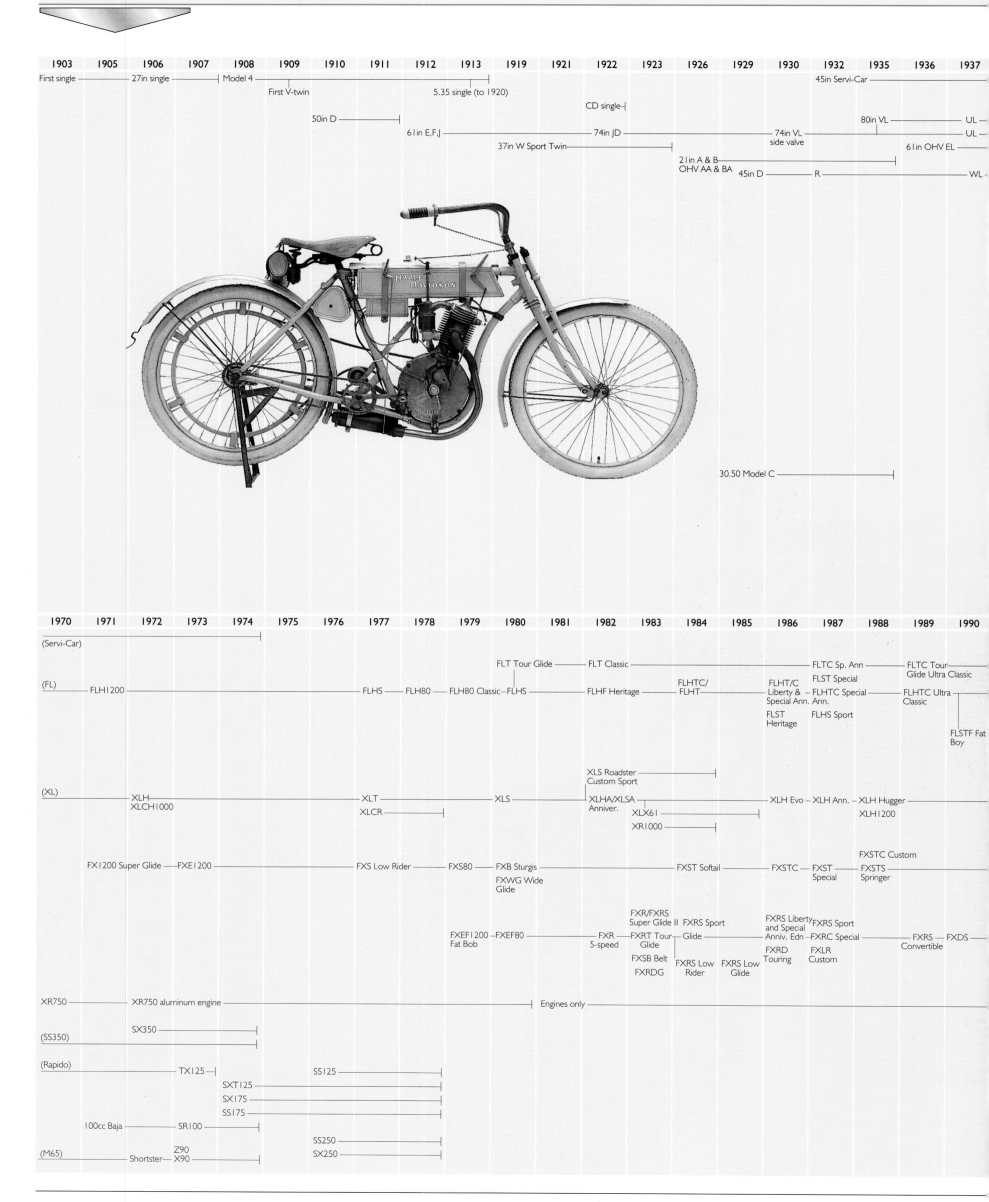

| 1941 | 1942 | 1945 | 1947 | 1948 | 1949 | 1951 | 1952 | 1954 | 1957 | 1958 | 1959 | 1960 | 1961 | 1962 | 1963 | 1965 | 1966 | 1967 | 1968 | 1969 |

74in FL

74in FL — FL Hydra-
Panhead   Glide

FL Duo Glide

FL Electra-Glide

WLA Army Special

45in K — 55in KH

XL Sportster

XA 750 Army

125 Model S ——— 125cc Teleglide 165cc engine ——————— Ranger trail bike

SS350 Sprint

125cc Hummer ————————— 125cc Rapido

175cc Pacer ——————— 175cc Bobcat

175cc Scat ————————

125cc Topper ———————

250cc Sprint C ——————— 250cc Sprint SS

250cc Sprint H (trail) ——— 250cc Sprint H

M50 —— M50S — M65

| 1991 | 1992 | 1993 | 1994 | 1995 | 1996 | 1997 |

FLTCU injection

FLH Road — FLHTC — FLHR injection
King   (fuel injection)

FLSTN Heritage
Softail Nostalgia

XL1200 Sport

XL1200 Custom

XLH 5-speed
belt-drive

VR1000

FXDB
Sturgis

FXDB Dyna
Daytona

FXD Wide Glide

FXSTSB
Bad Boy

FXD series
(new frame)

FXDC
Dyna
Custom

FXD Low
Rider

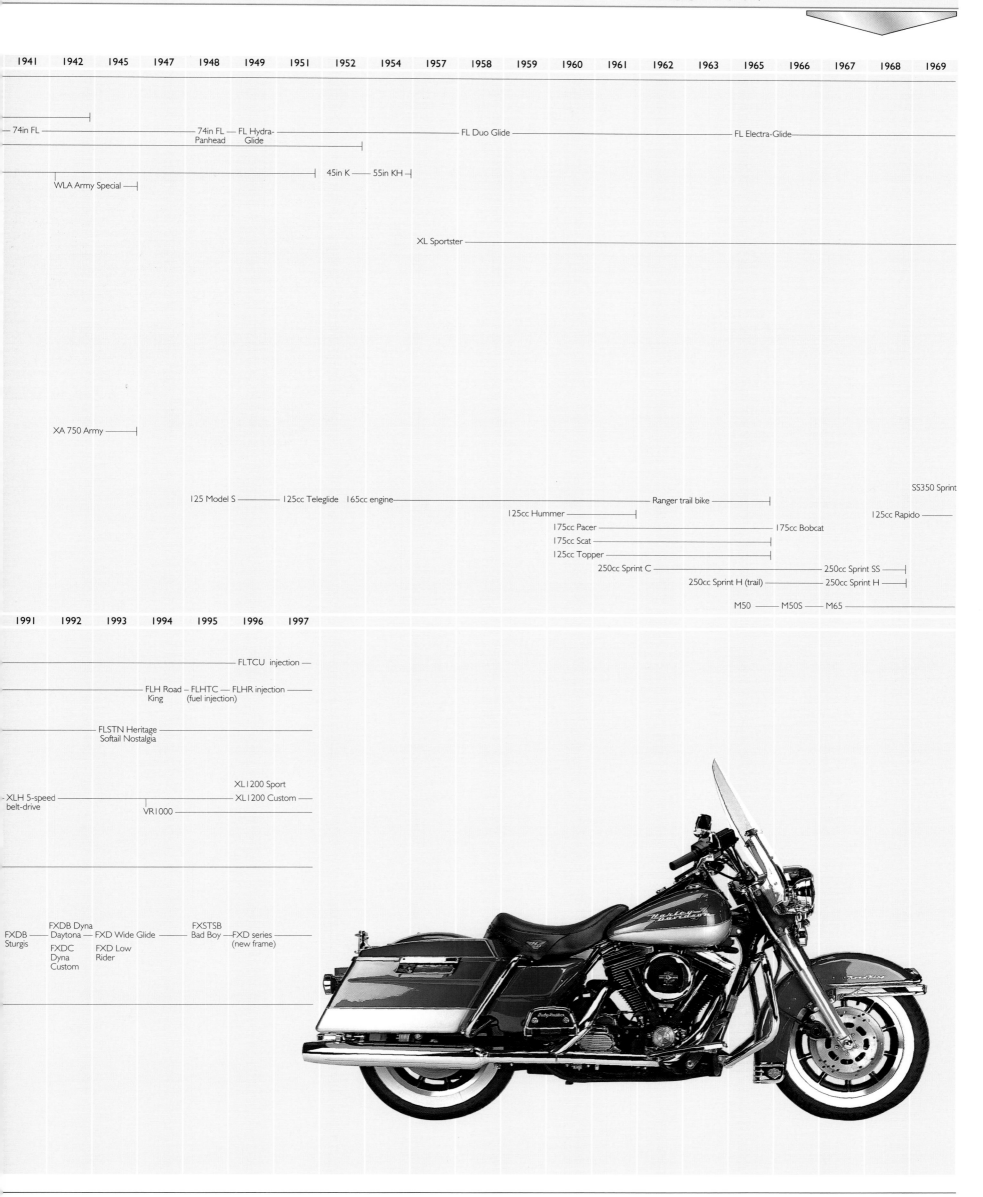

INDEX

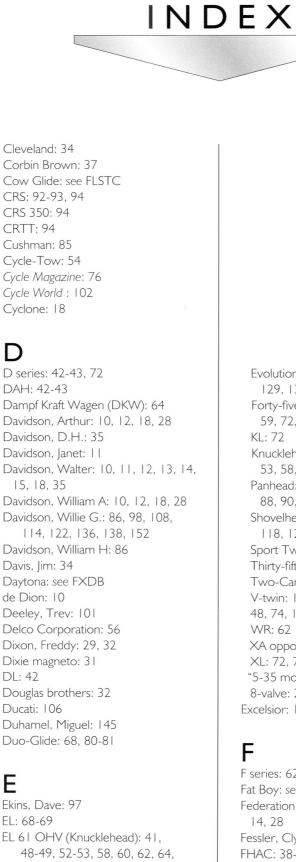

INDEX

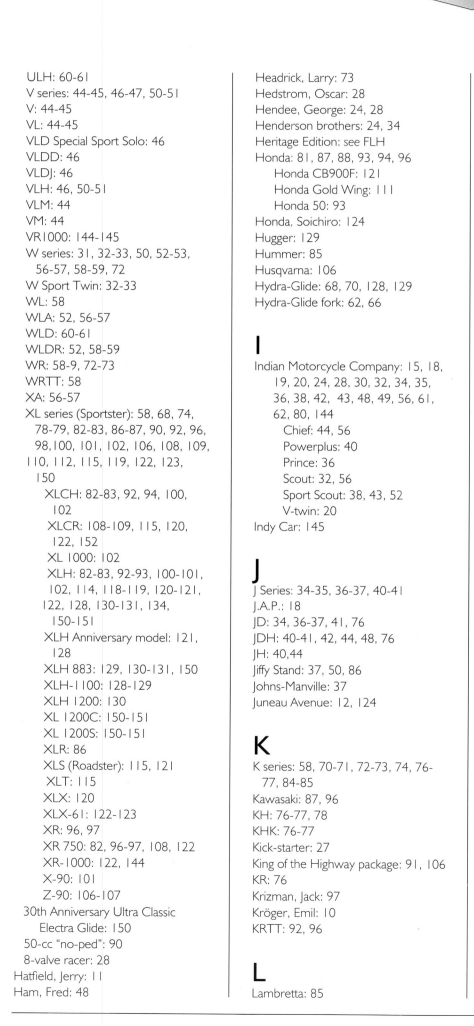

BIBLIOGRAPHY

Bach, Sharon & Osterman, Ken (Editors), *The Legend Begins*, Harley-Davidson, 1993.
Bolfert, Thomas C., *The Big Book of Harley-Davidson*, Harley-Davidson, 1991.
Briel, Dorothea, *Harley-Davidson*, CLB Publishing, 1992.
Buzzelli, Buzz, *Harley-Davidson Sportster Performance Handbook*, Motorbooks International, 1992.
Carrick, Peter, *Encyclopedia of Motor-Cycle Sport*, St Martin's Press, 1977.
Emde, Don, *The Daytona 200*, Infosport, 1991.
Field, Greg, *Harley-Davidson Panheads*, Motorbooks International, 1995.
Girdler, Allan & Hussey, Ron, *Harley-Davidson: The American Motorcycle*, Motorbooks International, 1992.
Ibid, *Harley-Davidson Sportster*, ibid, 1995.
Girdler, Allan, *Harley-Davidson Buyer's Guide*, ibid, 1992.
Hatfield, Jerry, *American Racing Motorcycles*, Haynes Publishing Group, 1982.
Ibid, *Inside Harley-Davidson*, Motorbooks International, 1990.
Marselli, Mark, *Classic Harley-Davidson Big Twins*, ibid, 1994.
Palmer III, Bruce, *How to Restore Your Harley-Davidson*, ibid, 1994.
Prior, Rupert, *Motorcycling: The Golden Years*, CLB Publishing, 1994.
Rafferty, Tod, *Harley-Davidson: The Ultimate Machine*, ibid, 1994.
Rivola, Luigi, *Racing Motorcycles*, Rand McNally, 1978.
Wiesner, Wolfgang, *Harley-Davidson Photographic History*, Motorbooks International, 1989.
Wright, David K., *The Harley-Davidson Motor Company*, Motorbooks International, 1993.
Wright, Stephen, *American Racer, 1900-1939*, Motorbooks International, 1989.